THE ONCE AND FUTURE CHURCH

COLLECTION

The Once and Future Church

Transforming Congregations for the Future

Five Challenges for the Once and Future Church

Updated and revised by

LOREN B. MEAD

AN ALBAN INSTITUTE PUBLICATION

Library of Congress Card Number 2001094862
ISBN 1-56699-248-6

CONTENTS

A Conversation with Loren B. Mead

The year 2001 marks the tenth anniversary of Loren Mead's book The Once and Future Church. *Since it was first published the book has become the Alban Institute's all-time best-selling book and was honored by the Academy of Parish Clergy as one of their top ten books for clergy in 1991. Two volumes that continue and expand upon the ideas behind* The Once and Future Church—Transforming Congregations for the Future *and* Five Challenges for the Once and Future Church—*appeared in 1994 and 1996 respectively and went on to similar acclaim and success.*

In May 2001, on the eve of the publication of this special commemorative volume of his trilogy of books, Alban Institute managing editor David Lott sat down with Loren Mead at his home in Washington, D.C. to discuss the origins of The Once and Future Church *and how his thoughts have changed and developed in recent years.*

DAVID LOTT: *Where did you get the idea for* The Once and Future Church? *What was the germ or genesis for the book?*

LOREN MEAD: The trigger was my fascination with the church and the sense that the parish or the congregation is where I wanted to put my life. When I was in a parish in North Carolina, the occasion came where I was asked to do an exchange with a church in England. Because my background was Anglican/Episcopalian, and because I knew that they did parishes differently than we did, I'd always been interested in the Church of England, so I took the chance. So going and living in and seeing an English parish, which is very much an establishment situation where the role of the church and the society is so different and is so territorial, made me start struggling with how we did things differently in America. The English talk about parishes, while back in this country we talk about congregations, and I started struggling with that distinction.

I think a lot of the book came out of that cultural tension. I tried to understand how the church in England was different and why it was different. I saw the English church as fitting into a particular social system; I saw England as living out what I came to call "Christendom," where church and state, schools and everything else is one entity. In the United States, on the other hand, there was a lot of separation between these things. Congregations were very much in competition with each other. In England it was very different. So I started struggling with that and I came to realize that in England people lived with a lot of the ruins of Christendom all around them. In the United States, although we had a similar background we actually were not as much in the world of Christendom as we were in something new that was changing.

That was the distinction that really got me thinking about *The Once and Future Church*, how church had once been one way and now it was different. Not because the people in it have changed their minds, but because society has changed, history has changed, and we're in a different place. And I came to think that people I worked with in congregations—pastors and laypeople—were beating up on themselves because they couldn't make the church work in this new situation. I wanted to convey that the church was built for a different situation and we were trying to make it continue to work in our new situation the same way it always had. That was kind of the basic scene.

Did you then start translating those experiences and that thinking into the other work you were doing, say with Project Test Pattern, and later with the Alban Institute?

Yes. Back in the '60s I got very involved with the World Council of Churches' study of the missionary structure of the congregation. I got in touch with them when I was in England. There were a lot of wonderful papers passed around, mostly mimeographed papers written by people in congregations. At the same time that I was trying to figure out how to bring these ideas into congregations. I began to find a lot of people around the country, right after World War II, who said, "the old system isn't working and we must start something new." People like Gordon Cosby in Washington, D.C., who started Church of the Saviour (which still goes on), Bill Webber in New York who was starting the East Harlem Protestant Parish, Bob Raines in Germantown, Pennsylvania, a Methodist, who was struggling with the use of small groups as the core of a congregation—they all had an enormous impact on me and a lot of others. There was a lot of yeasty kind of ferment going on. I just loved this and that's when I got in touch with Parishfield, out in Michigan, a bunch of people trying to figure out how to do parishes in a new way. These were the days of this kind of "urban mission" and "industrial mission." I was just fascinated by the conversation, I learned from a lot of them, and I tried out a lot of the ideas in my own congregation.

My understanding of parish ministry, which came out of Christendom, had been that the parish pastor organizes the activities and the worship of the church and people come to it, then go home and do other things. The critical event for me, doing my job as a parish pastor as best I could, happened when I was planning my Holy Week services one week in North Carolina. A member of my church, the senior warden, came up to me and said, "Loren, what are all these services listed in the bulletin this week?" and I said, "Well, this is Holy Week and we always have a lot of service leading up to Easter." And he asked, "Is this important?" and I said, "Yeah, I think so, it's pretty normal." And he said, "Well, I don't think it's fair. I work in the Research Triangle Institute, 10 miles out of town, and I have to be there at 7:30 in the morning, and all these services are at 7:30 in the morning at the church and I can't be there to worship." And I said, "You know, I hadn't thought about that," and I honestly hadn't. In other words, he was telling me that the parish, which I understood I was running, was missing something about ministering to its people. And he said, "If I arrange it, could you come out to the Triangle, and have a service for us out there?" There were six or eight members of our church who worked out there, I said, "Sure, I'll do it."

So on Wednesday he arranged for the auditorium for us to meet in, and I went out there, took my stuff along, and I did the service. There were 65 people there! I didn't know most of them—they were from Raleigh and Durham as well as from Chapel Hill and weren't members of my church. In fact, many of them were members of other denominations. And I realized the world I was living in did not fit the Christendom model of what the church was supposed to do. And that started our parish toward developing an "industrial mission" out there. But it also made me realize that the models I was working with and what I was trying to do as a pastor did not fit the life that the people in my congregation were living, and I had to make a lot of adaptations. Their work didn't fit my models; they wanted to carry out the Christian ministry through their work and I was not able to do that in the structures I had.

I remember the first time I ever taught that basic theory of the three ages of the church: the bishop of Indianapolis asked me to lead a conference for the lay leaders of his diocese, and the concept came to me as a way to frame the discussion. That must have been about 1980. Then in the early 1980s when I went to Australia and New Zealand I picked up again the echo of the European church system that they were trying to adapt to their churches. But what was fascinating there is they were caught between their fascination with the American culture and their fascination with the English culture. I could see almost a migration of ideas back and forth. Models of "parish" there experienced the tension I'd found in American churchs—in a more radical form.

Your concept of the meaning of the word parish *seems to have been shaped by your time in England and has become a key point in your work. Yet it is a somewhat foreign or misunderstood word still to many mainstream Protestants.*

There are three words that people use almost interchangeably: one is the *local church*, one is *parish*, and one is *congregation*. They each focus on a little different dimension. *Parish* and *congregation* are the ones I struggle with in particular. Parish really does mean turf, as in England—they have parish boundaries, and you don't cross those boundaries. For instance, if you live in this parish, you've got to be married in that parish, you can't go to the next one to be married. The whole business of reading the banns of marriage was to prevent people from committing bigamy. If you read the banns saying so-and-so is getting married then that was to inform people, and people in the parish would know whether that person was already married. That was the basic idea for it, it's kind of funny the way they use it now. But what I'm learning is that the concept of turf, having a particular area that sort of "belongs" to this church, is no longer as strong as it once was. The Catholic church has been the strongest in having bounds for a church; the Anglican church is probably the next strongest. We still have places in North Carolina and South Carolina where we still have Anglican parishes and in Louisiana you have Catholic parishes as geographical areas.

In Washington, for example, the parish I go to—we call it parish, that's the technical name in the Episcopal church—feels a sense of responsibility for people who live around the church, even if they don't have anything to do with the church. In our parish there tend to be a lot of retired, elderly folk, so we feel responsibility in church to provide midday meals for people who live in apartments and don't get out—so there's a kind of sense of parish. The other way I've discovered that parish hits us is that we also think of parish in terms of where our people work. Originally it meant where people lived; it was a neighborhood type of thing. But we have also come to think that our parish extends to the places where people work. Since a number of our people work in government—say, the Department of Agriculture—we have a kind of ministry through these other places. But that's a secondary meaning; the original is just geographic. Parish is a wonderful word. It's certainly not what it used to be, however.

When I was in England, living and working in the suburbs in London, I discovered that a lot of people in my parish worked in what was called the City of London, which was the financial center of the city, so they went up to the city on trains in the morning. I wanted to find out how they lived and what they did, so I started setting up lunches in the city. I would take the train up and meet a bunch of my people in London to have lunch. The first thing I did—since English people never tell you what they do and because I was an outsider they would be polite to me—I asked them to tell me what they did up in London, so I could understand it. They told me, and I discovered that they had never told each other, so I was really helping them make some connections between themselves about their work. Because of that, when I came back to North Carolina I stopped doing so much parish calling in apartments, where people lived, and started doing parish calling where people worked. I'd go out for a cup of coffee with someone in the pathology department at the hospital and started trying to connect that way. That's a different vision of parish, one that's around people's work lives.

As we become more of a commuter society, it would seem that secondary aspect of parish is growing.

I think it is. I don't put down the first one, because residence does mean something to people. But I think, from my understanding of what the ministry of the laity is all about, we need to pay heavier attention to the places where people work. That's also true in terms of where people are retired—where they are putting in their productive life may be around their home or neighborhood or in networks of retired folk—so they don't have a job as such. Or people like me—I work out of my home, so my workplace is my home. I suspect that is more and more true. People are connecting by e-mails and by other means to a very different kind of community. We're not limited by geography the way we once were. One of the strongest pastoral relationships I've had in recent years was by e-mail with a friend dying of cancer in New Zealand. Where does *that* fit with "parish" or with "congregation."

Are there ways that the positive aspects of parish can be rethought or recaptured for the church today? How has your thinking developed on how that might be applied to our current situation?

It's a terribly important question for a congregation to raise: What is our parish? The church I served for 12 years down in North Carolina was started at the same time that the university started its medical school, so a lot of the people who moved into town for the medical school got interested in this new church that was starting. Our congregation was heavily medical: medical students, interns, residents, people on the faculty. As a result, we started paying a lot of attention to St. Luke's Day, and we made a big deal about it, even though it's not a major festival, it's one of the minor days in the Episcopal calendar. We had a breakfast at church, we'd invite all the nurses and doctors and trainees, and it was kind of fun. The offering at the service was our professional work.

Another time the great pastoral theologian Paul Tournier was coming to town, so I started a study group at the hospital—not at the church—to study Tournier's work and I got the chaplain at the hospital to lead it. On the final day of the study Tournier actually came and sat down with them. Most of the doctors were not part of my congregation, but I felt they were part of my parish, to illustrate the distinction. The fascinating thing about that, I found out just a few years ago, is that there is a big conference in North Carolina every year at Kanuga, called "Medicine and Ministry." I understand that this conference grew out of that study group we had in Chapel Hill. I didn't know it was connected.

But that says something about parish, and I can't think of a better thing for leaders of a congregation to do than to spend some time struggling with that: What is our parish? And I mean, beyond what the congregation is. The congregation is a clue to what the parish is, and some of it is strictly geographical—our neighborhood. But where our people go—for instance, where they go on vacations, how is that related? I would encourage people have their members on vacation go to churches and find out something about churches and bring that back. Also overseas—go to churches, find out what's going on in those overseas communities and bring that back. *Parish* can have an incredibly large definition, I think.

When you put it that way, it also means to do something to get that concept into the people's mindsets.

That's hard to do, but it happens. It was interesting, after I did my exchange with this pastor in England, when I came back I helped arrange three or four other exchanges. There was a wonderful high school teacher in Chapel Hill who was Jewish, and I arranged for him to be on an exchange at King's College, Wimbledon; they'd never had a Jew on their faculty. I cared about him, and he was a good teacher. He was in no way a believing member of my congregation, but he was a part of my parish, looking at the larger meaning, and he became very close to some folk in the parish over there. And a couple of doctors did exchanges, as did a lawyer. But working with them to arrange those exchanges was seeing that this somehow related to the church.

Changing that consciousness—it's a double thing, like somebody who comes and worships where I do on Sunday morning, having a sense that when they go to work the next day that what they did on Sunday is connected to their work. They don't sit around reading prayers for the people necessarily, but somehow they come to understand that the energy for trying things a little differently, working a little harder, is related somehow to what they do on Sunday. That's what the emerging age of the church has got to be about, those people—a stronger sense of call into their day-to-day work.

Where does that go beyond the old stuff on "ministry in daily life"? What's the next direction in that?

We don't seem to be able to get anywhere with the ministry in daily life stuff—it's sort of hackneyed and dry and doesn't seem to capture people's imaginations. The ideas I'm describing are not that different—I've worked with these people who are developing things on ministry in daily life, and they're wonderful people. It may be that the undertow that comes from Christendom is so strong. Basically Christendom tells us that the church's supposed relationship to the world out there is to take it over and control it. What I am learning is that is not what we're supposed to be doing at all, just as—this is one I'll get in trouble about, I'm sure—everybody says that the thing we're supposed to be doing, according to the New Testament, is the Great Commission: "Go and make disciples of all nations." I think there's some very serious questions about that, both biblically and in terms of what that has led the church to be, which is basically an imperialistic institution. It sees its task is to win everybody into membership in the church and also to take over and make all the decisions about how the world is run. That image comes out of Christendom, and I don't think that's the image that fits the world we're living in today or in the next hundred years. Under that Christendom sense of mission we have justified terrible things we've done to other people—the American Indian, the Jews—the church has much to ask forgiveness for in the ways we've dealt with the world. I'll have a lot more to say about that in my next book, but that is certainly something I'm coming to see. We clearly must rethink our ideas about mission from the ground up!

In some ways it seems ironic that the churches that seem less established and less institutional, primarily the conservative and charismatic churches, seem to be the ones that really are pushing the Christendom concept, with the language they are using about America being a Christian nation and of restoring Christian ideals to the country.

The way that I've seen it, and I'm not sure I've ever said it very clearly, is that I think "my side" of the church—which tends to be the more liberal side, that's just my background—we tried very hard in the '50s, '60s, '70s, and '80s to try to get the world to adopt the church's agenda. We had a lot to say about how society ought to be run, and we raised the problems over race and Vietnam. We did our best, and the world didn't follow our suggestions that much. I think that then the liberals tried to rebuild Christendom with a liberal agenda, and what's been happening in the last 10 years is that now the conservatives are trying to restore us to Christendom, but this time it has a conservative agenda. I don't think that's the role of the church in the future, I don't think we're going to call the shots for society. I think we're also going to have to realize that we are one faith among a number of faiths. We haven't faced that yet very much. We've started to face it a little bit with the Jews, but I don't think we recognize how big that is.

When I was growing up I thought that by now everybody would be Christian. With typical arrogance, I thought they'd all be Episcopalians! When I was a kid in Sunday School I thought that was the way we were headed. I look around the world now and Islam is growing equally as fast as the church. Neither Hinduism nor Buddhism seem to be drying up and blowing away, they're strong and great faiths. I think God is calling us to a world where we have to live with these differences. I don't think the church is set up to do that. We don't have the mental equipment. So that's one thing I'd like the church to be working on.

How do you get that mental equipment? That's the tough part!

Well, I don't think that you get it without truly encountering the other. That's one of the things that has been happening between Christians and Jews. There are still Christians who think that what you do with Jews is you try to convert them, that the only way to deal with them is for them to become like us. But I think there has been much more willingness—I don't know if it's the majority of the people—but a strong willingness to recognize that the Jews are called to a different covenant and that we must respect and honor that. We must be ourselves in relationship to people who are different from us. God calls us to learn how to live that way. The great commission in my mind is not, Go make everyone my disciples, but "A new commandment I give to you, that you love one another." That is the big one—but it's not a popular one. And we certainly don't know how to do it.

Of course, when you talk about inclusiveness, it seems that much of what you talk about in your writing is currently encapsulated within the church's struggles over sexuality issues, particularly gay and lesbian ordination.

Absolutely. I haven't said a lot about that struggle. When I grew up, Christendom gave me an understanding of sexuality that was narrower than the reality. I remember the first person who came to me for counseling around homosexuality: basically, it was a pair of people who had split, and one of them came to me to consult with them about rebuilding the relationship. I didn't know how to do that—I didn't have any equipment to deal with it. It sounded to me, from what I knew, that this split was a move toward health. I had to do a lot of learning to realize that what I had learned was very inadequate. I had to meet people who were clearly other than me and to learn from them—I had to change to do that. But the church that wants to set the agenda that everybody else has to be exactly like us—I don't think there's a future for that church, even though they may have a lot of people in their pews on Sunday.

When I was helping a church in a large city find a rector, this was a very volatile issue for the congregation. I told them, first off, you've got to make up your mind about this issue in this search. It's one of those things that comes up, and you've got to be clear where you're at. I told them that anyone who is rector of this parish is going to have a large population of people calling on it for pastoral care, people who don't fit with the standard nuclear family model. And they came out with an interesting statement: they said, "We do not want a rector who is gay or lesbian, but we do not want a rector who cannot work with gays or lesbians." That's probably a way of living in that situation. But it's going to take awhile. And it's not simply theological ideas, but it's cultural ideas we've got to move through, as well as deep patterns of life.

I grew up in a racist community, I grew up in a sexist community, I grew up in a community that wouldn't even talk about homosexuality. My whole life has been trying to recover from some of those things and move out beyond those boundaries.

You talk about how the congregation has become a holy club, the focus of personal and family religious enthusiasm. The idea of the church as a social institution certainly changes the theological dimension of it. What does that mean for our leadership?

You go to a town and you can join the Rotary Club and you join the church. They do the same thing—they do nice things in town, it's a place where you can go once a week to have lunch. It's more a style of being than an intentionality. I believe that the issue is baptism. In the Protestant churches today I think we've gotten the message across that if you're going to be serious about being a Christian you ought to go for ordination, and I think that ought to be read back to baptism. I don't know what baptism means anymore—somehow that has lost its theological rationale. I mean, you baptize children—this is all medieval stuff to keep us from going to hell. It was almost "magic." And I think that is still what many people feel. We don't say it that way, or *think* about it that way, but it's back there. That works if you believe in hell, but I don't think a helluva lot of people today believe in hell. So baptism as an escape from hell I don't think makes deep, convincing sense today. But I believe what baptism is about is being called to make a difference in the world, to try to be something here in relation to the good news of Jesus, and that the church is a community that nurtures and calls us to that kind of life commitment. Some people are working on doing that—but I'm afraid we're still living with the emotional leftovers of a different understanding of what church was all about: baptism comes out of fear.

I think about the baptism of my children. I wouldn't have not done it for anything, but then my children were brought up in a family that was very much a part of the church. I am very nervous about baptisms where the family has a very tenuous relationship with the church. If it is a church as a social club, what can baptism mean? If, in some way, it has to say, we will somehow try to help this child put their life on the life for the Lord, and we'll back them up, and we'll stand with them—then it makes some sense.

This also suggests that we need to rethink what ordination is all about. Many have come to see that ordination is about power—who holds the reins of power in the church, and it seems ordination has been distorted toward the power issue, rather than the image of the servant leader.

I think recapturing the idea of what baptism is will also free us to think more about what ordination ought to be. I don't think it ought to be just the people who want to be serious Christians. Nowadays, the people who are going for ordination are frequently people who want to be on a religious pilgrimage. They're really searching and seeking—that's their motivation. They don't particularly want a job in the church. And to be ordained, I think it ought to be the people who want to help lead this institution.

I realize as I say these things that I'm not systematic in my thinking. I'm responding to the church that I've known and loved. All along, I've seemed to learn from people like Speed Leas, people like Roy Oswald and Celia Hahn. People I'm working with, people ask me questions, I often push farther than I intended to go. I'm certain that this realization of the church's relationship to the non-church, that is, how we face the other— that came out of work I'm doing right now for the Institute for Jewish-Christian Studies.

Doesn't the demise of Christendom and the church's minority status in society mean that the church itself now has to deal with being the other?

I think that's absolutely right, and we don't want to. We want to continue to call the shots for everybody else. There's a superiority written into us, that we've got something better than everybody else: "If you will just change what you're doing and do it just like us." There's a very interesting book I'm reading on constructing local theologies. The missionary endeavors of the church are reaching out and are realizing that we have done some things wrong. There's a big missionary enterprise now coming from Africa to Europe. When I was in South Africa, I asked the church I was at what their mission was, and they said they had a big one in Belgium. Well, I hadn't ever thought about that. The whole thing's being flipped on its head. Whereas we always thought that we were the wise ones who would be able to take faith to the poor and benighted—they had to be poor and benighted or we wouldn't have done it—and they had to take it on our basis. This thing about constructing local theologies is about how do you go out and help them construct a theology from what they know, because that has integrity. You don't have to just wipe it out and put ours on top of it.

The more I look at what's going on, the more I realize that the structures we have really have blocked us off from some of the big questions of the next century: How are we going to live with one another? It's easy to live with someone if you can conquer them and make them do what you want them to do. But how can we live with them when we say, "Jesus is the one way" and still honor the fact that they have another way? I don't know. So worrying about how a congregation works and how to make it work better pushes you eventually to these very basic questions. We think about God wrong. We have a false idea of what salvation's all about. And I hope to get at some of that in my next book. But on the other hand, I don't know if that's what Alban needs! I mean people don't go to Alban for basic theology. But what they don't understand is that *The Once and Future Church* is basic theology. People don't understand that.

Well, it seems that, particularly in Alban's early days, very few people were dealing with the practical side, and so Alban put the emphasis on praxis. We're continuing to do that, but I think there's a need to pull back toward theology in many ways. You can't separate the two as neatly as we might think.

I agree, but I have to tell you that I was heavily influenced by this guy who asked me to bring the Holy Week services out to his workplace in the Research Triangle. He was my senior warden, and once when we planned something at the church, he said, "Why are we going to do this sort of thing?" And I said, "Well, this is a program that we really need to have go; it's really important." He said, "It doesn't look that important to me," and I said, "Let me tell you the theology behind why we're doing this." And he stopped me and said, "Oh, for God's sake, don't—I've already got more theology than I'm using." *Bingo!* That's been an operating principle of mine—that I want to help people use the theology that they've got. I don't see any particular expertise in me to tell them what is the correct theology. So maybe that presupposition got into the DNA of Alban—we don't try to push people, but try to give them tools to use what they've got.

It seems like there is a sort of "congregational imagination" that needs to be captured and sparked today. Maybe that's part of what it means to be a pastor today.

That's a wonderful way of putting it. Maybe "imagination" is what the word *vision* is reaching for. Vision, in my experience, is a one-story word, it's a management tool, at least the way that it's used. But I think there ought to be something that's larger, that includes imagination.

Let me tell you about the night that Martin Luther King, Jr. was killed. A friend asked me to go to a lecture over at Duke University, and I had done a lot of work there in city and regional planning because I thought that somehow congregations were involved in the future of communities. The German theologian Jürgen Moltmann was speaking out of his then-new book, *The Theology of Hope*, and that night Martin Luther King was killed. Because of that, Moltmann's theology of hope just blew me out of the water—it was a fantastic experience to hear that and then over the next few weeks to read it, study it, and think about it in connection with my studies of city and regional planning. That's been the tension for me—the difference between planning and eschatology. When people ask me what I am, I sometimes say that I'm an operational eschatologist—trying to help the church respond to God's call for it to be something, and operationally, I'm trying to help people figure out what steps to take. I think that's a very important tension. Many of the words we have in the church have another, secular counterpart—like planning has eschatology—planning is a secular way of looking and trying to do the future. I think vision is that kind of word against imagination. We need to look at the larger word. It's like when we earlier talked about the word *parish*—I'm reaching for a meaning of parish that is so much bigger than what's been used by the church. I think that God broods over and calls us to that next generation of thinking. We can use these tools—and they're not bad tools. It's like conflict management— somehow beyond conflict management is the peaceable kingdom. Even as we're working at conflict management, we should be holding the dream of a world that's different than it is.

When you walk into a different culture, all the things you know and believe are different. You have to adapt to the situation, try to learn how they say things, and how it's connected to what you knew. It's basic com- munication—it's what happens when you've got a good consultation going in this country—you learn something new from the people who are involved in the problem. You don't go in with all the answers.

I want to say one piece about consulting, and working with parishes— because that's what I've done a lot. They say the most important thing about any consultation is knowing who is the client. When you are working with somebody and if you get confused about whether you're working with this group or that group or this person, you're in trouble. You need to find who's the client. One of the things we discovered is that we cannot consult when the pastor is the client. The congregation has to be the decision- making body, at least the way I understand it. So, for instance, Speed Leas won't take a consultation with a congregation unless the decision-making body agrees to it. One of the things you have to do in a consultation is that you have to meet the expectations of the client. If the board has hired you to do this, then they have to feel that you're really helping them to do that and going all the way through. Well, that can be—and I think for some consult- ants it is—an excuse simply to please the client and make them feel good. If you don't to some extent do that, they won't work with you and they won't pay you and they'll bad-mouth you to other people, and that's bad.

However, I have never been able to be totally happy with that. I have it in my head that when I work with a congregation, my client is *two* congregations—one is that one there that I've got to work with; I've got to keep them working and feeling like they're getting toward what they need. But the other client is that congregation as God is calling it to be. So there's a tension, and I feel comfortable putting a little tension and not just doing what they want me to do, but pushing them toward what God wants them to be. And I think that's the task we—whether it's the Alban Institute or it's Loren Mead—have with the church today. I work with this crazy, screwed-up institution and I try to deal with its craziness and screwed-upness. But I believe I am working for the church that God is calling into the future—and I think that's the orientation of what I am all about and what I'm trying to say in my books.

The Once and Future Church

REINVENTING THE CONGREGATION
FOR A NEW MISSION FRONTIER

CONTENTS

God is always calling us to be more than we have been.

In this book I will try to spell out some of the implications of that state- ment for the world I know best—the Churches. My reasons are very simple: It is my conviction that religious congregations are the most important car- riers of meaning that we have, with one exception. They are the most im- portant ground of purpose and direction that we have, with one exception. They are the most important source of an essential element of life—human community—with one exception.

The one exception is the human family. The reason the family is not the subject of this book is that it is not my area of expertise or calling. My thing—the thing I have been called to think about, struggle with, work on—is the religious congregation. For six decades now, I have inhabited them, enjoyed them, been frustrated by them, earned a living from them, and tried to understand them.

And, although I assume the primacy of the human family in all the ways noted above, I am also bold enough to note that even families—in my experience—run into trouble if they lose their connection to a religion- and value-bearing community—the kind of community I have experienced only in a congregation.

I come to this task from a very limited view; as a Christian and an Episcopalian, almost classically "mainline Protestant," I see what is going on through those lenses. I see more than that and my experience is much broader, but those are my lenses and they influence how I see whatever I see. I also have other lenses that limit me in one sense and give me perspective in another—male, American, white, southern, born during the Depression. In all these ways I bring perceptions and perspec- tives that help me see some things as no one else can, but that make me blind to other things. I have learned how to overcome some areas of blindness, but I remain sensitive to the limits of my vision.

Yet I am bold enough to say that even from a limited perspective what I have to say speaks of larger realities and a larger call, one much more universal than my experience, my perspective, or my vision. What I see of God's call in my portion of the vineyard is consistent, I believe, with the call of God in other parts of the vineyard and in other institutions in which we live and move. I do not think that God is calling just the Church or just religious congregations—God's call is for all of creation. And some of the groaning and travailing results from our having to deal with God's unsettling call in all of our institutions.

In this book I want to spell out the call that I perceive to be troubling the waters today. For I do see the turmoil and uncertainty, the civil wars and professional burnouts of religious institutions today as evidence of the troubled waters that always indicate the potential presence of God's healing powers. So long as we see those disturbing institutional issues simply as problems to be solved, we may miss out on the call that lies within them.

In the beginning I will talk about how mission has always shaped the life of the Church. I will try to point out the change in our way of thinking about mission that confuses much of what we are now doing. I will point to pressure points in the lives of congregations and religious institutions that shape the evolution of those structures toward new forms; I will describe the large shifts in religious consciousness we are experiencing; and I will point to dimensions of these changes that touch other institutions. Finally I want to spell out what I think the call is and what implications it has for the institutional structures we must invent to carry us into the next century.

God is always calling us to be more than what we have been.

Never has that been more true than it is today. Never has it been more true for anyone than it is today for those of us who are related to religious congregations. Never before have those in religious congregations had more—potentially—to give to the other structures of society.

In putting forth these ideas I want to acknowledge my indebtedness to those with whom I have worked these past four decades: lay persons, clergy, teachers of many denominations. I note especially my colleagues at the Alban Institute.

Celia Hahn has given the kind of support and encouragement that kept me on track when I wanted to quit. Mary Forbes performed miracles in deciphering my notes and locating things I lost on my computer disks.

Four others gave me specific feedback and criticism—Bob Isaksen, Lutheran bishop of the New England Synod (ELCA); Susan Heath, Canon Theologian of Trinity Cathedral, Columbia, South Carolina; Carl Dudley of McCormick Theological Seminary and The Center for Church and Community in Chicago; and Bill Craddock, lay theologian. Bruce Boston gave immense help in shaping the final manuscript. If anything is wrong with this book, as far as I am concerned, I am sure it's their fault!

CHAPTER 1

The Challenge of the Congregation

A cross the face of the country, no feature is more pronounced than the presence of places of worship wherever people live.

Small southern towns with only two roads crossing will have four fortress-like parish churches facing across the intersection. From a hilltop anywhere in New England, one can locate villages by the white spires of local churches poking up through the green foliage. Major urban centers house enormous buildings perched on corners, far more impressive than the few people who straggle through decaying streets to attend worship there. Ethnic neighborhoods boast houses of worship where English is rarely or never spoken by the older generation. Some ghettoes are home for great worshipping congregations whose membership is drawn from all over a metropolitan center.

Churches are found in the open country with no houses in sight, serving far-flung farm families. Others are behind urban storefronts serving very small communities in cities of millions.

A number, many in the Sunbelt, are major, fast-growing enterprises of publishing, worship, and service, dealing with congregations as large as small towns, led by corporate planning, and enjoying executive leadership of the most sophisticated kind. Some are called "megachurches" that carry on ministries through sophisticated media facilities and through hundreds of small groups.

Some are closed in upon themselves, while others eagerly engage the community and even the world with outreach or mission activities. Some are refuges of a narrow elitism; others work hard at breaking down barriers to become inclusive.

Some of them struggle from week to week just to survive, while others manage assets in the tens of millions. Some have no professional, paid staff, while others have rank on rank of professional and volunteer people-power. Some struggle to meet weekly, others have as much activity as a shopping mall seven days a week. Some are one-of-a-kind, accountable only to themselves; others are closely linked in regional and national networks.

Each one tends to be very important to many of its members. Each one also has within it members who are critical of it and who want it to be "more" or "better" than it is.

Over the centuries since 1607, congregations have been a special part of the social glue that de Toqueville described as characteristic of this nation. They have been a center of community life. They have been an anchor, a place of stability, holding up a transcendent vision of the meaning of life as a new nation struggled to understand and build a society. Congregations have grounded the nation in the biblical story that gave words and ideas to America's great moments—from the time of the Pilgrims to July 4, 1776, from Gettysburg to the Birmingham jail. Congregations contributed not only to the framing of statements but to people's ability to hear the messages of those critical times.

Congregations have also been places of refuge and identity for those from distant lands who spoke different languages, making possible the first steps of the immigrant into a new nation.

Less dramatically, but perhaps even more importantly, congregations have also been a place for retreat and regrouping in the face of hurt, distress, or injustice. They have healed and restored the spirits of those broken by deliberate cruelty and by simple human tragedy. To this day it is to congregations that people—even many who find formal beliefs and doctrines foreign to their style of life—come to face death, loss, birth, the discovery of love, the collapse of hope.

This book is about that institution, the congregation, because the congregation is at a critical point of change.

During the years in which refugees and pioneers came to America from Europe, then from other lands, congregational forms were imported, primarily from western and northern Europe. Churches of Reformation heritage—Anglican, Presbyterian, Congregational—became established in some colonies by law, in others by custom. When the founders of the nation, 200 years later, chose to reject the idea of a legally established church, they did so in a society in which the informal coalition of those three traditions made for a de facto establishment that still influences us today. That establishment expanded and changed many times as new partners first challenged, then were absorbed into it: Methodists, Lutherans, Catholics. Will Herberg, writing in the late 1950s, described the new establishment in the title of his book as *Protestant, Catholic, Jew*. Since he wrote, evangelicals and African-American Protestants have stretched the meaning of the establishment once again, and each component has become more diverse. At the same time, the earlier partners in the coalition have undergone change and diversification. The Episcopalians, the Presbyterians, and the Congregationalists of the late 20th century are distant cousins of those who sat in the Continental Congress and formed a nation.

Local churches were born into this culture of establishment, whether they approved of it and joined it, or disapproved and tried to remain apart from it. Denominations–those peculiarly American inventions–became families of identity for congregations within the larger community of the informal establishment.

The most articulate and self-assured of the partners in this establishment were those who came to it earliest, those identified as "the mainline" churches. The longer they had been accepted as partners in the establishment, the more mainline they tended to be. Evangelical and fundamentalist latecomers, although uncomfortable with the role, became more and more visible, establishment, and mainline as the original partners diminished in size and influence after the 1950s.

The much documented collapse of mainline religion was most visible as a collapse of denominational structures and agencies that themselves were born mostly in this century. The structure of agencies, boards, and commissions invented by the American religious denominations in the first half of the 20th century was the last flowering of a great and creative age when the churches were powered by a strong, clear, uniform paradigm of mission. The rich variety of national and regional church structures developed by 1960 were supported because thousands of local congregations knew in their bones that that was the way to support the mission that had been laid upon the church. The members of local congregations had a clear sense of what that mission was, and they supported it with some enthusiasm.

American denominations came out of World War II with a heady sense of how victory is won and with an unlimited enthusiasm for getting on with mission. Many of the denominations built their own Pentagons and formed a grand alliance to achieve mission goals. They expanded their training camps by enlarging their seminaries. Members were generous in providing capital funds and buildings. New congregations sprouted on the suburban frontier. Nowhere was there a more visible symbol of the consensus of the mission crusade than in the Interchurch Center, the so-called "God-Box" at 475 Riverside Drive in New York.

The dream of the new alliance for ministry and mission was never fulfilled. The National Council of Churches, a symbol of the great alliance, is today a shadow of what it was. The halls of the God-Box no longer bustle as once they did. New, separate Pentagons have sprouted in Chicago, Louisville, and Cleveland as old allies struggle for vision, clarity, and direction.

Historians, sociologists, anthropologists, and theologians are struggling right now to try to understand what happened. We may never know all of it. I try to describe in Chapter Two some of what I understand happened.

The result, however, was that in congregation after congregation, person after person, agency after agency, the one clear paradigm of mission stopped being clear. In one denomination after another, the consensus disappeared. Voices became discordant. Mission, which had once been both central rallying cry and basic assumption, became instead a subject of debate and disagreement. What had been clear simply was not clear any more. Instead of having a shared sense of one crusade in which all were engaged and to which all were committed, we began to be aware of different agendas, conflicting demands, and needs for ministry.

Perhaps the next steps were inevitable. People and congregations who were prepared to make sacrifices to support a mission consensus found it hard to generate enthusiasm and conviction for a more complicated reality. One need only look at the national capacity to make sacrifices for what seemed a clear crusade in World War II and the very different national response to the complex, confused, unclear tasks of the Vietnam conflict. In congregation after congregation, person after person, agency after agency, a consensus about mission ceased to have compelling power. The energy supporting the institutional infrastructure evaporated.

This book argues that three things are happening around us simultaneously:

First, our present confusion about mission hides the fact that we are facing a fundamental change in how we understand the mission of the church. Beneath the confusion we are being stretched between a great vision of the past and a new vision that is not yet fully formed.

Second, local congregations are now being challenged to move from a passive, responding role in support of mission to a front-line, active role.

The familiar roles of laity, clergy, executive, bishop, church council, and denominational bureaucrat are in profound transition all around us.

Third, institutional structures and forms developed to support one vision of our mission are rapidly collapsing. I argue that we are being called to invent or reinvent structures and forms that will serve the new mission as well as the old structures served the old vision. I believe that we are being called to be midwives for a new church, working to help our present forms and structures give birth to forms appropriate for the new mission of the church.

I am not sanguine, as I look around the churches, about the institutional response to this time of challenge when support for the traditional structures and roles is evaporating. All too often I see pessimism, depression, and defeat in the lay leaders, clergy, and denominational leaders we depend on for the reinvention of the church.

In recent years I have seen three kinds of responses in denominational systems:

1) Frantic effort to recapture the initiative, to get "ahead of the curve" and to develop a NEW PROGRAM so compelling that it will reattract all the eroded support. I see regional and national leaders, particularly, making more and more aggressive promises, holding up grander visions, calling their flocks to larger hopes. In almost every case the result is that the clock is not turned back, the resources continue to decline—with an occasional hiccup of growth—and those leaders end up with larger tasks, promises, and commitments but even fewer resources and staff.

Restructuring, relocation of offices, realignment of staffs—behind these names we try to hide what is going on. It is like fibrillation, in which a heart under stress, pumping more and more rapidly, but without coordination, actually begins to work against itself, pumping less and less blood to the body.

2) Holding steady and hoping for the best—if not for divine intervention—is a second strategy some are trying. The Catholic Church's attitude toward the crisis of a shortfall in priestly vocations is one example. All those denominational studies of how losses of members or money have "bottomed out" are other examples.

Still other signs of desperation are the periodic infusions of capital (through major gift drives, "major mission funding" efforts, etc.) which try to shore up programs that are dying because people are no longer convinced that they serve a mission at all and no longer support worn out programs with enthusiasm.

My point is that all too often these responses represent a vain hope that somehow things will change. They are ways of shoring up parts of a system that has stopped working. They keep our attention and resources from efforts to build a more effective system.

3) A third strategy, the one I obviously prefer, requires moving ahead into a new paradigm of mission, rebuilding and reinventing the church as we go. This choice would be simple to make if two things were clear—what the new paradigm really is, and how we determine which parts of the collapsing system we need to keep to make it in the new era. In this book I assume that we have no viable alternative to this third option, even though most denominational responses so far have been along the lines of the first two.

We face a significant problem: Our need for a clear consensus on mission from which we can construct the forms of a new church is no guarantee that we can find it. There is no certainty that we shall be led to a sense of mission as compelling as the one that drove previous generations. That time of clarity may be over. The denominational families with which most of us have had a love-hate relationship for years may have already become antiquarian relics. God may have a more challenging future in store for us, calling us out of these structures altogether.

We must also be aware of our temptation to expend all our resources and energy in shoring up collapsing structures, holding onto the familiar long after it has lost its possibility for new life. One inelegant rule of thumb I use in this area is what I call the "M-T-M ratio." By that I try to state how long I think a particular organization deserves to have mouth-to-mouth resuscitation practiced on it. Everybody need help from time to time, but I see all too many religious organizations that drew their last unassisted breath a decade ago.

Within all of this, the local congregation is critical. The congregation is where people touch the church and are touched by it. It is there that literally millions of people are struggling to understand their own personal sense of mission and to get the strength to pursue it. The congregation is where new people are brought into a faith-heritage that connects them to the biblical story and to the life of the people of God.

It is also there that urgency for mission is already being felt and articulated. It is there that the new structures and roles must be discovered to undergird that mission. Much of this book is about just that.

Our task now is to look at how our vision of the mission of the church came into sharp focus, shaping the way we organized ourselves and the roles we assigned each other to carry out that mission. After acknowledging what that vision produced, we need to look at how that clarity came to lose its sharp focus. Only then can we look at an emerging sense of mission and begin to forecast the kinds of changes that will require ordering our lives within the church.

CHAPTER 2

Paradigms Lost

Twice before the most recent change in its idea of mission, the church has been challenged to reorder its understanding of self and world. In the very earliest days it struggled about whether it was identical to or different from its Jewish roots. Simultaneously, it was trying to be related to and distinguished from the Greco-Roman world in which it spread. Looking back with the perspective of history, we see a paradigm emerge—the paradigm of the apostolic age. Generations later, when the new faith became the official faith of the Roman Empire, a reorientation occurred throughout the institution. Like the first, that reorientation was the church's attempt to relate to its social environment and accomplish its mission. I call the consciousness that developed out of that time the paradigm of the age of Christendom.

In our own time, that second paradigm is breaking apart. Its successor, a third paradigm, has yet to appear fully.

With each change of paradigm, roles and relationships change and power shifts. New structures develop. New directions emerge. Things that were of great value in one age become useless in the next. Times of transition between ages and paradigms are times of confusion and tumult.

But always, the focus is mission. The confusion and tumult, the upsetting of roles, structures, and relationships has the same purpose: to readdress the question of mission in a new time.

During those times of change, the confusion of the outside world was reflected in turbulence within the church, especially in local parishes and congregations. After generations of turbulence and change, a new self-understanding emerged so that the roles, relationships, and tasks focused outward to serve a new sense of mission.

This intimate conversation between a human group and its environment is characteristic of all institutions. It is in that conversation that the group reassesses what it is and what it values. But the conversation also helps it define its relationship or mission to that world surrounding it.

For two millennia the church has struggled with its image of itself and its image of the world outside. The church experienced a special pressure emerging from its belief that its Lord had given it a double-edged commandment—it was to engage with the world, to love the world, to serve the world, to convert the world. And yet it was also to maintain itself as in some sense "distinct from" the world. It was to be a "peculiar people," as Peter put it, but the peculiarity had much to do with caring for and serving that world for God.

The history of the church and its mission has been the struggle to carry out the two sides of that commission. Both the church and the world are always in flux, but usually we bring to that constant change a stable and unchanging paradigm, a mind-set that sometimes lasts for centuries. Sooner or later, however, the thousands of minute shifts and changes bring such pressure to bear that the stable mind-set cracks, shifts, or falls apart. That has happened to us.

Twice before in our history, a broad enough consensus developed about who the church was and how it related, in mission, to the world, so that a single vision became dominant (although it was never uniformly held). Twice before the church has faced such a complete upsetting of the old paradigm that life was disrupted and structures were reordered to form a new one. In our time, it is happening again. The importance of what is happening now, however, is that while we have experienced the disintegration and disruption of the old, the new paradigm has not yet appeared.

The basic idea of this book is that when that new paradigm does appear, it will emerge from a new sense of the church's mission, giving it a new clarity and focus.

THE APOSTOLIC PARADIGM

The first time of tumult was the first generations after Jesus. It resulted in the Apostolic Paradigm.

Jesus articulated a powerful call for people to be sent (*apostellein*, to send forth) to serve and convert the world, to care for the sick, the prisoner and the widow, the fatherless and the poor. As far as we can tell from the literature of the first and second centuries, different styles and different structures emerged in different places to carry out those tasks. Collegial and monarchical structures coexisted side by side. Communal experiments held sway in some places. Different functions and roles emerged—apostle, teacher, healer, bishop, presbyter, deacon, and a dozen more. Some fought to retain close links with the Jewish community; others fought to distance themselves from that community.

The turbulence came from the community's search for its identity in mission. Because these people knew they had been called and commissioned by their Lord to carry on his loving service in the world, they had big, pressing questions. They were driven to ask "Who are we in relationship to those around us? To whom are we sent?" They struggled with their answers as they worshiped week by week and listened to the stories about Jesus and his mission. It was out of their life in their world as they worked on these questions and stories that the paradigm of the apostolic age emerged.

The early church was conscious of itself as a faithful people surrounded by an hostile environment to which each member was called to witness to God's love in Christ. They were called to be evangelists, in the biblical sense of the word—those who bear good news. Their task was to carry into a hostile world the good news of healing, love, and salvation.

The central reality of this church was a local community, a congregation "called out" (*ekklesia*) of the world. It was a community that lived by the power and the values of Jesus. That power and those values were preserved and shared within the intimate community through apostolic teaching and preaching, through fellowship itself, and through ritual acts, preeminently the sharing of the bread and wine of the Eucharist. You gained entrance into this community only when the community was convinced that you also held those values and had been born into that power. The community was intense and personal. Belonging to it was an experience of being in immediate touch with God's Spirit.

It was no Pollyanna community. The epistles of the New Testament describe people and groups that experienced fractures and conflict, anger and division, as well as peace and joy.

The other side of this community image was an image of a world environment that was hostile to what the church stood for. The world was not neutral, it was opposed to the community. Each group of Christians was an illicit community, proscribed by the laws of the land. In many places, it was a capital offense to consort with or be a Christian.

A community formed of common values and shaped by a story within a larger, hostile environment: that was part of the story of the Apostolic Paradigm.

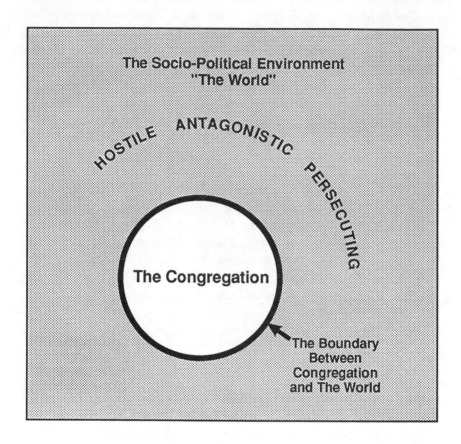

Figure 1

The other side of the paradigm, however, was the commission built into the story that formed the community. The community was called to reach out *to* the environment. The community was to "go into the world," to "be in the world but not of it." It could not be true to its nature and play it safe. Its marching orders were to engage the world, not withdraw from it. In spite of the world's aversion to what the church stood for, the church's people were required to engage with it, to witness to their Lord right in the middle of the hostile environment.

Put differently the congregation came to see that its front door was the frontier into mission. They were impelled to take the life they shared within the congregation and, in its power, cross over the boundary into the hostile world outside. They called it "witnessing," the Greek word for "martyr." The irony of their being is in that word.

The life of the church as institution was shaped by this paradigm. There was a clear "inside" and "outside." So great was the difference between them that entry into the community from the world outside was a dramatic and powerful event. In baptism the person dramatized a symbolic death to the things of the world and a new birth into the way of the cross. The leaders led the community in teaching and preaching the story and in recreating the community in the act of thanksgiving (Eucharist) that symbolized salvation to a new life in a new world. The roles of the congregation fit the mission to the world—servant-ministers carried food to the hungry and healers cared for the sick. Gradually, as the need arose, regional leaders were appointed or emerged to help connect the communities. Traveling teachers and troubleshooters like Paul and Barnabas became prominent.

An intimate community, whose being demanded that it serve and care for a world hostile to itself: that is a fuller picture of the Apostolic Paradigm. *(See Figure 2.)*

Much of the congregation's life was defined by its sense of being on the mission frontier to a hostile world. But it also perceived that the meaning of its life was to build up its members with the courage, strength, and skill to communicate God's good news within that hostile world. Its internal task was to order its life, to establish roles and relationships that nurtured the members of the congregation in the mission that involved each member. Members perceived that the power to engage in that mission—the crossing of the missionary boundary—came from the Holy Spirit.

The church that emerged from the first three centuries had adopted structures and roles to do that kind of mission. The Apostolic Paradigm was the mind-set the church adopted to understand its mission.

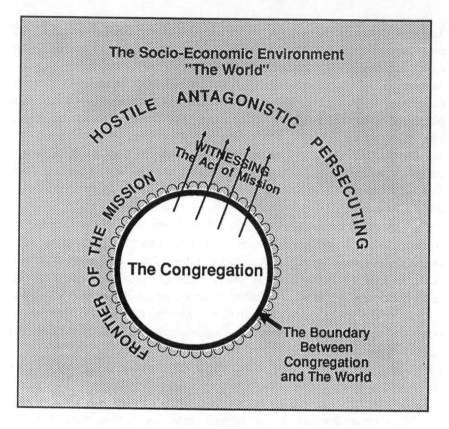

Figure 2

THE CHRISTENDOM PARADIGM

Beginning in the fourth century a new paradigm began to emerge. Again, the emergence of the paradigm took time. This time the change took centuries, not just a few generations. I call it the Christendom Paradigm. It was begun by the conversion of the Emperor Constantine in 313 A.D. and grew progressively as Christianity became in name and law the official religion of the Empire.

The critical difference, once this paradigm settled in, was that by law the church was identified with the Empire. The world—the world that immediately surrounded the church—was legally identified with the church.

There was now no separation between world and church within the Empire. The law removed the hostility from the environment but also made the environment and the church identical.

I want to say that again, in a slightly different way. Instead of the congregation being a small local group that constituted the church in that place, the understanding of the congregation had been enlarged to include everything in the Empire. The congregation was the church; the church was the Empire. There was no boundary between people on the local scene, defining one group as "church" and another as "world." The missionary frontier disappeared from the doorstep of the congregation and became, in effect, the political boundary of the society itself, far away.

Some implications of this change are obvious. No longer is the ordinary participant in a congregation personally and intimately on the mission frontier. The individual is no longer called to "witness" in a hostile environment. No longer is she or he supposed to be different from any other citizen. Indeed, citizenship has become identical with one's religious responsibility.

The other side is equally important. The missionary frontier on the edge of the Empire now becomes the responsibility of the professional—the soldier's job for the political realm and the specially designated missionary's job for the religious realm. In addition, however, the missionary understands that winning souls to the Lord is the same task as winning nations to the Empire.

The Christian in the local situation is called upon to be a good citizen and to support both Empire and church in reaching and overcoming the pagan outside the Empire.

This new relationship between church and Empire changed the structures and form of mission immeasurably. The commitment of the ordinary person to the Lord undergirded the structures of society that strengthened and enlarged the Empire. Several dimensions of that change are important:

1) The unity of sacred and secular

Within the Empire there could be no distinction between sacred and secular. Bishops were leaders in things we might call secular (raising and deploying armies and playing major political roles, largely as stabilizing forces); kings and princes were leaders in things we might call religious (calling religious convocations and influencing their theological outcomes, just as the Emperor Constantine did at the Council of Nicea in 325).

2) Mission as a far off enterprise

Because the mission field by definition was outside the empire, mission became a task of foreign policy. Therefore, the initiative for enlarging church and Empire became the task of princes and armies, of missionary orders and missionary heroes and heroines. Mission was no longer the direct responsibility of the ordinary person. The world hostile to the Gospel was the pagan world way over there, beyond the boundary of the Empire. The Empire had the responsibility for reaching out to the pagan world, to incorporate it into Christendom by conquest. The Empire also had a responsibility to protect the church from the "infidel" who would subjugate the church to the service of a false god. Imperialism and mission, in this paradigm, were inseparable. Because we in the twentieth century have come to see the former as one of the Bad Things of history, we have a hard time recognizing that the connection between imperialism and mission was inevitable. In its origins, it was driven by profound commitment to be faithful to God's command. Imperialism, bad as we now see much of it to have been, was seen as identical with the mission of the church. "Onward Christian Soldiers," the marching song of nineteenth century imperialism, expressed the sentiment perfectly. If it embarrasses us today, it is because the Christendom Paradigm no longer works for us.

3) Congregation as parish

Under the Christendom Paradigm, the local incarnation of church stopped being a tight community of convinced, committed, embattled believers supporting each other within a hostile environment. Instead, it became a parish, comprising a geographic region and all the people in it. Everyone within the geographic bounds of the parish became *ipso facto* members of parish and church. No place in the local arena was seen as "outside" the church. All institutions (e.g., labor guilds, schools, merchant groups) understood themselves as manifestations of a unified existence—at once religious and secular. The parish pastor became a community chaplain, a civil servant, and local holy person.

4) The drive for unity

The vastness of the Empire/church demanded a kind of administration and cohesiveness that the church, at least, had not needed under the Apostolic

Paradigm. For the whole thing to be managed it had to be unified. To assure unity in administration, theology, and politics, discord had to be minimized and standard structures developed. There was no space for differences. Ironically, it was this part of the paradigm that eventually began to pull apart, beginning in the break of the East from the West in 1053, gradually taking shape in the era of nationalisms and the national churches of the Reformation, and culminating finally in the denominational cacophony of American religious life.[1]

In Christendom there could be only one church within one political entity. To be outside that unity was unthinkable, impossible. To be outside the faith was to be *outside* the law and the community. Heresy and treason were two sides of the same thing. In such a paradigm people who were disloyal to the faith or the nation could be tortured, oppressed, or killed precisely because they were profoundly "other"; to be fully a human being was to be a Christian and a member of the Empire. To be outside either was to be outside the law—an "outlaw."

5) The religious role of the laity

The ordinary person did not join the church as a matter of will, but as a matter of birth; to be born into the parish was by definition to become a part of community and church. Baptism recognized what was already a reality. The life of the entire community was understood as the medium for nurturing the individual in the faith; community pageants and festivals told the story of the faith; the educational system was also the religious system; the legal system defined and enforced the moral code of the faith.

6) The calling of the lay person

The ordinary person had a responsibility as a Christian to do some well-defined things: to be a good, law-abiding citizen; to pay the taxes that supported religious and secular institutions alike; to support the efforts to enlarge the Empire and bring in the pagan world; to be obedient to one's superiors (disobedience was both seditious and heretical); and to support the whole system with one's prayers and, if necessary, one's life.

In spite of the flaws we see in it now, the Christendom Paradigm had inner consistency. It made sense of life, though at the cost of oversimplifying it. But for the Christian, it cut the nerve of personal involvement and responsibility for witness and mission. That personal engagement was re-placed with a sense of vicarious participation in a far-off mission carried out by heroes of the faith and armies of the nation-empire. It was difficult to see the ordinary folk of the village as a communion of the saints. Instead, the village became a support system for the saints of the mission, an outpost that sent CARE packages to the *real* mission.

A major difficulty of the Christendom Paradigm was its assumption that there was *one* answer, *one* way. Unfortunately, although the paradigm demanded uniformity, no lasting way was found to achieve it. For centuries ecumenical councils struggled to define the one statement that all could accept about various important matters of faith. But the one way was per-petually defeated by differences of opinion and conviction, and no way was found to enforce uniformity.

Loyalty and obedience were the primary virtues. But what to do about disloyalty and disobedience? The organizational implication of Christendom was a necessarily infallible hierarchy (where there is unity there can be no discord and therefore no error) with sacred and secular power united in one institution. That dream remains alive today for some in the religious world, and it undergirds the power of that religious-secular state, the Vatican.

Peculiarly enough, when the unity of life in Empire and church began to come apart, the Christendom Paradigm did not die. Instead, it continued to shape each of the fragments into which the world and the church broke. In Europe, today, for example, the Christendom Paradigm persists in each state (or provincial) church. The Church of England acted as if the English state and the English church were one, the parish system remained, the Christendom Paradigm was perpetuated as an English myth in the English colonies.

Within what eventually became the United States, the shattered Christendom Paradigm produced denominational shards, each of which perpetuated something of the paradigm within its own boundaries. There was a make-believe quality in each shard's assumption that its world was a microcosm of the whole world of which it was the remnant, as if nothing else exists.

We will discus other dimensions of the breakup of the paradigm later. For now I want to highlight the basic outline of the Christendom Paradigm and the strange way it fragmented at the end, with each fragment trying to continue to believe that it itself embodied the totality of the paradigm *(See Figure 3.)*

To describe the paradigm is to recognize that it never did reflect reality, nor does it seem very real to us today. It bespeaks a medieval world view with which we have many problems.

The paradigm's importance for us lies in the fact that most of the generation that now leads our churches grew up with it as a way of thinking about church and society. And all the structures and institutions that make up the churches and the infrastructure of religious life, from missionary societies to seminaries, from congregational life to denominational books of order and canons, are built on the presuppositions of the Christendom Paradigm—not the ancient, classical version of the paradigm as it was understood centuries ago, but the version that flourished with new life in the nineteenth and early twentieth centuries. This paradigm in its later years flourished and shaped us with new vigor, just as a dying pine is supposed to produce seed more vigorously as it senses the approach of its own death.

We are surrounded by the relics of the Christendom Paradigm, a paradigm that has largely ceased to work. But the relics hold us hostage to the past and make it difficult to create a new paradigm that can be as compelling for the next age as the Christendom Paradigm has been for the past age.

The final generations of the Christendom Paradigm have changed its six distinctive characteristics significantly, and all in today's churches have been deeply influenced by these changes.

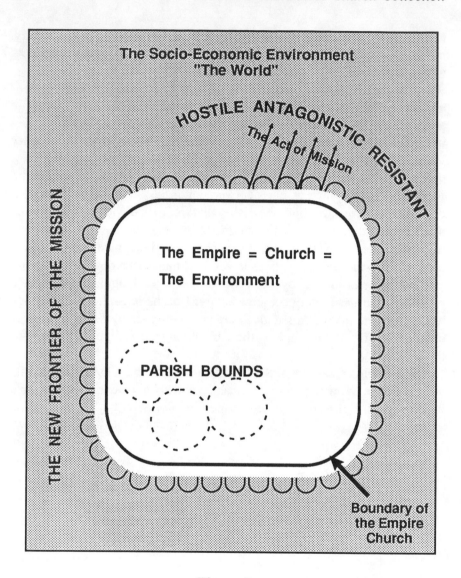

Figure 3

1) The unity of sacred and secular

Although our Constitution mandates a severe separation of church and state, in fact our nation has lived its own version of the Christendom Paradigm. An informal but fully operational religious establishment has held sway from the beginning—a creature of custom, never of law. National leaders have always been semi-religious figures. In the colonial years we experienced a confederated establishment of Congregational/Presbyterian/Episcopal leadership. The political and social pressure to live out the Christendom Paradigm led to a kind of cultural religion that pledges quasi-religious allegiance to flag and country. Religious people and institutions experience much grief when they challenge this part of the Christendom Paradigm by criticizing government policy. Such rebelliousness violates the sense of what is right and proper for those who grew up under the Christendom Paradigm. Thus, the emergence of the "Moral Majority" among conservative Christians in the 1970s and 1980s represented an attempt not to replace the Christendom Paradigm, but to substitute a conservative religious Christendom for a liberal one.

2) Mission as a far off enterprise

Mission to those far-off in pagan lands became an immensely powerful motivating and organizing factor for the churches in the nineteenth and twentieth centuries. Denominations organized themselves as missionary societies and their budgets were subscribed and oversubscribed because the people of the churches understood the priority of the missionary frontier. The clarity of the mission drove the pledging of the people. Local and regional groups organized to support that far-off mission. Education in churches was missionary education primarily, not theological education (education in matters of the faith and of the Scriptures was the function of the public school in reality, even though this contradicted the law). National bureaucracies and national buildings were structured to educate for mission and to administer mission-far away, primarily. The churches' concern for those in far-off lands continued to be connected with the nation's own sense of mission, i.e., the obligation to spread democracy (in a new manifestation of Empire) around the world. Imperialism and mission, born of the same paradigm, could not easily be separated.

3) Congregations as parish [2]

Local churches–particularly "mainline" ones–saw themselves as having territory or turf. Pastors felt themselves to be chaplains to an area, having a care for all the people, but a special care for those who "belonged" to the congregations. They tended to feel an obligation to "do" the children brought to them for baptism and the young couples brought to be married, without much thought to the religious preparation required. Those presenting themselves for membership were considered to have been converted already: membership classes were primarily orientation to a denomination's tradition. The ministry was carried out and controlled by the clergy. Because many denominations saw trained theological leadership as critical to the strength of its parishes, seminaries were invented and developed as special ways of building a professional cadre who could lead the churches. Indeed, the first institutions of higher education founded on these shores were begun primarily to meet the need for trained clergy.

4) The drive for unity

Each religious body or national church had a great sense of the oneness of the church and its mission, as if there were no others. Liturgies and theologies varied, yet people yearned for the certainties, the uniformity the Christendom Paradigm represented. The sense of difference disturbed many in church and state. For some, the differences led to feuds or strong competition for converts. In time the breakup of the unity began to lead some to attempts to rebuild an ecumenical entity and others to a firm loyalty to their own part of the truth. The overwhelming reality, however, was diversity and difference, not unity and coherence. The ecumenical bodies dedicated to unity never were as strong as the diverse alternatives. Indeed, the councils of churches have grown older, and they have grown weaker.

5) The religious place of the laity

Lay persons in the late period of the Christendom Paradigm continued to be seen as the loyal citizens of the realm, expected to be obedient to the powers, to pay their dues to church and state, and not to bother their heads too much about theological matters. They were expected to have a strong faith and a sense of commitment that they caught from the social institutions–the schools, the social groups, the community festivals. Those presenting themselves for membership were taught to be good citizens and loyal to their denominations. The lay person was not expected to have much to say or do about mission, except to support it vigorously with prayer, with generous giving, and by encouraging the young to go into "full-time Christian service" (meaning as an employee of the denomination, preferably overseas).

6) The calling of the laity

The ministry of the lay person was identical with being a good, law-abiding, tax-paying, patriotic citizen. One was to work hard and be obedient to the structures, institutions, and leaders of the community. One's sacred duty was to preserve the way things were and to avoid personal immorality, disloyalty, or disobedience to constituted authority. The Episcopal Prayer Book described the responsibility in these words: "to keep one's hands from picking and stealing." One's place in life was understood to be ordained by God, and one did not seek to change it lightly.

THE TIME BETWEEN PARADIGMS

Nurtured in this fractionating Christendom paradigm and living within institutions shaped by it, we have begun to awaken to the early stages of a new one. Neither the new age nor the new paradigm has arrived, so we are pulled by the new and constrained by the old without the privilege even of knowing fully what the new will be like. But as the new has begun to reveal itself, it has made us profoundly uncomfortable.

In Thornton Wilder's classic *Our Town*, the young wife Emily dies in childbirth. Given the right to return to some special day of her life, she goes back to a birthday she remembers as a child. When she returns she sees her familiar loved ones going about their ordinary routines, but they cannot see her nor do they see the terrible beauty visible to her from beyond the grave. She flees, glad to return where the pain is at least bearable.

Wilder has given us a portrayal of what it is like to have awakened into a new paradigm and how hard it is to communicate with those still living in the old one. Emily could not stand the pain. Many younger Christians today may be suffering a similar painful dichotomy—being born into a new paradigm and unable to communicate with those of us who inhabit the old, they may be running away from the pain.

Our situation may be even more desperate than Emily's. More and more we have lost our home in the familiar paradigm of Christendom, but we have no clarity about how to find a new home in the turbulence of the emerging world. The fault lines run through our own hearts.

William Willimon and Stanley Hauerwas describe their own experience of living in the earlier paradigm this way:

> You see, our parents had never worried about whether we would grow up Christian. The church was the only show in town. On Sundays, the town closed down. One could not even buy a gallon of gas. There was a traffic jam on Sunday mornings at 9:45, when all went to their respective Sunday schools. By overlooking much that was wrong in that world—it was a racially segregated world, remember—people saw a world that looked good and right...Church, home, and state formed a national consortium that worked together to instill "Christian values." People grew up Christian simply by being lucky enough to be born in places like Greenville, South Carolina or Pleasant Grove, Texas. [3]

Then, humorously, they describe the day the paradigm began to die for them:

> When and how did we change? Although it may sound trivial, one of us is tempted to date the shift sometime on a Sunday evening in 1963. Then, in Greenville, South Carolina, in defiance of the state's time-honored blue laws, the Fox Theater opened on Sunday. Seven of us—regular attenders of the Methodist Youth Fellowship at Buncombe Street Church—made a pact to enter the front door of the church, be seen, then quietly slip out of the back door and join John Wayne at the Fox.
>
> That evening has come to represent a watershed in the history of Christendom, South Carolina style. On that night, Greenville, South Carolina—the last pocket of resistance to secularity in the Western world—served notice that it would no longer be a prop for the church...The Fox Theater went head to head with the church over who would provide the world view for the young. That night in 1963, the Fox Theater won the opening skirmish. [4]

The Christendom Paradigm probably began losing its power centuries ago. Willimon and Hauerwas describe the change in 1963—when, as they put it, "the Fox Theater opened on Sunday...in defiance of the state's time-honored blue laws." Each inhabitant of a waning Christendom probably remembers a similar moment when the old way was irrevocably challenged and broken. But the break actually became unavoidable with the invention of an idea and a phrase—"ministry of the laity," which represents a change of consciousness. It recognizes the death of the old way, in which the laity had no direct call to ministry. Every time that phrase "ministry of the laity" is used, at that moment it is a little like the opening of the Fox Theater on a Sunday evening in Greenville, South Carolina.

"Ministry of the laity" is a cliché today, so routine that it's almost boring. Nobody questions it. Everybody understands that it is a Good Thing. It is also true that very few people seem to have much grasp of it and very little is consciously done about it in the denominations—other than talk about how important and good it is. For these and other reasons, it is hard today to recognize the revolutionary meaning in the phrase. Under the Christendom Paradigm no one would have thought to talk about ministry of the laity. People did talk about "the priesthood of all believers" as a theological concept, but except for some experiments of the Reformation (and even there, Milton noted that "new presbyter is but old priest writ large"), no one seemed to take seriously that the ordinary Christian person was called on to be anything other than simply a law-abiding citizen.

In spite of its familiarity to us, the ministry of the laity is very new in the church. I have found no use of the phrase prior to the late 1930s. The first great book about it in English was Hendrik Kraemer's *Theology of the Laity* in 1958 (Yves Congar's *Jalons pour une Theologie du Laicat [Staking Out a Theology of the Laity]* had appeared five years earlier). The 1930s, 1953, 1958 were only yesterday in the life of an institution that measures change in generations and centuries. It is a brand new idea still—an idea yet to have its full impact on us.

It is hard for us who are so used to it to grasp its radical character. The phrase itself breaks new ground. The first revolutionary thing the phrase says is that "a lay person" is not the same as "a citizen." That is brand new. If laity have ministry, then a Christian who is a doctor or teacher or laborer has something special that they are called to do or say or—that word again—witness to in their world. Someone who has a ministry has a citizenship with God that may conflict with citizenship in a particular political state.

There it is. If there is a ministry of the laity, then the church is no longer the same as the Empire. Somehow the world, the nation, the environment is no longer the same as the church. The former understanding no longer holds true. In some new way we are conscious of the world as separate from, different from the church.

The change in language is simple, but its implications are vast. First, we can no longer assume that everybody is a Christian. Everybody has not been Christian for a long, long time, but our Christendom assumption has not changed. We ask Christian clergy to preach baccalaureate sermons, for example, ignoring the fact that many in the graduation class are not Christians. We now have to deal with the fact that in any geographic area the majority of people may have no interest in church whatever. Congregation has forever separated from parish.

Second, people no longer assume that the community is a unit of the religious world, living out values derived from the Gospel. A new assumption has appeared, that something needs to be done to make a community "right" or "better." Further, it is assumed that the Christian who lives in a community has some responsibility for doing something about it.

Third, we are returning to one of the features of the Apostolic Age. We now assume that the front door of the church is a door into mission territory, not just a door to the outside. Everybody who goes through that door is personally crossing a missionary frontier and is involved in mission. This hearkening back to the Apostolic Age has an important qualifier, however, as we shall see.

Every one of those assumptions violates the mind-set of the Christendom Paradigm. Indeed, under the impact of such new assumptions the Christendom Paradigm is coming apart at the seams. All the institutions and patterns of life that grew up during Christendom are having their foundations shaken.

The crisis for congregations, Christians, and those who care about the Gospel is that the outlines of the new paradigm are not yet clear. Tested landmarks have disappeared, but we still lack enough clarity to know what new landmarks we need, much less how to find or fashion them. Indeed, it may be that the new paradigm may never become as compelling as either the Apostolic or the Christendom versions. The new paradigm may call for more diversity than we are used to or comfortable with.

Let us illustrate what we do see about the emerging paradigm:

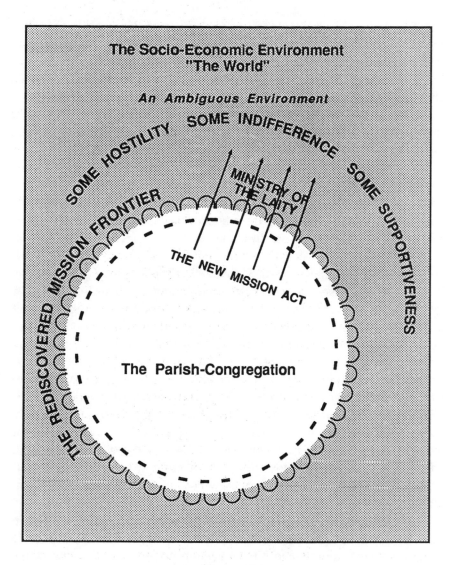

Figure 4

Note in Figure 4 the reappearance of the missionary frontier close-in to the congregation. The difference between this and Figure 1 is important, although here we note that the environment is "ambiguous."

How we read the environment, as we have seen above, says a lot about how the church sees itself and its mission. In Figure 2, the environment was hostile, leading the church to form tight congregations of people with high commitment. In Figure 3, the church sees itself as identified with the environment. Its perimeters are geographic, not boundaries of intent and commitment. In Figure 4, the environment beyond the boundary is "ambiguous." It is not always hostile, although sometimes it is. It is not identical with the church, although sometimes it still is. Much that is in the environment is somewhere in between; the school systems, for example, attempt to teach truth and justice, but are disconnected from their roots in the biblical witness.

The outside boundary of the congregation is porous and permeable, as in the time of Christendom. People move in and out with little sense of responsibility for mission and little knowledge of what the congregation is all about. The culture that used to pretend to teach faith no longer does so, but the congregation has not discovered patterns and disciplines for nurturing either its people or newcomers to the faith.

A very uncertain congregation, then, looks across an unfamiliar missionary frontier to an environment that appears less and less friendly and wonders. It often discovers that ambiguities from the environment have migrated into the congregation itself. It wonders how to constitute itself for the new mission that the new world calls for. It wonders what good news it has, how to deliver it, and to whom. It wonders how to differentiate itself from its environment. It does not know how to deal with environmental ambiguity in its own life and values.

At the same time, some members of the congregation see the shift in ages and paradigms and struggle to discover a better way. Right beside those persons in almost every congregation are some still living in the Christendom Paradigm, unaware of the changed age and unwilling to let go of the familiar past.

SUMMARY

The church has always worked out its self-understanding and ordered its internal life in dialogue with the world that surrounded it. Its sense of mission has provided the energy for its life, shaping the roles and relationships in its institutions. Where a sense of mission has been clear and compelling, the church has been sacrificial and heroic in its support of that mission.

Within the Apostolic Paradigm, the church formed itself in strong local entities or congregations and nurtured its people to reach out to a hostile environment to witness to the good news of the biblical story and of Jesus. There was diversity and pluriformity in the roles and relationships as shaped by local conditions, reinforced by a real effort to maintain effective linkages to congregations in other places.

The second great way of being church–the Christendom Paradigm–was born, flourished, and began its decline during the last millennium and a half. Here the identity of church shifted in response to a new understanding of how it should relate to its environment. Because the Empire was by definition identical with the church, and because the world outside the Empire was seen as a pagan environment, mission moved far away. Because the missionary frontier became the same as the Empire's frontier, to be a citizen was to be a churchman. The local congregation, previously characterized by high commitment and training in the faith, now became a geographic region within which institutions of society and government were assumed to support the faith and religious institutions were enlisted in the aims of society and government. In the end, mission became the responsibility of the professionals.

The third way of being church has begun be born, but its birth is not complete. Once again the church and the individual person of faith are beginning to discover a sense of a new mission frontier. But that frontier has not yet become clear or compelling enough; we see the horizon, but the path we must follow remains obscure. Worse, the church's energy for mission today is conflicted and at war with itself.

It is also true that the forms and structures, the roles and relationships of the churches we have inherited were formed by paradigms that no longer work for us. We live in the memory of great ways of understanding how to be church and to be in mission. Those memories surround us like ruins of an ancient civilization. Our educational institutions and our structures of leadership and service are likewise conflicted and at war with themselves.

How do we build religious institutions within which we can live out our calling to serve the world? How do we form ourselves for mission to the emerging age?

These may be our questions for the next age.

NOTES

1. Members of the historic "free" churches had experiences that distanced them from the full impact of the Christendom Paradigm. My appendix chapter describes the different dynamics of that paradigm. But *even* in those churches the Christendom Paradigm had powerful influence, particularly in their second and third generations.

2. Again, I refer to the somewhat different experience of the Free Church tradition as noted in the Appendix.

3. Stanley Hauerwas and William H. Willimon, *Resident Aliens* (Nashville: Abingdon, 1990, p. 16).

4. Ibid., pp. 15-16.

CHAPTER 3

Cracks in the System

Systems that seem stable and secure often have internal tensions and pressures that lead to dramatic, surprising changes. Most western Europeans and others were aware of what seemed to be monolithic, powerful governments in the communist East during 1988 and 1989. When the Berlin Wall came down, incredulous Westerners could hardly accept the evidence of the eyes.

In the aftershock, wise people have been able to point out the signs of change that were there earlier, but most of us did not see them. In fact, the walls and governments of the East seem now to have been a fragile façade. The people of the East had long ceased to believe in them and honor them. The stability and security of the structures were fictional. As I note in Chapter V, this particular illustration may say a lot about the changes in our denominational systems.

Cicadas know something about that. They grasp tree bark as they feel growth and change within themselves, then burst out of the old, unchanged carapace, leaving it hanging lifeless on the tree. They fly away. Geologists tell us that deep below the surface of the earth are immense tectonic plates upon which the continents ride, shifting slowly but with immense force across the globe. Fault lines mark the boundaries where these plates touch. As the continents shift, enormous tension and energy build up until with the lurch of an earthquake the tension is relieved for the time being. There isn't much you can *do* about a fault line, but if you know it's there and you cannot stand anxiety, you can choose to move somewhere else. Or you can learn to construct buildings to take into account the special conditions of unstable ground.

Changes as radical as those the church is experiencing as the age of Christendom disintegrates cause severe dislocations in some parts of the religious world, even while there may be no sense of movement or even tension elsewhere. For some there is the chaos of daily earthquakes; for others there is a sense that nothing much has changed and the earth does not move.

Changes of paradigm are, by definition, matters of perception, feeling, world view, consciousness; they are not external changes like the leveling of a mountain. As a result, one of the most difficult realities we deal with is the fact that two people, living side by side, may face the same phenomenon, yet their perceptions may differ radically. Even worse, one individual may see part of reality through the Christendom Paradigm and the rest of life in quite a different way. She or he may not even feel the fault line running through such behavior.

Al, a Presbyterian pastor, told me of a frustrating conflict he had with an elder when he tried to promote an antiwar initiative in his congregation when our national leaders were proposing confrontation with Iraq in the Persian Gulf. The elder was angry. She fought Al tooth and nail. "But the funny thing was," Al told me, "I couldn't get her to talk about 'war' and 'peace'; she simply was convinced that it was disloyal and wrong to question government policy." Al said, "She didn't blow up and quit the church until I said, 'The government's policy is immoral, and the church has got to stand up against it.'"

When I asked what the elder said in response, Al told me, "I am disappointed that my pastor would be disloyal to my country. I was brought up to believe in God and country and will not go along with what you are saying." Al reduced the problem to a political disagreement, but I saw an elder holding up the values of another paradigm—that the Empire and the church are one. Al had so much at stake in the political issue that he did not hear where his elder was coming from.

In that anecdote two ages were talking past each other. The elder saw the governing order as ordained by God, and that it was the task of the Christian to support the government at the same time that one worked to improve it. She couldn't conceive of the church as opposed to the Empire. She *could*, however, probably see the need to vote for another administration. But *oppose* the government? Heresy! Treason! Both.

Al, on the other hand, spoke out of the emerging paradigm or age in which one must make careful discriminations between those initiatives of government that serve the Gospel and those that are opposed to the Gospel. Al, as a matter of fact, was pretty extreme himself. *He* couldn't consider or even conceive of how the Empire sometimes can and does serve the Gospel.

I felt both were missing the boat and *needed* to be able to hear and affect each other's thinking. Neither the elder nor Al was willing to go beyond pre-set positions. Both were stuck in their own paradigms, unable to see or hear the other.

When paradigms shift, our battles get as confusing as the one between Al and his elder. Antagonists can argue past each other, fight each other because they do not realize that they are standing in different paradigms. That is why going to a regional denominational meeting can be a modern equivalent of visiting the Tower of Babel.

What I hear is people—clergy and laity—talking the same language, using the same words, but totally misunderstanding each other. Indeed, the speakers do not even speak consistently from the same worldview. The understanding of each has been shaped, more or less, by the worldview of Christendom. That worldview also shapes how they understand their roles and the church's role in society.

At the same time, each has been affected by the new age's consciousness of ministry and mission. Each is pulled in both directions. Miscommunication is to be expected!

It is therefore important to pay attention to the places where dislocations are occurring, where the tectonic plates are shifting between the two ages.

Most dislocations are occurring around the fault lines, and it is there that clear communication is most difficult. When pain and discomfort develop and when they lead to conflict, people living in different paradigms perceive the trouble differently and see different implications about what to do.

Today, there are four arenas of real dislocation in the way religious systems are operating: the role of the clergy, the role of the laity, that of the bishop or executive, and that of the congregation.

THE ROLE OF THE CLERGY

In the Christendom Paradigm, the role of the clergy was clear. It was strong, central, and unquestioned. It was a high-status role, carrying authority. Clergy were *the ministry*.

Clergy were chaplains and guarantors of community life, with power far beyond the walls of the church. As a thirty-year-old Episcopal priest walking the street of a village in southern England, I often had mayor and street-sweeper alike defer to me as "Rector." Their deference was not to me, but to the power the pastor carried in Christendom. For many people in churches today, that remains a very attractive idea. For many people the problem would be solved if we could return to that strong, hierarchical model, when Herr Pastor was Herr Pastor and the rector was truly the "ruler" (which is what the world meant in Latin.)

The network of clergy, operating within their strong, clear role at the center of the church's institutional life, built a formidable power system, designed to provide strong and consistent leadership of the institution for its mission. But the power the clergy gained was well-nigh impregnable. Aidan Kavanaugh, the Roman Catholic liturgical scholar, speaks of that power as "the hegemony of the presbyterate." That coalition of power in clergy hands was a fact in denominations regardless of their polities. The Free Churches fought against it more than those who had roots in the establishments, with Brethren and Quakers more consistently successful.

The fossils of that hegemony from the Christendom Paradigm make up much of the power system that rules religious institutions today, making change very difficult to effect. Its name is clericalism.

Clericalism—like sin—is carrying a good thing too far. The clear role and authority given to the ordained leader really did and often still does facilitate the mission of the church. But the development of the clergy into a special class with special privilege and considerable power to govern a large institution is what Kavanaugh's phrase points to. Regardless of the polity of the denomination, it is my impression that clergy have, effectively, a veto on every important issue. If they genuinely believe a course of action is wrong, it will not happen.

But the hegemony of the presbyterate, the all-powerful authority of the clergy as a class, is breaking down. Most church members, even clergy, welcome that fact, but they find the resulting arrangements to be confusing and chaotic. Hegemony was authoritarian and clericalist, but it was predictable. It is sometimes hard to know "who's on first" now that hegemony is disappearing. It is also surprising how the power of clericalism continues to influence and rule even as the paradigm changes. It is far from dead!

Along this fault line individual clergy have much less clarity about who they are and what their roles are. The reappearance of the frontier of mission on the church's doorstep has shifted mission responsibility more and more onto the shoulders of the laity, bringing their role to new prominence and power. Most clergy agree that that is right and good. At the same time, this shift has undercut the previously accepted role of the clergy. Consequently many clergy are double-minded: they give lip service to the ministry of the laity in the pulpit on Sunday, but jealously guard their prerogatives throughout the week and especially in denominational planning groups.

Many clergy are searching for roles that are clearer and less ambiguous. Some see themselves as social activists or spiritual directors, "enablers" or community organizers, educators or counselors. In some cases these new role descriptions are added onto the more traditional roles of preacher, pastor, and administrator. Without clear grounding, however, some clergy find themselves flipping back and forth, chasing roles as if they were fads. One man, whom I first knew in the 1950s, was then a pastor-educator. Next I heard, he was a pastor-counselor. Then followed in rapid succession human relations trainer, community organizer, consultant, renewalist, and most recently a spiritual director. I'm eager to see what comes next.

This loss of role clarity lies behind much of the stress and burnout among clergy. Most clergy come to their vocations from a deep faith and commitment. Trained in institutions that were generated by the mind-set of Christendom and ordained into denominations and congregations predominately shaped by Christendom, they discover that the rules have been changed in the middle of the game. Instead of being front-line leaders and spokespersons for mission, they now feel they are being asked to take a back seat to a newly awakened laity. The role they sought out and trained themselves for no longer fits what they have to do. Many are unsure how to give leadership in the new time.

The loss of power and role clarity sometimes causes depression, anger, and grief among clergy, making them more likely to seek scapegoats in "the seminaries," "the bishop," "lay people," or "the national church." Many clergy I know are bitter and angry at how the church has misused them, as they see it.

There is another important side to this. The clergy, as manager-leaders of the *institution*, badly need laity to help lead and support the institution (raise money, lead program, etc.). Clergy I know are already torn because they know institutional needs interfere with the genuine call of laity to be primarily engaged in family, job, and community. The result? Many clergy are painfully ambivalent—even schizophrenic—about what they want the laity to be and do. If they really succeed in getting laity invested in the mission frontier, it will disrupt the operation of the parish.

THE ROLE OF THE LAITY

The overwhelming majority of lay people in congregations 30 years ago understood what was expected of them. One of my senior wardens put it to me this way about 35 years ago: "My job is to back you up. Make sure the parish budget is raised and balanced. Make sure we're doing our part for the diocese and the mission program. Beyond that—my job is to keep my nose clean, pay my taxes, do my job, not run around, keep the booze under control, and support the governor and the president, especially if he's a Democrat!" Simple. Clear. Many lay people continue to understand their own ministry that way—most of the time.

But today the lay church member receives another set of messages, not all of which are consistent. These become points of stress and change as the paradigm shifts:

a. The lay Christian is told to support the parish with tithes of time, talent, and treasure. She or he is asked about this regularly and recruited to do things in organizations of the congregation, which, even in a small congregation, are many. The system makes a lot of noises that suggest the faithful member ought to be doing more than is usually the case.

b. The rhetoric from the pulpit urges engagement with the world and defines one's "real" ministry as job, community life, family, etc., all of which take place *outside* the church. Yet the bulletin, the parish organization, the pastor, and staff urge and reward engagement with parish *activities*. Ministry outside the church is rarely recognized and never rewarded. Ministry inside is recognized and rewarded. The pastoral calling that is done is generally done in homes, not in the workplace. Assignments to responsibilities in the congregation are generally made according to the congregation's organizational needs, not the expertise of the lay person. What is *said* at church undergirds the new paradigm. What is *done* tends to reflect assumptions left over from the Christendom Paradigm.

c. The lay person is often urged by the pastor to take positions on a series of complex, emotional issues (abortion, the civil rights of gays and lesbians, premarital sex, divorce, South Africa, war and peace). Generally the pastor advocates one position as "the" Christian position and provides educational opportunities supportive of that position. The lay member can be deeply distressed if she or he disagrees. Often there is no honorable space for disagreement. Passions and resentments may run deep.

d. The lay person hears of actions of the national or regional church on controversial issues. Sometimes he or she finds it hard to understand why the church is so focused on those particular issues and seems to ignore the things one was "brought up" to think to be important. Why worry about economic justice and seem not to care about divorce or premarital sex? Why get involved with foreign affairs when our children don't know the Bible? It is right to care for hungry people, but what right has the church to talk about agricultural policy or employment training programs? The lay person who brings up questions like these is often put on the defensive by clergy who seem more intent on winning an argument than helping their members make connections. The denomination's educational materials may reflect a paradigm that is out of touch with the paradigm the member lives in.

e. Lay persons sometimes do not understand why cherished parts of their religious past—worship forms, hymns, congregational customs and practices—need to be changed. People have a sense that they have no power in the decisions about those changes. Indeed, they sometimes feel that their strong concerns about those cherished parts of the past are ridiculed and denigrated by clergy and denominational leaders.

f. Although some articulate lay leaders today call for laity to be the primary ministers of the church, neither clergy nor laity are clear what that means. As a matter of fact, most lay people are already doing what they assumed they were supposed to do—working hard in their jobs and trying to make their communities better. They are surprised and hurt to find that their leaders consider those expressions of faithfulness somehow wanting. Indeed, committed laity sometimes feel their efforts in ministry are disparaged by church leaders. They feel patronized by the ordained. Many such lay persons really do not know what else is expected of them. All too many laity, nurtured in the Christendom Paradigm, simply have backed away from the painful experiences that continually face them at church.

If the clergy in the emerging age feel a sense of schizophrenia in understanding and fulfilling their role, so do the laity.

THE ROLE OF BISHOP OR CHURCH EXECUTIVE

Just as the roles of clergy and laity have become more problematical, the bishops and other denominational executives who serve in the regional office of the denomination feel the changes even more. Although different denominations have different names for these roles (bishop, superintendent, executive, general minister, area minister, etc.) each bears responsibility for what St. Paul described as "the care of all the churches." They function as coordinators, supporters, judges, spiritual guides, leaders, managers, chief pastors, teachers, and administrators. Their offices are the first place local congregations and pastors go when something goes wrong. The very real differences in the authority these roles carry from one denomination to another should not blind us to the very large areas of similarity between how they actually function.

Until now, the revolution in ministry has affected primarily clergy and laity. Judicatory[1] leaders *so far* have been affected by the change of ministry age in two ways: (1) They have received increased calls to intervene when clergy-lay friction erupts into a bruising battle, which happens frequently in these times of confused and conflicting roles and (2) they must deal with almost annual reductions in resources in regional budgets. Congregations genuinely trying to respond to the missionary frontier on their doorsteps naturally see a more convincing case to fund their own mission endeavor rather than support the judicatory. Both of these pressure points—the increase in congregation tensions and the decrease in resources—are more likely to increase than to decrease.

Few executives and bishops are aware that the new paradigm is threatening to marginalize further the role they played in the past. They have such increasing demands on them amid continually decreasing resources that few of them can focus on more than the here and now. As the old story tells it, it is hard to drain the swamp when you are surrounded by alligators nipping at you.

Once upon a time in Christendom, these executives had central leadership roles in the mission of the churches. They motivated, coordinated, shepherded the churches, and focused energy on building up a church for the far-off mission tasks. Their functions and practices were shaped for that task. They were our mission leaders. The excitement and energy that led to building national structures for denominations was fueled by Christendom's clarity about a far-off mission. National and regional structures proved themselves by their ability to bring individuals and congregations to participate sacrificially in mission beyond their borders.

But when congregations rediscovered a primary missionary frontier at their own doorstep, the judicatories did not seem to be as necessary; indeed, sometimes they seemed to be impediments. Congregations felt no need to ask the bishop before setting up a soup kitchen. Sometimes, as a matter of fact, they forgot to tell their executive that they had begun such a mission effort. The judicatory was seen as irrelevant to these strictly local expressions of mission.

I recently ran into a remarkable Lutheran congregation made up mostly of retired folk. They had carved out a special niche of ministry—doing laundry for one of the city's homeless shelters. I am not sure how they got started, but the effort is a very large one for them, and they are justifiably proud. When their bishop's assistant most recently visited to preach, he spent most of his time drumming up support for the capital funds drive to provide a camp and conference center for the synod. It seemed to the church members that the judicatory was only interested in funds to run itself and did not understand why a congregation might find its local mission effort more impelling. The people got the impression that their synod was not particularly interested in what they were trying to do in mission.

Unless judicatory leaders are able to shed this image and rediscover a central role in mission leadership, it is unlikely that they will again be as influential as they were in past generations. Christendom once gave them a central role because they were central to mission. In the new paradigm, they have been unable as yet to clarify their role, ground that role in the new mission frontier, or communicate a convincing case for a role in mission.

In many places loyalty to tradition and traditional patterns is strong and continues to support the denominations' systems and their bishops and executives. In other places those leaders, noting the erosion of traditional support, have responded by developing and marketing imaginative, often constructive, mission programs that attract both support and commitment. Imaginative marketing and programming cannot for long, however, obscure the need for a basic redirection of effort. The mission the judicatory has been most successful at defining is not the one that engages the people at the congregation's doorstep. What is worse, the mission the judicatory promotes most energetically looks more and more to congregations like the same old institutional baggage dressed up with new language.

The funding shortfalls in judicatory after judicatory are the logical result of what I am describing, and they have been getting worse for three decades. Although imaginative marketing, vigorous capital fund campaigns, staff reductions, and re-organizations can paper over the problem temporarily, the real concern is only postponed. People of the church will support what they understand to be mission. What they see coming from their denominational offices does not look like mission to them any more.

No number of bishops and executives will convince them that it is a duck if it keeps on barking. The church's people *hear* quacking in other places and want help from the judicatory. They are not particularly interested in supporting systems that do not seem to help them very much with what they want to be working at—their mission.

I believe the church of the new age or paradigm is going to need strong effective leadership and skill from its judicatories. But judicatories designed for Christendom will not be sufficient for the new church.

I believe that the ministry role crisis, which has been so painful for clergy and confusing to laity over the past half-century, will, in the next generation, make the work of the denominational executive or bishop extraordinarily difficult. Some judicatory systems may not survive. Some national systems are already in serious trouble. A wise friend states the case more dramatically than I do: "It seems to me," he says "that what God is doing right now is dismantling the denominational systems as fast as possible."

Action for mission has always driven people in the churches, whether or not they have a clear (or even right) target for their mission concern. Most congregations now see little connection between what their judicatory or denomination proposes as mission and what they themselves identify as mission. Fewer and fewer will find it compelling to support staffs and budgets they feel to be only marginally in touch with mission.

Despite these serious shortcomings, an important case remains to be made for the importance of judicatories within denominations. Potentially, they can still provide a wider view of mission, offer important challenge and support, provide connections to resources, and make available technical assistance for launching new ventures. Even more important is their role in providing a stable back-up system, just "being there" to help the congregation when it hits a bad patch or gets overwhelmed by an opportunity.

On the whole, they are not now making a convincing case to most congregations. Their increasing impotence is a serious matter for the health of all congregations.

THE ROLE AND WORK OF THE CONGREGATION

All the uncertainties and changes of the emerging age of ministry come to a head in the life of the local congregation. Once a stable center and guarantor of community and family life, it witnessed to the deep values and commitments that made life coherent and whole. Today, the local church has become merely one institution alongside all the others, competing for time and energy and often less sure than the others about its basic reason for being.

Clergy and laity alike struggle with two realities in congregations today:

1) It is harder and harder to maintain the congregational structure and systems that have served so many generations so well. The institutional framework of congregations is not working efficiently in many places. The financial system undergirding congregations is overwhelmed by rising costs and hemmed in by uneconomic assumptions about professional leadership and organizational structure. Clergy and lay leaders have overwhelmingly difficult tasks.

2) It is becoming clearer that urgent needs are calling for *more* caring ministries. Every congregation is faced with increasing needs for ministry on its doorstep. The need for imaginative, caring ministries that reach out to the community is greater than ever. But both laity and clergy face the new challenge unclear about their roles and unclear about how to move ahead. In short, the need for strong congregations comes at the very time when congregations are most fragile and uncertain, and when their primary support system is threatened.

In this climate, many respond by trying harder and harder to do the old thing better. They try to turn the clock back to the familiar dream of the Christendom Paradigm, working to resurrect an antiquarian institution. I am reminded of a apocryphal church board whose embers all died in a church fire because they could not figure out the proper way to use *Robert's Rules of Order* to adjourn the meeting.

A variation on this theme is the response of the evangelical, more conservative denominations and like-minded wings within liberal denominations. These groups seem to be trying to rebuild a Christendom that is a "holy club" of personal and family religious enthusiasm in, but not engaged with, the church's social environment. It responds to the mission frontier of the individual, but not of the community. This response arises in spite of the pioneering history of these groups, who were the first to perceive the gap between the demands of the gospel and the policies of the state in areas such as slavery and child labor.

Historically, the more liberal among and within the denominations were the last to recognize the gap between church and Empire. Their establishment roots made it difficult for them to differentiate between the values of state and society on the one hand and those of the Gospel on the other. Yet, once convinced of the problem, as I believe they were through the upheavals of the civil rights movement and Vietnam, liberal religious leaders seem to focus on building a liberal political realm in which theologians called the tune, a new Christendom where liberal theologians call the shots of the Empire.

The conservatives' much noted "great reversal" at the turn of the century led them from engagement with the world toward a Christendom of personal religion. The liberal "great reversal" half a century later led their elites—but not their people—toward a Christendom that looks for all the world like a liberal Empire, a secular version of Calvin's Geneva.

Some in both the liberal and conservative camps respond to the tension of role confusion and anxiety by buying into society's utilitarian values. They design marketable churches and search for things that "work." Ten steps to this and twelve dynamics of that. I am embarrassed that many of the purveyors of this line call themselves consultants; I find some of them hard to distinguish from snake-oil salesmen flogging the latest miracle cure.

I speak harshly about these aberrations because I am attracted to something in every one of them. Yet none does justice to the radical demands of the new mission frontier; all are patchwork responses. I believe that the discomfort of the congregation is a call to something genuinely new.

Congregations—like clergy, laity, and executives—are living in a time in which landmarks have been erased and old ways have stopped working. We also live in a time when the answers have not yet become clear. It is a time that calls for steadiness and perseverance through uncertainty. Such a time generates energy for change, but it also generates intense anxiety that makes partial answers attractive, so long as they are quick.

The church—its laity, clergy, congregations, executives, and bishops—has organized and structured itself for one mission. We have awakened to a world in which the mission frontier has changed. The organization and the structures of church life, formed for that one mission, now need to be reoriented to face the new frontier.

The task ahead is the reinvention of the church.

NOTE

1. "Judicatory" is one of those awful invented words that no one has been able to get rid of or improve upon. I understand the Presbyterians inflicted it upon us, reflecting as it does their understanding of levels of the denominations as different "courts." I will use the word as infrequently as possible, primarily to denote the regional entity of a denomination that relates to local congregations. Technically the word is used for any entity of the denomination larger than the local congregation.

CHAPTER 4

The Reinvention of the Church

What does all this mean? It means that God who called the church out into the apostolic world two thousand years ago is again calling the church out, this time into a secularized world where its mission and its life must be once again redefined.

In the days of the formation of the Jesus movement, the forms of Mediterranean Hellenistic culture did not fit a people who had heard the radical Gospel of Jesus. The followers of the new way responded with close-knit community cells informally and loosely linked together. Centuries later those structures for that marginal religious movement proved inadequate for the official religion of a world empire. In that second calling out, the church was led to a structure of parishes within an imperial system.

For the most part, those forms have now stopped working. God is calling us out of them to systems that will support our life and mission for the coming age.

The dilemma of the church in this transitional time is that the shells of the old structures still surround us even though many of them no longer work. Some of the structures are institutions, some are roles, some are mind-sets and expectations. At one moment they mediate grace to us and at the next they block and confuse us. Sometimes some of them actually support and nourish us, while others get in the way of the new structures we need.

Our task is no less than the reinvention of the church. It may take several generations. We will not see the end of it, but we must begin now.

In this chapter, I want to talk about the reinvention as a process that will engage those of us who care about the church for the rest of our lives. In doing so, I will touch on three key polarities with which we will struggle and then identify some structural issues we will have to solve. I shall also note some resources for the task and some threats that lie ahead.

THREE POLARITIES

By definition, polarities are differences you live with but never resolve. Polarities are particularly galling to religious people who want a clearly defined "right" and "wrong." But in fact, the history of the church is the story of many polarities. The catholic spirit and the protestant principle. The push toward the charismatic and the struggle for ordered life. The tension between law and grace, faith and works. Flesh and spirit. The elect and the nations. If there is a lesson from this history, it is that one is always tempted toward one of the poles, but that none of them is complete by itself. Fanaticism seems to be, almost by definition, the establishment of one pole as absolute truth and the absolute rejection of the polar opposite. Some polarities come into play as we think of reinventing the church for the next generations.

Parish vs. Congregation

The words "parish" and "congregation" reflect important meanings with deep roots in the church's experience. While the former was the dominant form of Christendom and the latter of the Apostolic age, the concepts are larger than either of these.

Parish means turf. Place. It includes within it a sense of the responsibility of the church for the people of the neighborhood, regardless of their relationship to the faith. Parish includes the farms and businesses within the area. It spreads over environmental, social, and economic relationships as well as personal, family, and moral concerns. The word stands for the fact that the church cannot separate itself from its social context, from realms of politics and economic life. It is engaged indissolubly with the world. The idea of parish also assumes close linkage to other parishes in a network of relationship.

At its best, parish stands for the church's commitment to serve and strengthen the fabric of the community and society. Its patron saint is Jeremiah who, when his Empire was crashing about his shoulders, went out to buy a field, grounding himself (literally) by showing he belonged to the land.

At its worse, parish signifies a comfortable accommodation between religious life and political forces. Parish understands what it means to be "at ease in Zion," accepting the protection of the state's powers by muting the cry for justice.

At the other pole of meaning is the concept "congregation." As parish focuses on turf, congregation focuses on people—believing, committed people. Congregation refers to those who choose to engage with and accept a life within the framework of faith. Where parish implies first a relationship to society, congregation implies first a separation from it. Congregation speaks to the need for a deep, nurturing religious community based on commitment and mutual support. More easily than parish, congregation can stand alone without depending on linkage to other congregations.

At best, congregation nurtures an intensity of faith-commitment that can result in personal, moral, and spiritual growth at the same time it impels individuals to minister to social ills. At best, congregation is able to recognize the injustices of the political realm, often because of the consequences to specific persons. At worst, congregation turns ingrown, fostering religiosity and narrow personal moralism. It becomes unwilling to bear the burdens of those outside the congregation. It can ignore the responsibility to build a just social order.

Jesus called upon the church to be "in, but not of" the world. Both parish and congregation at their best approach that high calling. Parish, however, leans toward the sin of being exclusively "in" the world; congregation is similarly tempted to be "not of" the world. We need parishes and congregations that are able to draw energy from both poles.

In the church we have to reinvent, these two polar realities will remain in tension. During the time of the Christendom Paradigm the predominant form was parish, although the reality of congregation was reaffirmed by the Reformation and through the Free Church tradition (see the appendix). Parish is the heritage of the mainline denominations, even those who call themselves congregational—those who have been close to the establishment. Congregation is the gift and heritage of the Free Church traditions.

In the reinvention the pendulum will swing toward congregation. In fact, a swing has already begun. The external linkage system of every parish has eroded significantly. The sense of responsibility for turf has been stunted as the shortfall of resources has made parish focus all too often on members more than mission.

In the pendulum's swing, we must preserve the best of what parish means and also seek to avoid the worst of what congregation has meant.

It will not be enough to shore up what we have known as parish or as congregation. What is already at work is a difficult interpenetration of the two, an irresolvable tension of polarities, neither of which can be abandoned. What we need in the age to come is not parishes of civil religion or congregations of the righteous, but a new thing.

Servanthood vs. Conversion

A second polarity has to do with the church's understanding of what its mission is. This polarity is reflected in the two ways the church has described its work—conversion of the world or serving the world. Both terms are drawn directly from Jesus' ministry. He called his followers to go to the ends of the earth to convert, but he also sent his disciples to be servants even as he had been one who served them.

At no time has the church ordered its life exclusively to one or the other pole, although the predominant public model of both Apostolic and Christendom Paradigms was conversion. I note that as the public model, the one that drove the engines of the institution, although I suspect the predominant private model has always been servanthood. Literally millions of ordinary folk have acted out their faith in caring for their neighbors and for those in pain around them, often without even thinking of it as mission.

Conversion, at its best, leads to bringing the stranger into life-giving relationship to the Gospel and to a nurturing community. It has always been an imperative laid upon those who follow Jesus. More than an imperative requirement, it has been the natural response of the believer, reaching out to share the source of his or her own new life.

At its least attractive, conversion has led past generations to religious and military imperialism. In our day the imperialism has been more likely that of psychological coercion and manipulation, all too often masked as crusades or evangelistic campaigns. My skeptical friends call it "religious scalp-hunting."

Servanthood, the other pole of mission, reflects the way Jesus lived as a servant among others. Millions have followed his example, giving their lives for others. Teachers, doctors and nurses, agricultural specialists, and engineers have expressed this meaning of mission across the world as they have given skill and insight into improving life for others. Ordinary folk have done ordinary caring things for those around them because of Jesus. The fruits of this servanthood are impressive—school systems around the world, health and medical systems, the ability of tribes and peoples to communicate with one another through taught language, and a growing world-wide consensus about the value of the individual's well-being.

Servanthood's temptation is not, like conversion's, to coerce and manipulate, but to lose its depth and grounding. It can degenerate into mere activism and "do-good-ism" when it loses its intimate link to the story and example of Jesus. The worst of servanthood is seen in the mindless bureaucracies that institutionalize good intentions without preserving the call to serve. It can be found as easily in church programming and institutions as in the public sector.

The local religious community of the future will have to move beyond the simplistic either/or we experience today. Servanthood vs. conversion is not a choice to be made; it is a polarity that must be built into the structures we create for the church.

Exclusive or Inclusive

A third polarity relates to the church's image of itself. Is it to be exclusive or inclusive? Is it to uphold tight, demanding criteria for membership or open its arms as wide as possible to bring in the stranger and sojourner? Both poles reflect important parts of the Christian heritage.

There is strong precedent within the church for strict enforcement of clearly stated boundaries. At times the boundaries are primarily moral (acceptable moral behavior), at times they are creedal (right belief according to specific belief statements); at times they can be tribal (belonging to the right group). Where there is a strong consensus about those standards, it is possible to assure considerable conformity. But where the standards cease to represent compelling inner convictions, the exclusive community collapses. "Temperance," for example, served as a strong behavioral boundary for religious groups such as the Methodists for decades. When lay leaders came to accept the fact that even some Methodist pastors occasionally took a social drink, the moral boundary eroded. "Inerrancy" of Scripture still serves as a powerful boundary for many, but even some of them now wonder about the story of Jonah and the whale. The more they wonder, the less strong the boundary is. And the increasing stridency of those who support the boundary suggests increasing anxiety about it.

At its worst, exclusivity becomes rigid and legalistic, separating the righteous from the unrighteous according to manmade standards. (A friend has told me that one of the laws of religion is that "All people are divided into two groups—the righteous and the unrighteous; and the righteous usually do the dividing!")

But exclusivity is important because it speaks of something more important than these limited boundaries. Exclusivity states that there must be a place where a decision, a belief, or an action marks the difference between who is "in" and who is "out." Exclusivity demands that one who identifies with the Christian community stands for something, not for everything. At its best it engages and focuses energy and anchors community life.

Inclusivity goes in the other direction. It opens its arms wide to the diversity of the world, inviting the stranger into community without question. At its best it represents hospitality and prevenient grace—acceptance before it is asked for or earned. It points to the acceptance of the unacceptable.

At its worst it degrades the meaning of membership to a laissez faire "anything goes."

As churches seek forms for living in the coming age, the polarity of exclusivity and inclusivity will continue in tension. Because the structures of the parish tended to fall over backwards in the direction of inclusivity, local churches with an "establishment" heritage and orientation are likely to be working to discover how to fix boundaries that help members and nonmembers differentiate from one another.

These three polarities, then, are the fields of force within which the church must build new structures and processes of what it means to be the called-out people—the *ecclesia*. It is within the tension of these polarities that the church will be called on to address the formation of its laity, the new roles of the clergy, the function of oversight, and the locus of theology. It is to those issues that we turn now.

FOUR PRESSING ISSUES

The Formation of the Laity

During the time of the Christendom Paradigm, the formation of the laity was a matter of little concern. The entire social order was supposed to be so rooted and grounded in the Christian faith that ordinary community life produced a faithful people. There was no subcategory of education that was called "Christian" education—all education was that. When Sunday Schools were invented—almost exactly two centuries ago in Gloucester, England—they were invented for educating working class people, especially children, in how to read and write. They were probably more akin to today's Head Start than to what we call Sunday School. In no way were they thought of as providing specifically religious education. The gradual transformation of those institutions into programs for religious instruction indicates how the assumptions of the Christendom Paradigm were disappearing. All the signs pointing to more specifically religious education are signs that people were beginning to experience a gap; community life was not providing a religious environment.

As the Christendom Paradigm collapsed, a widespread need for better formation of the laity in the faith thus became increasingly clear. Wesley's genius invented the class meeting for adult training in discipleship. To this day, no better model of lay formation has been invented. The religious education movement of the late nineteenth and early twentieth centuries, probably the largest movement of laity in American churches, led to Sunday Schools in almost every congregation and to strong adult Bible study classes. Immediately after World War II, many denominations put great resources together for national Christian education programs that had wide impact.

A wealth of efforts and programs have been mounted in the half-century since World Ware II: the explosion of education programs that followed the Baby Boom children up through public school age, the attempts at house churches, the lay witness weekend movements and their cousins, Cursillo, Faith at Work, Serendipity, as well as the growth of formal retreats for laity. Even parish leadership weekends have become a standard, focusing partly on formation of lay leaders and partly on planning parish life.

But the future church will have to be even more intentional in formation of its laity. Living in the world's ambiguous environment and attempting to act faithfully there, every church member is on the front line, frequently alone. The canned information about the faith produced by denominational publishing houses will not fill the bill. Lay people in an uncertain environment will be called on for independent decision and action. Memorized answers will not be enough. Every local congregation will be called on to develop processes and programs to support laity on a life-long basis.

The systems of pastoral care and nurture built into the denominations are, for the most part, splendid expressions of Christendom. They provide a liturgical framework that nurtures people through the classic life-cycle events and crises: birth = baptism; puberty = confirmation; family = marriage; illness = laying on of hands; death = burial. In each case the believing community provides the human caring for those crises; the religious ministry is controlled and administered by the pastor. Although the denominations vary in how they name those crisis-repsonses, the processes are similar. The pastor acts as chaplain at the event, presiding over the transition from one state to another. The community, by definition, surrounds and supports the life of the one going through the life-change, grounding the whole of life in religious meaning.

Two things make this Christendom perspective more difficult in our time. On the one hand, life is now more complex, with many *more* key transition points than ever before. The worldview that our pastoral system reflects has no space for such profound personal changes as divorce and remarriage, yet a significant part of our congregations have experienced it. Today's lay person may make two, three, or more major professional changes during their life. The churches' response to these life-changing events is weak. Nor do we adequately respond to the mobility of our people. And today we are much more aware of the significant developmental crises of men and women moving through life. A pastoral care system that responds to this complexity, bringing the faith fresh to those many change points, is a real need. We do not have it yet. Formation of laity in the future church needs such a system.

On the other hand, the community of faith itself–the congregation–has lost some of its capacity to be a reliable ground for initiating, educating, and nurturing each person in faith.

Several issues in the formation of laity seem inescapable:

Catechumenates: Obviously the "new Christian" needs more intensive training than has been the habit of Christendom churches. We can no longer assume that the community has engaged people in any serious contact with the tradition. Near total ignorance of the biblical story and of the faith is more and more the norm. More and more new members of the church start at ground zero. Young people and adults now come to churches with absolutely no previous experience with any religious group or tradition. An acquaintance told me with astonishment of his own daughter–brought up in a "good" family, regular attender at church and Sunday School, university graduate and recipient of a Ph.D from a first-class university–who had never heard the story of Joseph and his coat of many colors! My acquaintance was astonished. I was not. The cultural environment of our younger generation is much more distant from even the stories and illustrations of the faith than previous generations. This same acquaintance noted, "When Martin Luther King said 'Let my people go,' almost everyone who heard him knew what he meant." "I wonder," he said, "if King could get away with it today?"

The traditional name for this initiatory training, coined to describe entry into an apostolic congregation, was catechumenate. At times such entry processes involved several years of preparation and study.

Churches are already responding to this need. The Rites for Christian Initiation of Adults (RCIA) in the Roman Catholic Church is such an attempt. Churches such as Episcopal and Lutheran who have long had some kind of confirmation preparation are beefing up their programs and reemphasizing them for adults. In some cases they are even calling them catachumenates. A remarkable program called "Education for Ministry" developed by Charles Winters and others at the University of the South has been designed as a basic course in theology available across the country, to be used in congregations anywhere.

Local congregations will need to discover the system that fits their own situation. But each needs to understand the strategic importance of training for entry into the faith. Congregations in the church of the future will have to have strong entry processes, assuming very little previous knowledge or experience of religion or Christianity. Such congregations will have to set aside the time and energy to put first class attention on this need, year after year after year.

Turning-Point Ministries: More important than the program for preparing the new member, each community of faith must rethink all of its ministries to take on the character of training for formation in ministry. Many of the members who were "cradle members" entered their churches—at whatever age they entered—pretty much as one entered Christendom. One got in by being born to a family in the congregation. Individual preparation received at the time might be adequate for one who is a back-bench supporter of mission, but it is unlikely to have been adequate for one charged with front line mission responsibility.

Life-crisis ministry for the future church will be seen as opportunities for formation of the laity. Each such moment will also be important for remedial education for those of us who come to it as Christians inadequately formed by earlier experience in the Christendom Paradigm. Each life-crisis will need to be seen as an opportunity for growing deeper in faith—not just getting through the crisis. Job-change, divorce, marriage, remarriage, retirement, going to work after retirement, breaking up from a relationship that was not a marriage, discovery that a friend or a friend's child has AIDS, going into a nursing home—each of these crises is a personal challenge. It is also an opportunity for the community of faith to help a person go deeper into faith and into a new stage of ministry. Pastoral care in an age such as we inhabit needs to be catechumenal care as well.

The adult and children's education programs of local churches need enhancement in two particulars. Because adults and children receive less of the Christian heritage from the social order, our ordinary educational programs need to concentrate on the basics and assume less. Secondly, these programs need to take very seriously a study of the social environment as a field of mission. For adults and children alike we need to develop "mission training" to help each person to cross the mission frontier more responsibly. Case studies, story-telling, and community analysis need to become staples of religious engagement for church members. I would love to see congregations develop programs of "field work" in mission—sending members out Monday through Friday conscious of being on a mission and using class time on the weekend to reflect and report or to share cases of mission they had attempted during the week.

Every congregation also has a major opportunity in this mobile society to provide membership training for everyone who moves to town and seeks to join. Regardless of the newcomer's former involvement or noninvolvement in church, *every* time she or he enters a new faith-community is an invaluable time when training should be mandated.

In the time of Christendom, infants were assumed to be born into and nurtured by a parish that was a community of faith. Baptism of infants made sense in many different denominations, including my own. In this age, when we cannot assume that a child will be nurtured within a faith community, we simply have to rethink what the churches mean by baptism and how they structure their life to bring the young to faithful maturity. This rethinking involves deeply loved practices and long-held theological positions. It requires something more than tinkering with the age of baptism and admission to communion. It requires more than a Saturday afternoon hour with lovely pagan godparents! The problem is acute right now for those who practice infant baptism, but it is no less important for those whose practice is different.

The Reformation of the Clergy

Clergy are a critical part of our problem. Many of them are uncomfortably aware of that fact, but believe someone else is responsible for their pain. During a thousand years of Christendom the churches built a power system controlled by the clergy—a clericalism that now distorts power relationships. In the beginning I am sure that was not the intent; the intent was to use talented people to strengthen the church's life. The call for ordained leaders to shape and guide the institution was needed and was remarkably effective.

The power system that nevertheless developed continues to be in place, but it has less and less to do with the church's sense of its mission. A layman once told me how it feels to him: "I didn't know the church existed as an employment system for clergy."

In the Church of Christendom, the clergy were assumed to play the primary role in mission and ministry. In the emerging church, the laity are the primary ones to cross the missionary frontier and undertake the missionary task. Many clergy feel displaced and have difficulty accepting the new lay authority. What is more, they do not have a sense of what new role they should bear.

Thus, no one faces a greater change in the future church than clergy. In the past four decades they have already experienced more change than they expected. From being a high-status/low-stress profession the clergy has become a low-status/high-stress profession. The number of congregations who can afford to pay their pastor a living wage has declined.

In the next generation we must produce clergy who can support the ministry of others and train them, rather than act out of a need to control their ministries. Clergy leadership must be unabashedly religious and spiritual, but they will also have to be flexible and creative managers of institutional structures, coping with all kinds of changes. They will have to become imaginative stewards, frequently operating with decreasing resources. They must be single-minded in commitment to building up and equipping the people of God for their new mission in the new age.

Clergy are, I believe, a key resource for the future church. They are badly needed to ground the new structures in which lay people will gather to be formed and sent. They are critical training officers for the church of the future. The educational systems we have for training clergy, however, were invented to produce pastoral leadership for a Christendom Church.

Those systems know how to add or change course offerings, but they still—as educational systems—prepare for a role and a world that parish pastors no longer face. Seminaries face the need for major changes while facing escalating costs and decreased resources.

It may be more important that we develop the tools, resources, or energy constantly to retrain clergy *after* seminary. I emphasize *constantly*. We seem to be able to gather the energy for any kind of exciting experiment or program even when resources are scarce. But what is needed is long-distance attention, the ability to establish and continue to support training year after year as successive classes move out from theological education, using their experience as the curriculum for retraining.

The Shape of Church Oversight (*Episcopé*)

The structures for providing oversight of the churches have long been a cause of infighting in denominations. Rethinking the location of the mission frontier forces us to rethink the functions of oversight. That will require each denomination to rethink the structures so they will serve the functions more adequately. Here the issues are not about what you *call* them, bishops or presbyteries or conferences or conventions or superintendents; I am talking about what those people or groups *do*.

In the Christendom Paradigm, that function was mostly exercised by talented professional staffs and bishops who administered programs or processes larger than of those at the congregational level and that linked the local congregation to far-off concerns of mission.

If I am right, every congregation will face major stress in the coming decades. More, not less. Power will shift. Financial systems will be affected. Relations with congregations will change. Basic frameworks may have to be redesigned. The old model of oversight will not be adequate. In many places even today it is in crisis or collapse already.

Episcopé, the function of oversight, is the sum total of how each denomination makes available all the help they can give to those on the local scene. Congregations of the next few decades face needs that are greater than ever, and their need for help from their system of *episcopé* will far outstrip the capacity of the systems.

As the clergy face daunting tasks of retooling for a very different kind of ministry than most of them thought they had bought into, even more so will those providing oversight be challenged to change and adapt.

Just keeping up with pastoral care for clergy overwrought by stress will be overwhelming. Beyond that is the larger task of retraining the clergy and providing a steady, dependable institutional framework.

One particular point makes the new role of oversight difficult. In the age of the Christendom Paradigm, the flow of resources was from the congregation through the regional structure to the far-off mission frontier. As we think about organizations, that was a flow "up" from the local situation to the "higher" office and then to the frontier. That set relationships in one direction. In the age of the future church, with the mission frontier close to the local congregation, the flow of resource and attention needs to be reversed. Those in oversight need to shift emotional and functional relations with congregations by 180 degrees. If resources are to flow to the mission frontier, they must be flowing primarily toward the local congregation, not away from it. That is an enormous change.

Here I worry about several things: the increasingly severe financial constraints at the regional and national levels of the denominations, the almost total lack of training and retraining models for these key persons, and the almost total lack of support systems for them. There is virtually no research on this critical leadership function in the churches.

In all the denominations, by whatever names we call it, we badly need a better functioning system by which local churches, clergy, and laity are strengthened and encouraged into their ministries. The old system of oversight approaches collapse.

Theology in the Future Church

In the age of Christendom, the work of theology became more and more an enterprise of the academy and its professions and less and less relevant to everyday life. The theological frontier was addressed in learned study and in the library, but the ordinary Christian had little knowledge of its usefulness. As a matter of fact, even among professional theologians usefulness was not often a high-level objective. A decade ago, a colleague had occasion to do a study of decision making at a group of theological seminaries concerned about their future. He discovered that in no case in his sample did anybody in those seminaries make reference to a theological idea or principle in the decisions that were being made. The same thing can obviously be said of theology's relationship to most parish debates and decisions, most family decisions, or the decisions we make about our work.

Theology has become a classroom exercise just when we need most to have it available to guide us on the new mission frontier.

In the new *ecclesia* the primary theologians have to be the laity because they are on the missionary frontier. They will need to be theologians for two reasons: First, because as our primary mission officers they will be engaging the world, making judgments, and seeking God's direction. Second, because it is on that frontier that God will be revealing God's nature, opening doors to the new theologies of tomorrow's world. The laity will be on the front lines of theology as well as mission.

Clergy and theological faculties need to be retooled to become resource persons *to* lay theologians. I have sometimes characterized the current system as a "trickle down" system of theology: We try to get extremely good theologians to teach in seminaries, hoping they in turn will somehow get "enough" theology into their students that they will somehow preach and teach "enough" into the lives of the laity so they can get by. To say it is to recognize its absurdity. Yet, there is something in our system that operates that way.

Clergy and theological faculties are not trained to do it backwards, as I am suggesting they must. If the laity are to become the functioning theologians on the mission frontier, they will badly need well-trained, deeply grounded specialists who know not just the historical tradition, but how to ask questions and probe today's experience. I have seen models for this in the training being given to mentors in the Education for Ministry course—lay people and clergy being taught to help laity reflect theologically on cases of their own experiences in work and community life. There are gifted educators using supervisory skills to help laity elicit learning from experience. Some cell groups put a high value on exploring experience theologically.

In our present system most of our theological training for laity frankly looks like watered-down seminary classes. Gregory Baum, the Canadian theologian, once described it to me as a kind of "Super Sunday School." The curriculum, the methods of teaching follow seminary models, but the work is less demanding. Perhaps we should not be surprised that the net effect, often, is that we simply underline the thing we hope to avoid. We reinforce the old idea that the only "real" ministry is ordained ministry. The people going through the lay training systems get that deeper message and more and more present themselves for formal theological training. The last state is worse than the first.

The development of this new kind of theology really depends on partnership between clergy and laity. We need clergy and theologians to mine the Scriptures and the theological traditions and discover new ways to use those resources in listening and questioning the laity about the mission frontier. We need the laity to take authority as the church's operating theologians, acting on the frontier with confidence in the power of the Spirit, but also searching and reflecting to discern God's purposes. I believe this requires a new kind of partnership in learning between clergy and laity.

The future church demands a new locus of theology, a change from the library and university to the place where the baptized person encounters the world, the place I have called the missionary frontier. The future church demands a new actor in the work of theology: the baptized lay person. The future church demands a new kind of training center for theology: the local church.

What the seminary has been for ministry in the nineteenth and twentieth centuries, the local congregation must be in the twenty-first.

If this really happens, theology as an enterprise will be vastly changed. Many clergy and theologians will feel this as a loss of their power and their special role. They may feel very threatened, unless they understand that power expands as it is shared.

THE CHURCH UPSIDE DOWN

I am describing a church turned on its head. Upside down. At least it seems so. Although roles, relationships, and centers of organization and power seem to be turned around, the orientation to the mission frontier is the same. It is just that the frontier has moved from the far-off edge of Empire to the doors of the local congregation.

I have a friend who once asked me over to watch the Super Bowl. We sat in his den, my wife and I, he and his wife. At the half time his four teenage children roared in with Cokes and pretzels and six friends. We could no longer fit into the den. We had to move the TV to the living room, shift all the furniture around and reorganize ourselves to see the second half. We had to change nearly everything to go on doing what we had already been doing and wanted to continue.

The church is always focused on its mission. In the Christendom Paradigm it understood that mission one way and organized its life to accomplish it. We have awakened to find out that the mission moved on us. To keep focusing on mission, we have to turn the furniture around and face a different direction. We may have to move into another room. For many of us, it is going to feel very different, as if the world were turned upside down, but the function and direction of our calling demands that we turn around.

The Church of Christendom structured itself to address mission beyond the Empire. That meant that it built parish systems, regional structures, and national entities that could gather and deploy resources to the critical point on the missionary frontier. Because that frontier was far away, it required the kinds of logistics and organization it takes to mount a military campaign in a far-off land. There were lots of training camps to prepare the key troops, special training for the leaders, airplanes and ships for transport, policy decisions at high levels at meetings of the generals and the prime ministers, and total support from the citizens at home.

That's the church we built. It served well—for that understanding of mission.

But the missionary frontier has changed. It's gone local. In the above analogy, it is as if the far-off battle ended and a new one emerged on the home front—let's say an epidemic of drug use and addiction. Our impulse would be to attack *that* crisis in the way that worked before. We would announce a War on Drugs and appoint a national czar. We would develop great strategies and even train new armies. We might call out the army and the National Guard. We would try to develop more sophisticated weapons.

The example makes the obvious point. The same approach does not work if the problem is that different. The misuse of drugs is predominately a local problem, involving decisions and individuals, the life of families and neighborhoods, and schools and playgrounds. Bombs, even *smart* bombs, won't work. We can't even use them on the parts of the problems that *are* larger than local.

That's what happened to the church.

The structures designed for one mission do not work in the new mission. The church upside down has not changed at its heart. Its focus is still mission, but the mission location has changed.

A system designed to deliver resources far away must redesign itself to address a missionary frontier at home, one that literally surrounds the local congregation. The national and regional structures designed to send resources far away must change to face the thousands of local situations where the mission frontier touches each congregation.

The leaders in this mission are the laity. The first-line resource people and trainers are also laity—experienced, theologically solid laity. The laity are supported by the clergy.

The clergy and the laity are the strategic teams, but they have to learn a new way to work together. The regional structures—bishops, executives, conferences, presbyteries—are the strategic reserves. They must have the tools and the flexibility to get resources to the congregations in the thick of the mission when there are challenges, opportunities, or breakdowns. The region may also be able to see farther down the pike and be aware of dimensions of challenge that local people have not noticed. The national structures become the second line of reserves, focused on training systems and research.

IMPEDIMENTS TO CHANGE

I have tried to be honest about the significant resistance I see to the changes that lie ahead in building the church of the future. Now I want to address several specific areas in which we must be prepared to work with or around impediments. I see them as of two types: structural and personal.

Structural resistances refer to characteristics built into our systems by the successes of the Christendom Paradigm: strong, conservative, institutional frameworks, leadership patterns, dependency-affirming relationships, and financial systems.

The institutional frameworks we have inherited from the Church of Christendom were built over centuries to provide stability and predictability. Systems of church order had those values built into their warp and woof. The primary value was the ability to hold settled communities steady on a distant unchanging goal. Flexibility was discouraged and uniformity encouraged. Books of order of the different denominations reflect this bias. Such systems work where the environment is stable and the need for inventing new responses is low. Such systems affirm fixed patterns of congregational life and discourage efforts to do things that are off the norm. In many areas of church life, these patterns continue to have high value. But in the places where new life emerges and new challenges to ministry are developing, the books of order make it difficult to be adaptive. Attention needs to be given now to opening up, even in the books of order, space for zones of experimentation where for a time the official rules may be suspended to allow something very different to be tried.

We have laity and clergy who are ready and willing to make such pioneering efforts. From past experience, I expect many of them to fail, but at times of paradigm shift like ours, we need to encourage the scouts to search out territory that lies ahead. Some will succeed. Our systems of order need to encourage their ventures, but not many do.

Inadequate leadership is also an obstacle. I make no criticism of the people in leadership roles in the denominations. I fault the denominations for the system of leadership that sets impossible tasks without adequate support and training, and without clear delegation of authority. Our leaders reflect the inadequacies of our systems. But there are several areas of specific inadequacy.

We and our leaders have a poor theology of institutions. We do not see the very structure of institutions as possible servants of God and gifts for ministry. In consequence, we look at our institutions as albatrosses hanging about our necks and dragging us down. I contend that institutions and specifically the church as it is, warts and all, is one of God's most graceful gifts to God's people. Without a biblical theology of the spiritual power of the corporate, modern church people are at the mercy of a shallow individualism that is cultural and not scriptural. Indeed, without such an understanding and without the spiritual power of the community of the church, we are helpless to deal with the substantial and ambiguous corporate powers of which St. Paul warned us. Without such a theology and commitment on the part of its leaders, the church has little power to address the profound issues of change that it faces.

There are specific areas in which this poor theology penalizes the church that attempts to work for the future. The unwillingness of clergy as a group to face their profound ambivalence about money acts as a barrier to their own financial stewardship and that of the church's people. The common wisdom passed about among the clergy that parish endowments are the creature of the devil is a case in point. That "wisdom" is profoundly unscriptural and gets in the way of the desire of many church people to contribute financially to the future church.

But the issue of inadequacy of leadership is far larger than ambivalence about money. The inadequacy of the leadership reflects the inadequacy of the membership. The invasion of the church by cultural values about money and its relation to success and effectiveness is the broader frame of reference needed to work out what has happened—the erosion of the church's clarity about what it is vis-à-vis the environment.

The dependency system fostered by the Church of Christendom remains a barrier to building a church for the future. The hierarchical arrangement that grew in the institution through its life was a response to the worldview of its leaders. It was reinforced by the leaders' interpretations of history, and it facilitated responding to the missionary frontier at the edge of the Empire. These reinforcing systems contain unhealthy structures. In an earlier generation we described this as a classically Parent-Child institutional arrangement, locking the child into permanent dependence. In today's language of Twelve Step Programs we describe this as a co-dependent system. Whatever the language or image, we are pointing to the fact that the church has a culture that encourages some to take responsibility for the lives and behavior of others, with loss of authority and independence to those others. System that continue as Parent-Child or co-dependent systems will block the development of the kind of individual responsibility and authority that only can shape a church responsive to the new mission frontier.

Personal resistances to change exist within everyone. I see them within the framework of the behaviors Elizabeth Kubler-Ross used to describe another kind of grief. Indeed, facing the changes of leaving one age of the church and discovering another may be most analogous to a kind of death. Following Kubler-Ross, then:

Denial is the behavior I see used most often as a barrier. I see denial in congregations continuing to operate as if nothing has changed. Churches or congregations in denial look at downward patterns of membership and finance and talk about how it seems to be "bottoming out." Denial can be seen in the congregation that gradually eats up it reserves in deficit budgets year after year, with no thought to what comes next. Denial is a good word to describe congregations who put off capital needs for future generations to face. Denial exists in denominations using scare tactics and crisis methods to generate temporary support for continuing on a collision course with disaster.

Denial also exists where clergy and executives put their heads down and slog ahead, doing the same thing, sometimes a little bit harder. Denial is what prompts two or three congregations (or seminaries or agencies) to merge, refusing to deal with the very difficult dynamics involved, with a simple faith that something will intervene to make it work. There is a lot of denial around. So long as it is around, it will be difficult to generate energy to face needed change.

Depression is almost equally present in congregations and judicatories. Depleted energy, listlessness, and a lack of imagination or leadership sucks people into a slow downward spiral. In depression there is often a sense of the depth of the disease but no capacity to respond. Depressed congregations may quietly hope for a miracle, but they do not expect it. Depressed clergy and executives doggedly hang on by their fingernails, trying to make it to retirement. They no longer expect to make any difference.

Bargaining is the arena of the "the new program will fix it" people. Sensing the loss of the familiar, such people latch onto some new action they can take that will turn back the clocks to the golden age. A new program of evangelism, a new hymnal, a new bishop or denominational president, a new prophetic issue solved—all are potential options for the bargaining response to the loss of certainty.

Anger is the most visible response. Much of the bitter anger in the theological and political conflicts in our denominations comes from the depths of persons who have a sense of loss of the church they loved. The conflicts may be about substantial concerns, but often the anger that surrounds them comes from those feelings of loss. I see this anger in bitter debates leading to the firing of some pastors. I see it in the way clergy scapegoat their executives or denomination. I see it in the way clergy talk about their lay people and the way lay people talk about clergy. I see it in the way people at all levels engage in civil wars or try to purge one another for one reason or another. I do not deny the fact that there is often truth behind many of the angers, but our age of change and the loss of the familiar puts a bitter edge to the anger, often violating the spirit of community. Building a church for the future will take all the sense of community we can get.

But if we are to move beyond these barriers, we must move in the direction of the dying patient toward the one stance that can truly deal with the monumental change from the old order of death to the new order of acceptance. The era of Christendom is over. Change is our future. How do we bring it about?

RESOURCES FOR CHANGE

When we look at the need for major changes throughout the religious systems—indeed, the reinvention of the churches—we can be overwhelmed, but there are substantial resources available. Let me name and describe some of the most obvious:

Theological Seminaries. Nearly 200 accredited theological seminaries are spread over the face of the land. Of course they vary enormously in strength as institutions and in their financial and human resources. Some are barely surviving. Others are strong with imaginative leadership. Some have two or three score students, some number their matriculants in the thousands. Each seminary is a pool of talented thinkers and scholars, and each has made significant contributions to religious leadership.

We sometimes forget that theological seminaries themselves are testimony to the adaptive capacity of American churches. Less than 200 years ago, faced with the expanding need for clergy to lead congregations in the new nation, American church leaders invented seminaries. Those seminaries met the need, and they still produce well-schooled pastors, scholars, and denominational leaders. The seminaries exemplify the inventiveness of American churches.

If we become overwhelmed by the problems of reinventing church structures, we can take considerable comfort in how American churches have already demonstrated remarkable adaptability in their invention of a national system of theological education, generating really massive resources to make it happen.

What is disturbingly clear, however, is the difficulty seminaries are having in adapting to the changed conditions of church life as the twenty-first century approaches. The costs of the theological education escalate geometrically. As inflation has led to shrinking endowments, more and more of the costs of theological education are being carried by student tuition.

Churches are called to supply more and more financial resources for candidates who provide significantly less service as professional leaders. The typical seminary graduate of 1950 could be expected to serve forty years before retirement; a typical graduate of 1990 will serve only twenty-five to thirty years or less—meaning that the cost of educating clergy *per year of service to the church* is twenty-five to fifty percent higher in *hidden* costs over the past half-century, to say nothing of the escalation of the visible costs in budgets.

The ability of the churches to sustain that model of education in the face of dwindling "job openings" is questionable. A letter from Princeton Seminary to Presbyterian leaders in 1991, for example, notes 152 entry-level job openings for which there were a total of 1,500 applicants; the Episcopal Church reports that in 1955 the number of total available seminary graduates to open positions was in a ratio of 1/1; in 1990 it was two graduates per job.

Several seminaries, however, suggest that imagination can redirect seminary resources into new forms of service to the church of the future:

* In 1939, a small Presbyterian seminary in upstate New York faced a dwindling need for its traditional services. Instead of accepting a long, slow demise, the trustees took a bold step. They sold the property and moved, lock, stock, and barrel to New York City. There they kept their name, formed a partnership with Union Seminary, and started a new life. There Auburn Seminary developed new services for its constituency, becoming a center of continuing education and a support system for Presbyterians at Union Seminary. Even as this is being written, Auburn, led by Barbara Wheeler, is expanding its role by developing a center for research in theological education.

* Hartford Seminary (United Church of Christ) faced similar dynamics and a reduced pool of students in the 1960s. Under the leadership of a courageous board and president, Hartford transformed itself from a "standard" seminary into an institution that focuses on research and continuing education. The move was painful for many and required major changes. Hartford has become, however, a significant resource for those attempting to build a new church. Its research has broken new ground for religious life, especially for the mainline denominations.

* A number of seminaries run by Catholic orders in the Washington, D.C., area, shattered by drops in vocations to holy orders, chose to band together in a Theological Coalition under Dr. Vincent Cushing. Instead of several marginal and dying institutions, they have fashioned a living coalition.

There is clearly a limited pool of funds with which to fund theological seminaries. The dramatic increase in the cost of seminary education per year of professional service rendered already is forcing the churches to reexamine their investment.

Yet, as the Auburn, Hartford, and Washington examples show, theological seminaries can be remarkable clusters of imagination, leadership, and financial resources. Where they can find a vision of new contributions to the emerging church, they may successfully address options for the future.

One worries, however, that the pain of change and the inertia of old ways will trap too many seminaries in continued downward spirals. Tenure systems alone make it difficult to change directions with any speed. It takes strength, courage, and resources to change. Those who wait too long may use up the resources and have no energy left for even essential changes.

Our Current Structures

From local church to national denominational board our religious organizations and structures and the people in them represent enormous resources, energy, and experience. I do find mindless bureaucrats in some church offices, but they are the exception. On the whole I find imagination and commitment when I meet executives or program directors and their staffs. When they are frustrated—and many of them are—it is usually because they see how unproductive some of the patterns and programs with which they work are. One fact that most of them live with is that they have been experiencing declining real income for two to three decades while local congregations and clergy have not reduced their expectations. They are expected to operate fully in the model of Christendom while at the same time helping congregations and regional structures realign themselves to the new mission frontier.

One great strength these systems bring is the flow of financial resources—by far the greatest philanthropic phenomenon in our society. This flow is supported by the dedicated stewardship of ordinary church members, but it has been developed, organized, and stimulated by careful denominational efforts over the generations. This flow has funded the extraordinary set of buildings and institutions through which churches do their work—from modest rented store fronts to majestic cathedrals and modern office buildings.

There are offsetting and severe problems in the financial area. In many places, funding increases no longer keep pace with inflation. Local congregations face a squeeze, regional institutions face a crunch, and national agencies face near catastrophe as people first fund the religious structures that deal most closely with their perceptions of need, with their understanding of where mission lies.

Crises multiply. Maintenance on great buildings is deferred. In many places the buildings are far more expensive than their current members can sustain. Increases in medical insurance and utility costs play havoc with budgets. Current needs outrun the availability of current funds.

The problem is really a double-bind. The church is torn by well-deserved guilt when its budgets simply support a comfortable, self-concerned congregation. But both economic shortfall and the concern for "outreach" make the church neglect its infrastructure, allowing its institutions to erode and lose their vitality. Churches—local, regional, or national—invest nothing in research and development. This is a serious lack. One must note, however, the critically important role played by several foundations, most notably the Lilly Endowment of Indianapolis. Established by a caring and devoted Episcopal businessman, this foundation supports more research on religious life, as far as I can tell, than all the denominations put together!

The need is urgent for two things: more *imagination* in helping every congregation, judicatory, and board begin radically restructuring its life and *significant new resources*, certainly the development of resources that can support experimentation and study, trial efforts, and skilled advisory services to those attempting change.

Changing church structures in any significant way takes time, energy, imagination, and money. Change takes *more* than is needed to maintain the steady, slowly declining state. If significant time, energy, imagination, and money are not allocated for change, the future is clear; gradual depletion of resources, using up of assets, and dissipation of energy. There are already too many national systems, theological seminaries, regional judicatories, and congregations where that downward spiral has become irreversible.

The People Themselves

People of good will and deep commitment fill our churches today. They are there because they believe in what the church proclaims. They are there because they want to be there. They are there to give themselves to a cause larger than themselves. They are there to be fed and to grow.

One cannot say enough good about this asset.

Over recent generations the giving of committed people to their churches has increased substantially. Actual declines in giving to religious institutions come from decreased numbers in the pews; the evidence is that those who remain behind are more and more generous with their giving. They give money and time, although life-style changes (particularly the increased number of women in the labor force) have made a difference in how they can give time. The demographics of this group have changed, too, with increased age a part of the picture in mainline denominations.

A New Breed of Change Agents

The church is generating a new asset base in the band of change-agents, entrepreneurial organizations, and talented consultants who can provide back-up resources for those who *want* to change. There are many kinds speaking languages of change. Stephen Ministries works with congregations to develop lay pastoral ministries. Paul Dietterich and his colleagues at Chicago's Center for Parish Development bring revitalization skills to pastors, lay leaders, and executives. The Institute for Church Growth in California does research, teaching, and consulting focused on helping congregations expand their membership in size and depth. Lyle Schaller exemplifies the peripatetic consultant across the country, meanwhile turning out an unprecedented flow of books and articles to help those engaged in leadership. There are several score of similar itinerant consultants, none of whom approaches Schaller in written production. Herbert Miller and the National Association of Evangelicals provide resources and expertise.

The Congregational Studies Task Group, an informal gathering of religious leaders, teachers, and researchers, has now spent a decade developing resources and books to support change in religious life at the level of the local church. Their best-known and most widely used resource is the *Handbook for Congregational Studies*, published by Abingdon in 1989.

The Alban Institute provides research, education, publishing, and consulting across the continent from its home office in Washington, D.C., and through its national network of consultants.

There are more. One characteristic of this time of change seems to be the proliferation of resource people.

These people and agencies exist because people facing change in their religoius systems need help. They seem, more and more, to be eager to get help wherever they can get it, whether it comes from within their denomination or not. The rapid growth of these groups in the last two decades is testimony to how serious church leaders are about rebuilding the structures they have inherited. These groups also model how the role and function of *episcopé* may emerge in the next generation or two.

Anybody who wants to begin rebuilding toward what God is calling the church to be can find help.

Summary

We are at the front edges of the greatest transformation of the church that has occurred for 1,600 years. It is by far the greatest change that the church has ever experienced in America; it may eventually make the transformation of the Reformation look like a ripple in a pond.

That transformation is occurring because of the persistent call of God that our whole world be made new, and that the church's mission in that world be itself transformed in new patterns of reconciling the world to God.

There are enormous tasks and daunting challenges for those who intend to follow that call, but then the Lord never said it would be easy.

Principles and Strategies for Building the Future Church and Some Signs of Its Presence

PRINCIPLES AND STRATEGIES

B ecause we cannot know the exact shape of the future, it is all the more important to identify principles to hold onto as we work toward it. If one cannot see the land, it is all the more important to understand how to use maps and compasses and to know the currents of the sea and how the wind blows. Today, as never before, we are aware that the future is blowing in the wind.

The new discipline of congregational studies describes four dimensions of congregational life that need to be probed by those who would understand or change congregations:

— *program* is the sum total of the things a congregation does, including what is on its calendar;

— *process* is the way the congregation does what it does: how its leadership works, how its people and groups make choices and relate to one another;

— *context* is the setting in the community and the denomination, the external forces that constrain or influence what the congregation and its members are and do; and

— *identity* is that rich mix of memory and meaning that grounds the congregation, defining who it really is in its heart.

Most of the attempts I see to change congregational life in response to the dislocations I have described seem to be in the area of tinkering with program. Denominations develop new program emphases, regional judicatories announce "this year's crusade," which usually coincides with the annual pledge campaign. Nobody expects much to change. There is a conspiracy of silence, hoping that things will be no worse next year than last. In places where rapid growth is occurring, there is increasing pressure to strengthen and broaden program offerings and staff for new needs. When growth is not happening, the pressure approaches desperation. The assumption seems to be that the answer is to get the best program ideas and put them to work.

The attention paid to context is primarily to find out how to market the program already adopted or how to adapt the program to be a better fit with the population in the area of the local congregation. At its best, this tinkering produces better program, better connected to its potential audience. At its worst, it falls captive to the kind of marketing that simply repackages old goods and flogs them to a new audience.

If we are, as I am convinced, in a time in which the paradigms are changing, a cosmetic approach to change, the kind that deals with surface appearances, in inadequate. Organizational specialists distinguish between "transitional" and "transformational" change. By transitional change they mean the adaptations and shifts brought on by temporary dislocations and discomforts, moving to a new stability. By transformational change they mean the shattering of the foundations and the reconstitution of a new entity.

Churches that tinker with program and marketing are barely beginning to be on the edge of transitional change, but the building of the future church requires transformation at its very core. We are not looking for cosmetic changes or the kind of "fixes" that come in annual program cycles; we are looking for several generations of struggle with our identity as people of God, with how we live together, with what our environment really is. As we do that struggling we will have to generate program, revise our structures, and adopt new roles.

To mount that struggle with identity, process, and context, however, requires that we start where we are in the church we have, caught as it is in the time between paradigms. As we do, there are some principles and strategies that we can hold onto. It may be that none of these principles and strategies is new or unique, but they are the distillation of experience accumulated from two decades of listening to and working with people in several hundred congregations, several scores of judicatories in several dozen denominations.

Looking for Learning Points

Change in an evolutionary time does not occur everywhere at the same rate. Most organizational structures, as well as our own expectations, assume that it is the same everywhere. Our denominations develop approaches intended to fit every situation and every congregation as if they were the same, and as if they all lived by the same schedule. That approach often produces answers that therefore fit nowhere.

At the Alban Institute we have pioneered a strategy that seems to work. We look for what we call "learning points," those moments special to a single congregation when those particular people feel a challenge to change and are ready to act. These points are unique. Sometimes they do not last long.

We find that effort to work toward these learning points doubles and redoubles the effectiveness of the change effort.

Some learning points are cyclical and almost predictable, like the change of pastors. Others are quite unpredictable, like the unexpected collapse of an institution or a person, or even a building. Almost any kind of crisis within the system can be a learning point. We find that the break-out of a severe fight or a major economic change in the community can precipitate such an opportunity.

Whether these learning points—predictable or unpredictable—lead to change or not depends on a number of things. If the people in the situation are overwhelmed by the moment, if they are unwilling to accept the opportunity within the challenge, or if the outside resources are not responsive and available, the moment may pass with nothing to show but a papered-over crack in the wall. Similarly, if the people are burned out emotionally or have used up all their resources, they cannot rise to the occasion and use the learning point as a moment for change. The opportunity will pass and may not recur for some years.

Moments like this are scary and threatening to the people who lead congregations. They bring out all kinds of defensiveness ("Nobody can tell us what to do"), anger ("If so-and-so hadn't messed up, we wouldn't be in this boat"), depression ("I give up"), and a host of less palatable behaviors.

Moments like this call for strong outside support. This is the opportunity for imaginative oversight by whoever has the call to the function—whether bishop or executive, judicatory staff person, lay leader from the next parish, or consultant. If consultants are called in, they frequently ask the question of oversight in a proposal—"I think the problem is this, and I suggest these three steps to deal with it. It will cost this much. Do you want to work on it?" For the congregation that may be the moment of truth. Some congregations take up the moment. I know many who say "No" to the consultant, but nevertheless act on the problem. Others say "Yes," but do not make a real commitment. But that moment is an open opportunity.

I have also seen judicatory staff exercise oversight at such moments ("I'll send you our guidelines for dealing with that, but how about letting me come out to talk to the group to help you figure out what to do?"). I have known a lay leader from another congregation to be the one exercising the function ("That is a mess. We ran into it last year before our annual meeting. Let me tell you how we dealt with it and where we got help.")

I think the most important function of the judicatory is to provide that kind of oversight. It requires careful and continuing listening to congregations and their lay and clergy leadership. It means interpreting attacks, not getting defensive. It means reading the bulletins and listening to the scuttlebutt at meetings, being prepared to step in when a learning moment seems to have arrived. It means hearing the issues behind the griping and complaining. It also means working to increase the kinds of resources that are appropriate to different learning points. No judicatory in these days can afford to have a staff that is prepared to respond to all crises. The best judicatories, in my opinion, operate primarily in intervention, providing a wide menu of trusted resources with which the congregation can address its issue. A judicatory that does this well will discover that there is no need to mount independent judicatory programming efforts.

There are political implications to working strategically as I suggest here. Expectations that judicatories have of themselves, and that many congregations have of their judicatories, are that program is equally accessible to all. If you take seriously the importance of learning points, you know that those expectations are wrong.

The alternative to the focused use of resources on congregations that are at change-points is a wasteful scattering of resources. Bureaucracies tend to try to make everything available to everybody, with the result that no one's needs are met. Denominational offices have to think and act strategically in their use of resources in a way that focuses those resources on the individual.

Let me address the judicatory with my naked point: "Put all your energy into congregations that are at learning points. The others? *Leave them alone!*"

Working Experimentally

Under the Christendom Paradigm, churches have structured themselves for uniformity and permanence. Congregations in one place think they need to be like congregations in other places in style, program, and behavior. They and their program need to be relatively unchanging. Nothing gets started that is not intended to become permanent.

Thinking that way helped when their mission was primarily to produce resources for the far-off mission frontier. That mission did not change much over the years, and the prime need was for steadiness and predictability in responding to that mission.

But in a time of change, when pressure and opportunity for change are not the same everywhere, we badly need innovators, people and groups who will take a stab at a new way with the freedom to fail.

The structures of the church, formed as they were for stability and endurance, mitigate against innovation. How many experiments in the churches have worn themselves out trying to get permission from the legal entities of the denominations? Where the experiment did get off to a limping start, often the suspicious requirements for reporting and justifying the change wore down the innovative enthusiasm. Of course, when that happens, the system says, "There! We knew it wouldn't last!"

The churches must learn to encourage innovation and even fund it, rather than handicap and punish it. We must encourage innovation to find some new paths and to get models of innovation widely known. Eventually every congregation will need the capacity to approach its uniqueness with innovative energy. Meanwhile, in times and places where change is rapid, our most important asset is the pioneer, the one—or the many—who is willing to break new paths. We need to honor them, even when they fail, recognizing that even though some may fail, we can still learn from the attempt.

I am aware of two ways in which we undercut the effectiveness of experimentation. In the first case we do not make a commitment that is sufficiently long. Change in religious institutions takes time. I remember one presbytery that authorized and funded an exciting new effort to start a congregation. In only six months the leadership of the congregation discovered that they had to start defending what they were doing on the presbytery floor. The presbytery really had made inadequate commitment to experimentation. They counted on fast results in an area in which fast results are not possible. They were unwilling to give the experiment enough time. Experiments do not work if you keep pulling them up to look at the roots.

Denominators and congregations also undercut experimentation by excessive turnover of leadership. Many small church projects that are started with real enthusiasm by one group of judicatory staff and leaders founder when a new group of leaders comes in or a key staff person changes. Two areas in the Episcopal Church with outstanding experimental support for small congregations—the Diocese of Nevada and a deanery of the Diocese of New York around Upper Boiceville—owe much of their success to continuity of leadership. Two bishops in succession saw the strategy the same way, and one archdeacon has stayed put for two decades. It is not easy to find one judicatory leader who is willing to support the basic strategies of her or his predecessor. It is even more rare to find a staff person who stays in place long enough to give a framework of policy stability.

Even more painful to me is the way we negate experiments by neglecting to capture and communicate what is learned. The church all too often walks away from pieces of its work with no effort to share its successes and failures. This is enormously wasteful. There are file cabinets in the basement of every judicatory and every national denomination full of information about important attempts to solve problems or install change. Nobody opens the files or even remembers who did it. Those of us who have been around for a while often run into projects that are being announced as "the first ever," and we remember others who worked hard on the same issue perhaps a decade ago. The new pioneer is often unaware of the trails others blazed in earlier generations.

Working experimentally is key to making some of the changes we need to make for the future church.

Paying Attention to Boundaries

In 1976, the Alban Institute was attracted to a concept that has become foundational for us in understanding and searching for the meanings of change. The concept was the "boundary." We believe the concept has broad usefulness for those seeking to build the future church.

The concept of the boundary came to us as we studied what happened when a seminary student moved from the seminary into her or his first assignment. We wanted to find out why the dedicated efforts of seminaries across the country to help their graduates become better prepared for ministry in congregations all had the same result—graduates, with varying degrees of anger, saying "Why didn't the seminary prepare me for this?"

We discovered that the problem was not a lack of information or anything of that sort. Nor was it a lack of imagination or effort on the part of seminaries. It was a matter of two cultures, seminary culture and congregational culture. They were different, including different ways of thinking and working, different reward systems and values, even different languages. Our study (some results of which were published in Roy Oswald's Alban monograph, *Crossing the Boundary*,[1] and in Harbaugh, et al., *Beyond the Boundary*[2]) focused on the extraordinary experience people had when they moved from one institution to another. It was frightening and invigorating; it was also a moment of potentially extraordinary growth and learning. We decided that boundaries were worth watching as important definers of change.

We found many other boundaries, each one of which has unusual potential for growth—in emotional and spiritual depth, and in relationships. Each also provided an unmatched opportunity for learning new skills and abilities. Some of the boundaries we have since worked with others to explore are these:

- the boundary one crosses in choosing to go to church;
- the boundary a pastor crosses in moving from one congregation to another;
- the boundary a person crosses in moving from one town to another; one job to another;
- the boundary between work life and retirement;
- the boundary shaped by angry leave-taking or firing;
- the boundary from a congregation into a seminary;
- the boundary from one stage of life to the next;
- the boundary of death.

The important point for us has been the use of boundary as a metaphor for a learning opportunity. We clearly find such boundaries have very high learning potential, but in most cases the persons involved are so busy they do not stop to learn. Indeed, their very busyness is the escape mechanism most people use to avoid the pain of learning and change.

Let me give an example. The Alban Institute did a lot of research on the process by which people enter a congregation, discovering different ways congregations helped or hindered that movement. Since that research began we have held a number of conferences about what we learned; we have published numerous books and articles. What may not be obvious is the fact that all of this activity centered on the concept of the boundary. We saw that the newcomer, somehow, makes a decision to cross a boundary from not-in-the-congregation to in-the-congregation. We tried to find out what changed for them. How were they helped to learn the language of the new community? What barriers did the new community have in place that it might not even be aware of? We also recognized that the boundary-crosser generally sees things that natives do not see, so we asked the newcomer to help us map the congregation as they experienced it.

Any congregation can do what we did and learn a lot about itself from its newer members. The exercise would be more valuable than taking our findings and applying them second-hand.

In this time in which the paradigms are changing, the boundary between the congregation and the world outside has become more important than it has been for 1,600 years. Every lay person crosses that boundary twice a week. To be conscious of this is to be aware of one of the most exciting opportunities for research and for training that one could ever have. I believe that the concept of the boundary gives us a framework for developing some of the lay training we need for the church of the future.

The concept of boundary, however, is larger than this particular one, important as it is. Those who seek to build a church for the future will find it pays to pay attention to boundaries.

Steadiness

The discomfort of church structures with all the disruptions and changes of the present age has made church leaders anxious for new answers. That anxiety feeds what I call the "Tyranny of the New." There is a sense that only The New has value, so all our energy is used up inventing the new and marketing it. We rarely take time to install it well or to do the painstaking work of adapting it to the local situation. Rarely is time taken to see how what is new relates to what has been before.

When the new way is considered the only way, there is no continuity. Fads become the new Gospel, and in Paul's words, the church is "blown to and fro by every wind of doctrine." Particularly at times that require innovation, we need structures that hold steady, grounding The New, not allowing it to become erratic and impulsive.

We badly need church leaders, pastors, executives, and institutions that hold steady for the long pull. Without steadiness at the core, a steadiness that supports and studies the changes and innovations and then transmits the good to the next generation, the structures merely fibrillate anxiously and aimlessly.

I think this is a major concern for whatever paradigm we construct. Our fascination with The New and our faith in the rotation of leadership has eroded our ability to hold steady. The value we place on novelty is at war with our need to examine each novelty, discarding the useless and holding onto the valuable. In the past, steadiness frequently came from denominational identity, from institutional loyalties, and from trusted, steady leaders. None of those claim us as once they did.

Institutions have been an important source of steadiness in the past, but many of those we have known and trusted–like denominations–have lost some of their ability to hold us together. What new kinds of institutions do we need? Can the denominations themselves be reconfigured? Can seminaries rebuild themselves as the kind of institutions that can prepare leaders for a post-Christendom world? Can we find institutional frameworks through which to develop and deploy training and consulting skills to congregational leaders? Can the new institutions (e.g., the Alban Institute, the National Catholic Pastoral Center, the National Association of Evangelicals) find the resources to support congregations in new configurations? Will they be able to renew themselves?

What other institutions and leadership do we need for building the future church? Who will hold us steady on the future?

Accountability

The structures the churches developed in the first two-thirds of the twentieth century were fueled by a clear sense of mission to the far-off frontier. The financial and human resources needed for that frontier flowed into the churches because people who believed in mission saw the connection between what their churches did and what they understood mission to mean.

When that concept of mission began to shift in the 1930s and 1940s, the connection between local church and mission lost its clarity. The people in the denominational structures began to press for mission needs *they* perceived, but they did not make the connection clear to those in local churches. The message became something like: "You really cannot understand what mission really is; trust us and send us the resources." The people trusted and sent the resources. Floods of resources. But accountability suffered. Denominational program did reflect what denominational leaders deeply believed that mission was, but people in local churches were less and less convinced that it was what they understood as mission. Loyalty and trust held the system together for a long time. But loyalty eroded. Many committed Christian laypeople no longer trust that what their national denomination is doing is mission. And they do not trust what those people say.

I believe an analogy can be made to what has happened in Eastern Europe over the past fifty years. A cadre of leaders took power, assisted by the Soviet Union's armed forces. Those leaders had a clear sense of how a good society should be built, and they took the steps to do it. The citizens, by and large, accepted the painful consequences of a society and an economy that did not work very well in hope that their sacrifices would eventually produce that good society. Also, they did not have access to power or ways to change things.

At some point though, things stopped working. The people became unwilling to continue. They lost hope that things would get better. They stopped whatever support they had given to their governments out of previous loyalty or hope. At some point, in country after country in Eastern Europe, the establishment was challenged, and the socialist power structure blinked.

From the outside, the fall of the Berlin Wall was a dramatic surprise. In fact, the Wall had lost its strength a long time before, but nobody had pushed it. The will of the people had been withdrawn as they lost their trust in the system.

In Europe, people are finding answers very difficult to come by. Pushing over one ineffective system was deceptively easy. But what do you do *now*? Even though that system did not work, there still must be a system—an economy, a set of political parties, a way of making decisions and enforcing them.

I believe the societies of Eastern Europe foundered for the same reason that many of our denominational systems are in trouble. Leaders, committed to a real vision of what the mission of the state (church) is, shaped the life of the state (church) toward those ends. They lost the hearts and the trust of their people.

I believe we have been seeing evidence of similar disaffection for several decades in the denominations. The certainty of our leaders that they are leading toward mission has not been convincing to ordinary church members for some time.

For two thousand years Christians have sacrificially tried to get their best resources to the missionary frontier. Today that frontier has moved. Many members of congregations feel that their judicatories and denominations are using rhetoric about mission to secure support for activities that the members themselves do not understand to be mission. The nerve of trust has been cut.

Equally important in the long run, the judicatories and denominations have been slow to recognize how mission frontier has shifted. That may be because to do so is to raise serious questions about how and where the church spends its money. And until the churches begin seriously to make their structures accountable to the new missionary boundary, they will face continuing declines.

Those who work to build the future church will need to put energy into developing systems that promote clear accountability between those in congregations and those who assist them in mission. In the Alban Institute we have found the use of clear contracts between parties to be helpful in maintaining trust and accountability. We really believe a congregation ought to be able to fire us if we do not produce. Is the idea of a contract between a congregation and its judicatory out of the question? Are there better ways for accountability to be initiated once it has been damaged? Real work and imagination are needed at this point if congregations are going to get the kind of help they will need increasingly to face their mission frontier. Similarly, those in denominational structures may need to work through contractual systems to develop their ability to provide oversight and reestablish trust.

Building Bridges and Seeking Allies

The process of building the new paradigm is already happening in countless communities. Five or six congregations (some members of whom would not be found dead or alive inside one of the others' churches during worship!) band together to address a community need—care for the homeless, support

for local schools. Several denominations form a consortium to develop television ministries neither could handle alone. Lay people from different denominations and faiths band together to address drug problems.

In time, these connections may become as strong or stronger than the
bonds of denominationalism. Most of them will be local or regional, not
national. The national and international structures (councils of churches,
etc.), which grew out of Christendom and linked denominational structures,
may have the potential to make the kinds of connections needed, particularly on the local scene if they can move beyond fixation on survival.

Every Christian will need to seek allies in the mission into which he or
she goes every week in the ambiguous world. Every congregation will need
to build bridges to others to accomplish its mission.

Valuing Failure

A church or congregation that moves ahead must be ready to value its
failures, to expect many things not to work.

Many more things must be tried than can be expected to succeed.
Building a climate that welcomes that kind of effort is not going to be easy.
The church tends to honor only those who succeed and has been known to
shoot its wounded.

If the church is going to meet the test of the next century, finding new
vigor for its new mission, it simply must learn to honor and learn from the
pioneers who do not make it over the Great Divide.

Faithfulness in the church has always been faithfulness in following the
call. It has rarely meant winning.

SIGNS OF THE FUTURE CHURCH

The church of tomorrow is not yet visible. How it will configure itself we
cannot know. What we can do, however, is note some signs of what it may
be like—signs in the here and now that point to the character of what it may
become in God's time. Each of these is a pointer toward something of what
I believe the future church will be like:

- a Baptist congregation joins a Lutheran congregation and a Church
  of God congregation in establishing a watch program in
  neighborhoods where drugs are sold;

- a group of lawyers in a congregation issues an invitation to other lawyers in town to discuss forming a guild to start talking about the role of law, faith, and community life;

- a group of Christians and nonChristians forms a local group to build homes for the homeless through Habitat for Humanity. Mission is fully present, but it begs questions of local religious structures;

- a seminary in a nearby town works with a group of Catholic congregations to develop a four-year night-school course for preparing parish lay workers. The lay workers take over major responsibilities in three parishes without resident priests;

- a group of skilled church professionals forms a partnership to provide consultative assistance to congregations and nonprofit agencies facing difficult changes in their state. Soon they find a demand for their services in corporations and government agencies;

- a national denominational mission agency decides to focus on providing services instead of developing programs. It develops contracts with judicatory offices;

- people seeking depth and growth form a variety of twelve-step programs, many meeting in local churches. The spiritual power released in lives of individuals and families bypasses ordinary congregational programming. Local churches feel the power, but have a hard time knowing how to relate to the new life;

- an agency unrelated to any denomination builds a network of thousands of pastors, executives, and lay leaders committed to building better congregations and begins to broker knowledge among them;

- a seminary professor invents a way to give basic theological education to lay leaders and designs a way to deliver that education anywhere at nominal cost. Many congregations build their own lay seminaries as a result. Some of these become community seminaries of ministry, linking several congregations;

- pastors starting new congregations demand help from their denominations—and get it;

- a congregation, formed to be experimental, collapses after six years, and the members do a careful post-mortem for the denomination;

- a group of pastors with the unusual role of interim pastor decides to take responsibility for their specialty. They form a national support group independent of their denominations. They develop training and professional standards;

- executives and bishops from ten to twelve denominations take a full week each year to engage each other in learning how to carry out their jobs;

- a congregation joins one of another ethnic make-up in a tutoring program for elementary schools;

- a group of doctors, nurses, and medical technicians forms at a research hospital for weekly lunches and discussions of "the ministry of healing." No clergy are invited;

- a congregation facing the retirement of a pastor invites other congregations into a study of community needs of the next decade;

- a congregation just over a disastrous relationship with a pastor who sexually abused three members of the congregation hires a family therapist to help them grow and learn rather than avoid and hide;

- a congregation's board appoints one of its members to attend all city planning sessions;

- six congregations of different denominations set up a training program on new member ministries and coordinate their work for unchurched people of the community; and

- a congregation spawns four house-churches over a six-year period, and receives back members of two house-churches that came to an end after two and three years.

Each of us has probably seen signs like these. When they appear singly, they are not particularly dramatic. Each however, points beyond the Church of Christendom. Each is the tip of a possibility being born around us even now.

My hunch is that your congregation has some visible signs of the church that is being born. I would love to hear about them.

NOTES

1. Roy M. Oswald, *Crossing the Boundary* (Washington, DC: The Alban Institute, 1980).

2. Gary Harbaugh, William H. Behreus, Jill M. Hudson, and Roy M. Oswald, *Beyond the Boundary* (Washington, DC: The Alban Institute, 1986).

CHAPTER 6

Where in the World Is the Church Going?

A new church is being born around us. That is my thesis.

It is a church with deep roots in the past, shaped by the past. Its forms and roles and structures and institutions were formed to serve a great, but flawed, vision of its mission. On the whole, that past church—in spite of the faults and sinfulness intrinsic to human structures—served mission as well as it could. Looking back on it, there are many pages of history that we would change if we could, but I doubt that we would have done it better than they did.

The Christendom Paradigm is now rapidly fading. The great mission that undergirded its strength and fueled its growth is no longer clear. It leaves behind, however, powerful structures still shaped by it—structures of denominations and theology, hierarchy and priority, roles and relationships. Those structures still surround us, supporting us and frustrating us at the same time. The thought patterns of that church also continue to have power over us, for they shaped our consciousness as well as our institutions.

It is as if the magnetic North Pole moved from Greenland to Alaska, and our compasses keep flickering between the remembered pole and the new one. Our institutional compasses still point to Christendom while flickering toward the new orientation, the new pole. In such a world it is hard to keep one's bearings. The same is true of our own consciousness of our mission. It, too, flickers back and forth, making it hard to chart a straight course.

I have written this book because I believe we are called to engage with God in the process by which the new church comes into being. I believe the wisdom of lay leaders across the church, the faith of church people, the commitment of clergy, bishops, and executives, the skills of all leaders and members—*all* are invited and needed for the new to be discovered.

I do not expect clarity about the new church for several generations—I shall not see it, even though I work for it. This is true for most of us, I think. But perhaps there may be some of the young among us who will, like Moses, be led up to the high mountain from which at least to see the Promised Land.

What I have described as paradigms of the church and a changing paradigm of religious life is connected to equally radical changes of paradigms going on throughout the world. Our evolution is part of a cosmic evolution of nations and of consciousness, one that is reshaping evolution of East and West, of humanity and environment. What is happening to the church is part of the entire work of God, making all things new.

The evolution of the church is imbedded in and related to those great changes. God's call to a new world is the context of the call to the church.

The church's call is also very special within that larger framework. The evolution of the church holds up the pole of meaning within cosmic evolution. It holds up some key theses: that there is meaning and purpose in creation, that at the heart of creation is a loving, self-disclosing and self-giving Presence that broods over it all, breathing life into the whole of it. It holds those theses and witnesses to them against the antithesis of meaninglessness inherent in a mechanistic view of the story of creation.

It is that dialectic—meaning vs. meaninglessness—that is the driving power of history, not the minor dialectic of communism and capitalism that political economists have argued for the past century and a half.

It is no small thing to be part of an affirmation of meaning and purpose in the midst of chaos. The church hears the call to the new world as a call from the God who promises, not as the grinding of mechanical forces of necessity, moving inexorably to a determined denouement. The church hears the call as a call requiring response, commitment, and choice from a God who will not leave us comfortless.

But it is no comfort to speak of evolution. The word in recent generations has hidden a smug, simple faith in inevitable progress, a faith contradicted by scientific research as well as by the Christian faith. Modern science—from paleontology to physics—holds no brief for predictability, certainty, or progress. Those simple confidences, the legacy of Newton and Darwin, have not survived the vast uncertainties of quantum physics and fossil studies of the Burgess Shale.

What we know now is that when change occurs, there is much that is unpredictable and uncertain. One cannot plan how to handle the next great California earthquake. One cannot know which species will survive the next cataclysms of nature. That mankind survived at all is not, science now tells us, the result of some innate superiority, but it is an extraordinary mystery. As Christians, we would say that it was the working out of grace, not of immutable forces.

As we take little comfort from an erroneous concept of progressive evolution, neither do we hear good news from our tradition. The story of the Hebrew people and of the New Testament people is a story of a troublesome pilgrimage. Rebellious, cowardly, treacherous, undependable, fractious, the biblical people have been a constant trial to their God. Their path is not a succession of great moments and great achievements. Their constant theme is the building of golden calves whenever things get difficult.

Why do we expect now to be any different? Why do we worry that "mainline" declines and "conservative" grows, and each envies the other? Two generations ago it was the reverse. Why do we wonder who will sit on the right hand of Jesus in his kingdom? Why do we make our theologies or political correctness the touchstone of our orthodoxy when Peter was told that all the animals in the great bedsheet let down from heaven were clean? Why are we surprised by the disappointing moral behavior of good Christian people—and, horrors, their pastors—when we read how the people in the Corinthian church lived?

Neither the concept of evolution nor the story of the faith gives us any confidence whatsoever that we shall make the right choices in moving from the Church of Christendom to the church God is calling to serve the world of the twenty-first century.

None whatsoever.

Those of us who share the biblical faith look at the uncertain future with normal human anxiety and fear, but also with a strange confidence that springs from knowing in Whose hands we are. We can look back at what our forebearers did and how they carried the faith. We can look at the institutions they built to house their life of faith. We can look at the shape of community that nurtured them. In what they did we can see flaws, but we can also see that there was a Presence with them in their wildernesses—in their false starts as well as in their successes. We can act now trusting in that same Presence. There is no other way for us.

A new church is being born. *It may not be the church we expect or want.* The church of the future may not include our favorite liturgy or hymn, our central theological principle, or even our denomination! God's promises always arrive with surprises in them. The form of the new world and new church is not in our hands.

What is in our hands is the chance to respond to God's call. To put our skills and our wills to the tasks of discerning the opportunity points, the places and times for change effort, and to add our gifts to God's church in this time of change. How God uses our gifts we cannot predict.

God is calling people across the face of this country and the world. God's call is to newness for the whole world, not just the church. Those of us who are called into the church have a special vocation to work for the renewal and refreshment of the church, not as an institution out of the past, but as a centering presence from which we may serve the new world that God is creating around us. We have been told that God is making all things new. God is calling us to participate in that new creation.

We have also been told that God's time is now.

The Free Church Variation on Christendom

Many American denominations lived a significant variation on the paradigm I call "Christendom." All of the "free" churches—those whose life is structured congregationally, including families such as Baptist and Congregational—have an order and a self-perception distinctly different from the model I have described in Chapter II.

In this appendix I want to speak to that difference and yet still argue for the strong influence of a "Christendom consciousness" within even those religious bodies that rejected an establishment role and a connectional polity (a system that makes congregations into federated or confederated families). The denominations that grew out of the European "establishments" and those that are "connectional" find the Christendom model more in their tradition.

In Ernst Troeltsch's distinction between "church" and "sect," Christendom speaks more to the experience of the continuum near "church."

First let me speak to the difference.

The appearance of groups of Christians who differed from the state religions was part of the ferment that gave rise to the Reformation of the sixteenth century. I want to focus on the experience in the churches of the British Isles for two reasons—it is the experience I am closest to and it is an experience that illustrates well the distinction I am driving at. Let us look at the situation as it developed in Anglican parishes *after* the Reformation, after the Civil Wars of the seventeenth century.

The English parish found within itself a different religious group, organized, worshipping, having fellowship in opposition to the local parish church. During the turmoil of the seventeenth century those religious differences had fought for domination, beginning with the assumption that the winner would replace the loser. The Pilgrims went to Holland and then to Massachusetts to get out of the oppressive religious climate of the English Parish Church and to set up a community in which their religious practice could be dominant. By the end of the wars a kind of exhausted, fairly distrustful truce had been established whereby the winners—the Anglican party in England, the Presbyterians in Scotland—accepted the fact that the losers existed and probably were around to stay.

Over several generations the majority community's perception of "the others" changed. From the seventeenth to the twentieth centuries it progressed from fear and suspicion, to grudging but careful co-existence, to a reluctant tolerance, to collaboration and cooperation. The government's attitude toward these establishment religious groups changed from legal proscription to a kind of grudging second-class citizenship (the Act of Conformity is *important* because it granted the right of *existence* to the nonconformists). Today, the nonchurch of England citizen is not under legal restrictions because she or he is Methodist, Catholic, or Baptist.

But for our purposes, the issue is how the experience of being in a nonconformist congregation shaped relationship to society and to one's sense of mission. *(See Figure 5.)*

What has happened is that the nonconformist congregation inside the parish discovered a new boundary that separates it from the parish. It was a boundary of *religious practice* and *personal behavior.* Being part of the "chapel" rather than the parish, as the difference is still described today, stood for religious practice involving more attention to preaching and Bible, a more enthusiastic worship and singing, and sometimes theological justification of the same. The lay person of these congregations saw this boundary as a requirement for more demanding personal piety and higher morality in business and community dealings.

Only the Quakers consistently witnessed that the boundary of mission was more dramatic, more all-inclusive. Only the Quakers from the beginning saw that the boundary of faith required them to witness against the laws of the state. For that reason they were the least tolerated of the nonconformist groups. The state couldn't care less how one prayed or sang if she or he still paid their taxes and served in the army. On those scores, Quakers—but generally not the other nonconformists—stopped preaching and started meddling.

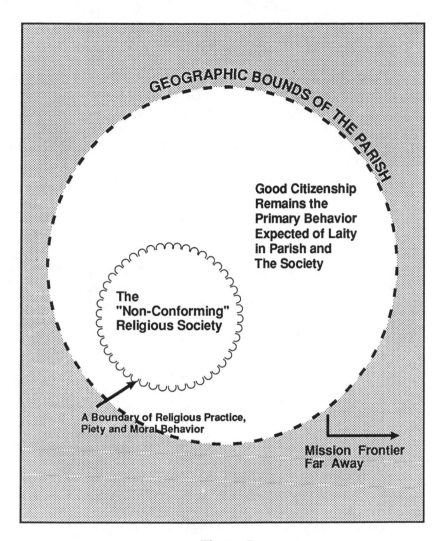

Figure 5

Over time the appearance of that *religious* demarcation line between congregation and parish became a critical turning point in the paradigm change this book is about.

Most of the American evangelical denominations drew important sustenance from the demarcation line. They discovered the importance of being different from the bland, inoffensive, subservient religion of the establishment.

Over time that ability to make *religious* differentiations from society led those people to understand the more radical differentiation of the people of faith from the political state.

Because people of congregations began to say, "we are different from the parish in how we study the Bible," they also were first to see and then say, "We are different, as Christians, from a government that permits slavery."

The boundary, once experienced in terms of religious practice, more and more became a boundary between one culture and another.

It is no surprise that Free Churches and evangelicals were the first to recognize social ills—slavery, the inhumanity of prisons and insane asylums, etc. What remains to be understood is how two extraordinary reversals took place—the first much discussed, the latter less so. The first reversal is how the powerful social activism of the evangelical and nonconforming denominations and groups reverted almost entirely to personal religious values early in the twentieth century, becoming quite subservient to the Empire.

The less-discussed reversal is how the establishment churches, late in coming to an awareness of any boundary—religious or secular—between the Gospel and the Empire, developed a political infrastructure that became so intent on the boundary between the Gospel and the social and political realities that it lost touch with its religious constituency. There are books to be written about both, but not this book.

For our purpose, it is important to note that the more a person or denomination has experienced the boundaries described in this appendix, the less compelling will their experience of Christendom have been.

Yet I argue that the climate of Christendom has affected the thought-patterns of the Free Churches nevertheless. The Christendom paradigm has been the dominant background thinking, the cultural myth. Even when personal experience rejects it, the culture has supported it.

There is another point. Within even the freest of the free denominations there seems to be a sort of gravitational pull toward what here I call

"Christendom thinking." A Pentecostal friend from the Assemblies of God said to me, "Your description of Christendom sounds like a lot of stuff that keeps creeping up on us!" Troeltsch noted the tendency of sect over time to begin to adopt the behavior, structure, and stance of church.

This book describes the "church" experience. Those who have grown up in the churches of the great informal American establishment will identity most with the argument. Those who grew up in another experience of congregation will find some elements over- or under-emphasized, but I believe they will find important implications for their religious systems.

In the final analysis, the issue is one of mission. How do we as Christians—whether mainline or sideline, liberal or conservative, connectional or free—find a community that forms and sustains us in an authentic faith and move out bearing that faith into the structures of our ambiguous society? How do we pass those forms of community on to the next generation?

Transforming Congregations
for the Future

In gratitude to four of my teachers

Miss Carrie Cain,
Pinopolis,
Terry Holmes,
Nashota and Sewanee
Andy Penick,
Chapel Hill
Verna Dozier,
Washington

Each pushed me
further than
I wanted to go.

CONTENTS

Everyone I know who works in churches knows there is trouble. Churches do not "work" the way they used to. Roles of leadership have become more confusing and frustrating to those who hold them. What we remember as being crystal clear in church life a generation or two ago now seems muddy, uncertain.

What has gone wrong? many wonder. Who is to blame? The strong, confident, even triumphant institution that they remember from their youth—or that others tell them about from just a few decades ago—is not what they or their children experience in church today. They now see an institution exuding self-doubt, with leaders who seem less able to lead than to mimic the least common denominator of public opinion. Their vision of prophetic justice sounds suspiciously like the latest liberal definition of political correctness.

Church people talk about membership losses and cast covetous eyes at the burgeoning membership rolls of other churches that have a different theological stance or seem better at reading the market. Without a clear sense of what they ought to do, they have grown unsure that what they are doing is the right thing. If you are not sure of what you should be up to, then why not do whatever is selling best?

The people I talk to are not terribly confident as they voice these concerns. They know that these questions are not in a league with those about peace and war and justice. Yet what's happening to the church is something that touches them very deeply. It's easier to get more exercised about and involved in local church issues than about Bosnia or Somalia. Their concern about their congregatons—in today's language—is not politically correct, but it matters a lot.

It matters a lot. A simple statement with deep roots. Religious congregations do matter. They matter personally to millions of people who find a source of meaning in a congregation. They matter to those who week by week make their way to their religious observances and contribute more money to churches than to any other set of institutions in the country. They matter to those who take the values learned in those congregations into their business relationships and continue to make possible an economic system that is dependent upon promises and the keeping of one's word. They matter to those who work hard to build caring relationships—in traditional families and in new forms of community. They matter to those who build towns or counties or nations that do what is right for most people—without being coercive to those without power. They matter to those who care about the development of the next generation of the young—those in families and those who have no families.

People raised in religious congregations make this a society that cares about justice, although it often falls short. People raised in religious congregations make this a society that recognizes a responsibility in Bosnia and Somalia, although we may be confused about precisely what we ought to do there. People raised in religious congregations help us have a healthy skepticism about human perfection, reminding us of how our own society has permitted practices leading to near genocide of Native Americans, condoning African-American slavery for more than two centuries, exiling Japanese-American citizens to concentration camps, and allowing radioactive experimentation on other citizens. Religious congregations condition us to ask questions of right and wrong about public policy. Through our history the first questions about injustice often have been raised in congregations. After attempts to justify injustice as God's will, those congregations led us to debate and finally reject the practices.

Congregations have power and that power can have enormously creative influence in leading us toward an ever-more humane society. Critics and observers of American society since deToqueville have noted this role of congregations. We do well to remember, however, that they do have demonic potential. Congregations can care and teach us to care, but they can also be places where prejudices are nourished and grudges passed along to future generations.

Yes, congregations have power, enormous power. They matter. I do not plan to argue this point further, but you deserve to know that I start with this assumption.

Against this background, the fact that our churches and the congregations that make them up are in trouble is a concern not just to the religous community. It is a matter of concern for the health of the society itself.

In this book I contend that the storm buffeting the churches is very serious indeed. Much more serious than we have admitted to ourselves, and much more serious than our leaders have yet comprehended. The problems are not minor, calling for adjustments or corrections. They are problems that go to the roots of our institutions themselves. What I am describing here is not something we will fix. It is a state of existence in which we must learn to live even as we seek new directions for faithful response.

In my earlier book *The Once and Future Church,*[1] I explored some reasons for our being where we are. In my subsequenty book *More Than Numbers,*[2] I gave perspectives about and tools for congregations in this time between two ages. In this book I want to take up the argument of *The Once and Future Church* and push further ahead, delving deeper into the nature of the storm we are in and making suggestions for the future. Everything I say has been influenced by the hundreds of people who have worked with me in conferences and corresponded with me. Many have asked questions or given me feedback, making points I had never though about. I can therefore claim little in these pages as being original with me.

In Chapter 1 I begin with a discussion of the serious storm I see buffeting the churches. The storm is so serious, I believe, that it marks the end of "business of usual" for the churches and marks a need for us to begin again building church from the ground up.

The heart of my argument will be in chapters 2 and 3, in which I begin to restate for our time the basic functions of congregations—what the religous enterprise in congregations is really about. I will give the best clues I have about the process that is at the heart of congregational life—a process I call transformation. I am aware that I am calling for a radically different understanding of mssion, of evangelism, and of how individual congregational members are called to live it out.

That is followed by a chapter about the implications for regional judicatories and a chapter that identifies roadblocks in and guideposts on the road ahead. I have tried to include practical suggestions throughout. The first appendix is an educational design I use to help people work on some of these ideas. The second appendix gives the raw data for the graphs I use.

If my final chapter feels sermonic, forgive me. I deeply believe that the storm we are in presents the greatest opportunity the churches and religous leaders have ever had. Bar none. I also believe it is a deeper challenge and threat than religious leaders have faced in many centuries. We are in serious trouble that we will not get out of soon or easily. When we get clear of this storm, our religous institutions may bear little resemblance to those with which we grew up.

I have two other comments about what I am doing and why. In my books I have never used much of the language usually found in theological works. Some readers have complained that I am not adequately "theological" in my approach. That particular criticism confounds me. The substance of my concern and my method are both firmly based in a deep theological framework, but I approach things inductively, doing theology, as Terry Holmes and I used to describe it, "from the ground up." In another context, I described the way I work and think as "operational theology."[3] I do not plan to change that approach now, but I apologize if my language about congregations does not fulfill your expectations. In this book I am inviting you to do ecclesiology "from the ground up."

Finally, I want to invite you into this book as into a conversation. You know things I do not know, and I beg you to bring your knowledge to the table. Let your ideas work with mine, test them, argue with them. I know I have a limited point of view and that you have much to add. My insights come out of my life experience and bear the values and limits of their origin. Althought I wrote *The Once and Future Church* out of my own experience (primarily mainline Protestant), I was delighted that so many from very different backgrounds found it helpful. Those who have found it most helpful did what I hoped they would do: They translated it into their own situations; they used it to ignite questions they had about their own congregations. I have had rabbis tell me how helpful my use of the term Christendom was to them in understanding the relationship of their congregations to their world. Pastors of independent congregations have told me about the "connectionalism" they have discovered among congregations that were technically "nonconnectional."

So join me in a conversation. I hope that what I have to say out of my life, experience, and commitments will help you illuminate points of your life, experience, and commitments. My experience will not tell you what to do, but you can hold your experience up to mine, test my ideas to see how they translate—or if they translate. If you do that work, I think our conversation will help you discover things that should be on your agenda.

I speak out of my own faith, too. I often use words of that faith because they are how I know to express what I perceive to be true. I have tried not to use language that will offend those of other faith positions, but I have not tried to homogenize my language to do so. If my words do cause offense to your way of understanding or speaking your truth, I ask two things of you–that you accept my apology for any insensitivity and that you go back to what offended you and try to reach through the words to what I am trying to say.

I deeply believe God calls us severally to move into the future. I believe we need one another if we are to hear our own call clearly. We hear best in dialogue with one another as well as with God. I will say what I mean as clearly as I can, but I know my vision is distorted, no matter how hard I try. I hope you will discover things I do not know as you interact with what I have to say. I hope you will discover things you did not know. For both of us this dialogue is likely to hold surprises. This is intrinsic, I believe, in the process of revelation.

This is not an optimistic book. I see much that is difficult ahead of us. I do, however, speak from a deep and abiding hope. The faith I learned in a congregation in South Carolina in the 1930s is desperately needed in the 2030s. That faith has been built up and transformed by life experiences, by relationships, and by learning, but in many ways its basics are unchanged. But the faith I received in the thirties was clothed in a world view of a now-past age, and its institutional "delivery system" reflected that age's understanding of how to do things. The institutional forms in which I learned faith and the structures for carrying it on have been hard to change. Many of them continue as today's structures, although they stopped working in some places years ago. Many of us have worked hard to reinvent those forms–with mixed success.

God calls us to a daunting task: to take those structures and those resources of faith and re-present them in forms that will carry them into the next century. I am astonished that God would invite us into such a task of co-creation. God obviously sees potential in us that we have a hard time accepting. And I believe that potential can be approached only as we in our differences enter into dialogue with each other. This book is my attempt to work at that task.

LOREN B. MEAD
Washington
Ash Wednesday, 1994

NOTES

1. Loren B. Mead, *The Once and Future Church* (Washington, DC: The Alban Institute, 1991).

2. Loren B. Mead, *More Than Numbers* (Washington, DC: The Alban Institute, 1993).

3. Loren B. Mead, "Operational Theology" in *Patterns in Parish Development*, ed. Celia Allison Hahn (New York: Seabury Press, 1974), pp. 157-58.

CHAPTER 1

The Storm We Are In:
It's Worse Than We Thought

THE STORM ABOUT NUMBERS: MEMBERSHIP LOSSES

Those in what have been called mainline churches are feeling particularly defensive and sensitive about membership losses. Fast-growing congregations and denominations look on the traditional bellwethers--Methodist, Lutheran, Episcopal, Presbyterian, Congregational--and say, "Main? More like sideline these days." Mainliners wince. Sometimes we try to kid ourselves about the number by talking about how we think they've "bottomed out."

Reasons for the declines are as numerous as the commentators. I have heard reasons ranging from "it's because of all the social ministries the mainline got involved in in the sixties" to "it's because the mainline is not as aggressive in its social ministries as it was in the sixties." The polarization between social liberals and conservatives plays itself out in this debate--with conservatives seeing the problem as too much liberalism and the liberals seeing the problem as too much conservatism. Each side accuses the other of divisiveness.

"Too much concern for political correctness," scoffs the conservative. "That's why everybody is leaving!"

"Fascist pietism," accuses the liberal, "turns off the people who want to make a difference at this point of historic change."

Respected researchers state that the church-membership losses illustrate a universal law of American religion: Sect-like religions sells; church-like religion dies. Their critics reply, loosely translated, "Horse-hockey." (I am sure you can recognize the high intellectual level of and deep philosophical basis for this debate.)

It is hard to get clear data that is not filtered through someone's ideological presuppositions. It is also clear that "church numbers" is a fluid crap game. Many people consider themselves "members" but are not listed in the church statistics. Many people feel free to tell a census report or survey recorder that they are Presbyterians or Catholics, but they have never happened to mention it to the local Presbyterian or Catholic church! Kirk Hadaway, research officer for the United Church of Christ, has a felicitous name for the group: "mental members"![1] More recent research by Hadaway and his colleague Penny Marler of Samford University indicated that perhaps only half of the people who tell pollsters they go to church actually show up on Sunday. So we are in a land of much data, some of it conflicting, much of it closely touched by strong biases in interpretation. Further, words such as *member* and *attender* have ambiguous meanings. In our work we have located people who never darken the church doors, but they have strong emotional ties to a congregation or denomination for which they care a great deal. Still others somehow crept onto the church rolls and simply do not care a fig about the church. A number of these people, for reasons of church administration, have been taken off the rolls. Some who are on probably ought to be taken off, and some who are off probably still ought to be on. Some, who have been off for years and years, discover in a life crisis the need to reconnect.

There is ambiguity in what we know. Not all mainline congregations are losing members, and not all parts of the country are losing to the same degree. Mainline denominations can boast some rapidly growing congregations—the match for almost any specific local growth claimed by any other denomination. In some judicatories growth occurs routinely almost across the board. Statistics get skewed when one judicatory with two large congregations and many small ones reports significant growth—which was limited to those two congregations while sixty others each experienced losses. The truth one experiences locally is more complicated than the statistics.

The fact remains. Membership loss is the overall picture in the mainline denominations. There is no question. Denominational executives and leaders announce membership initiatives, "decades of evangelism," programs with aggressive growth targets. In spite of that, the curves continue downward.

The overall statistics as reported annually in the *Yearbook of American and Canadian Churches* show remarkably consistent curves in several denominations over the past few decades.[2] For simplicity I will illustrate with curves for the Episcopal, Lutheran, Presbyterian, United Methodist, and United Church of Christ denominations.[3]

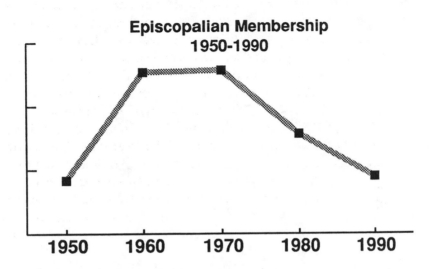

Episcopalian Membership 1950-1990

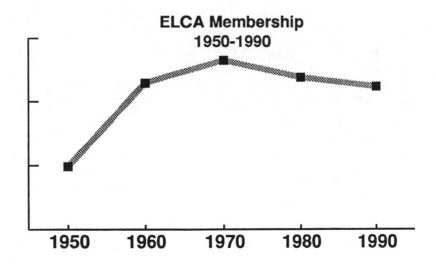

ELCA Membership 1950-1990

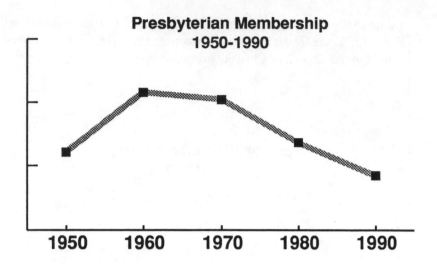

Presbyterian Membership
1950-1990

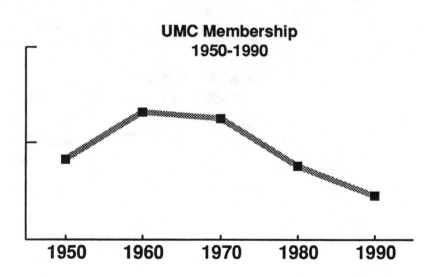

UMC Membership
1950-1990

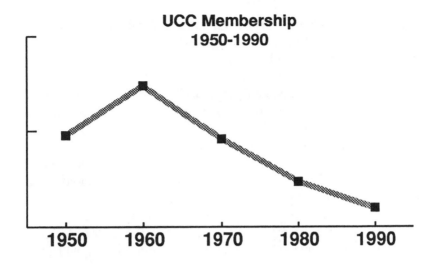

**UCC Membership
1950-1990**

Note that the curves are relatively congruent in shape and direction. They go up and down at similar points along the scale.

That is not to say that the denominations have similar numbers of members. The Methodist curve begins at well over nine million members while the United Church of Christ begins at a bit under two million. Methodists can take wry comfort in the fact that they are failing from a higher beginning point than the Presbyterians and Episcopalians. They have a bigger cushion underneath them.

As I have shown these five graphs to people of many denominations around the country, I have sensed their surprise. You see, before seeing all these *different* curves, each group was aware only of its own downward curve. Each had generally thought that it alone had a problem: that it alone had done something wrong. Cause-and-effect thinking had led each to find someone or something to blame to explain the problem they thought nobody else had. Episcopalians blamed a social ministry program called General Convention Special Program (GCSP) of the late sixties. Or the new prayer book. Or the new hymn book. Or the ordination of women. Presbyterians are still blaming the controversy about Angela Davis. Or the move to Louisville. Some Methodists are still blaming Bishop Oxnam or the racism program of the World Council of Churches in the sixties. I imagine UCC members probably still blame Governor Winthrop for his policies in the

Massachusetts Bay Colony! Lutherans are sure it's because they reunited and moved to Higgins Road.

Closer to home, people blamed their own pastor, bishop, or executive, if not some particular practice they disliked. "It's the new hymns!" "It's that motion they passed at the general assembly!" "Our minister uses the new version of the Bible. That's the root of it."[4] Still others blamed the usual catchall—permissiveness.

The five curves together suggest that we are involved in something larger than we had thought. An analysis of the problem carried out internally within a single denomination is simply not adequate. Solutions designed as one denomination's response to its problem will overlook what may be the key factors because the most important factor in the declines may be outside any of the denominations. It may even be that efforts designed to deal with one denomination's problem—any program designed for one denomination—will simply be wasted effort. Something is going on that is bigger than any of the denominations. It is this "something else" that makes me talk about the storm we are all in.

An interesting book from an earlier period—*Understanding Church Growth and Decline*—differentiated between four sets of variables that affect growth curves.[5] It claimed that making sense of the curves themselves requires us to analyze each of four quite different factors: (1) national contextual trends—factors related to the changes in the social and intellectual character of the larger community, the nation; (2) local contextual trends—things going on in the local community and shaping the lives of local residents; (3) national institutional trends—national changes specific to each of the denominational families and often different from those of other denominations; (4) local institutional trends that involve what is happening specific to the congregation one is looking at.

These researchers suggest that growth or decline curves need to take account of all four variables. They argue against too simple or too quick a judgment about where "the trouble" may be.

Church leaders have had all this information before them for at least a decade now. In the nineties articles in *Time*, *Newsweek*, and many local newspapers have made American laypeople aware of the problem. This awakening of the ordinary congregational member has moved the membership issue onto the front burners of conversation and action and put the professional denominational leaders on the defensive.

I am reminded of the similar kind of public outcry early in the sixties following publication of John Robinson's popular paperback *Honest to God* and the subsequent interview in the Sunday *Times* of London. Ideas that had been bandied about for a generation or two in theological seminaries of England were suddenly dumped into the public arena. The laity was shocked and upset.

Losses of membership have moved out of the private preserve of the researchers and the church's program professionals and suddenly become public property. And the public—church members—is concerned. Clergy and denominational leaders, particularly among the mainline denominations, are on the defensive.

What can be said about these curves of increasing and declining membership?

Right after the Second World War the mainline denominations experienced a remarkable growth of membership, almost across the board, and that increase peaked by the early sixties. Since about 1965 there has been a strong and continuous decline in membership in mainline denominations; some have lost from 20 to 40 percent of their members.

That is not the whole story. Statistics can mislead, and these curves do. They present a picture significantly more optimistic than facts warrant. They measure the sheer number of members on the rolls of these denominations, not the relationship of the number of members to the number of potential members. Three researchers raise this question in their interesting book *Vanishing Boundaries: The Religion of Mainline Baby Boomers*.[6] It is misleading to look at the sheer number of members without comparing them to general population statistics. It is as if an automobile company were to tell its stockholders how many of its cars were currently on the road without telling how many were sold in relationship to the number of potential buyers out there in the market.

In *Vanishing Boundaries* Hoge, Johnson, and Luidens raise the additional questions of what is happening in the social environment in which the churches exist.[7] That information is even more unsettling for people in mainline churches than the raw membership charts.

Again, the graphs I included earlier in the chapter point to rapid growth of the mainline churches after the Second World War, followed by a period of rapid losses. No one likes to see reduced numbers and strength. That would be true even if the population remained stable. If the membership losses occurred at a period of rapid general population growth, the losses would be much more serious. And that is what happened.

But as far as we know, no one until Hoge, Johnson, and Luidens ever talked about it. Once the *Vanishing Boundaries* manuscript became available, other researchers have made the same point.[8]

In the years charted above, the number of potential members of churches did not remain stable. Actually it increased significantly. The actual population of the country grew by considerably more than a third in those years. Had the denominational membership curves increased by a third they would have been holding their own. The downward curve speaks for itself. But their actual losses when compared to the potential in the population are at least 30 percent worse than the graphs. The graphs we have, disturbing as they are, are misleading and significantly more optimistic than the facts warrant.

Let me put it baldly. What appeared to be a clear decline in numbers begins to look more like a nosedive. There is the curve that describes the population of the United States between 1950 and 1990:

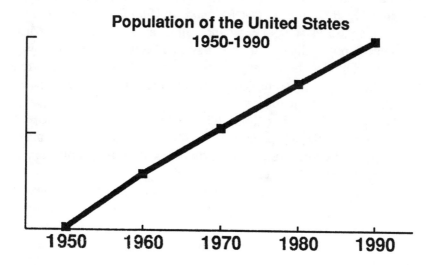

Population of the United States 1950-1990

1950   1960   1970   1980   1990

For a period—roughly 1945-1965—the Episcopalians and the Presbyterians experienced a significant period of unusual growth, growth without precedent for them. Although all the denominations I cite experienced solid growth in the years following World War II and the baby boom, the growth of the Episcopal and Presbyterian churches outstripped the population growth for a few years. For a while those denominations experienced comparatively more members—and consequently more money—than previously. (Later I will comment on many consequences of this period of unusual growth.)[9]

Episcopalian Membership as a Percentage of the Population 1950-1990

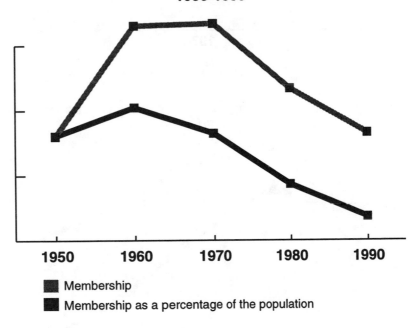

■ Membership

■ Membership as a percentage of the population

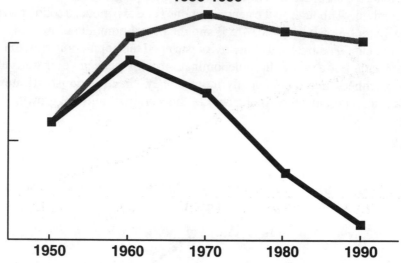

**ELCA Membership as a Percentage of the Population
1950-1990**

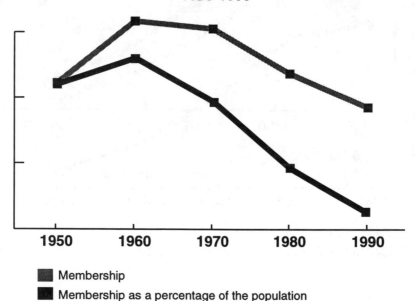

**Presbyterian Membership as a Percentage of the Population
1950-1990**

■ Membership
■ Membership as a percentage of the population

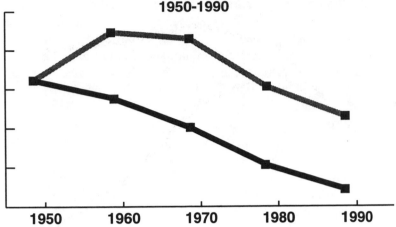

UMC Membership as a Percentage of the Population 1950-1990

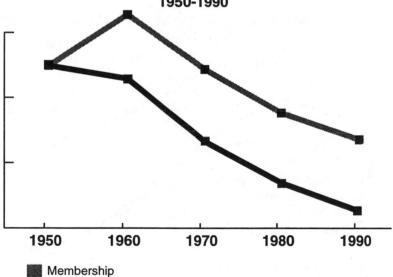

UCC Membership as a Percentage of the Population 1950-1990

■ Membership
■ Membership as a percentage of the population

The postwar increase of the general population had two main ingredients—the baby boom and immigration. And neither of these gives much comfort to mainline churches. Research indicates that postwar members of mainline churches had fewer children than members in previous generations, and the congregations are not adequately holding even those diminished numbers of young members.[10] It is also true that the mainline denominations have not generally been in the forefront of effective evangelization of immigrant populations.

When all is said and done about the numbers game, the mainline denominations face significant bad news. I believe the news as reflected in market share is considerably worse than we have let ourselves believe. As one looks at numbers of members, it is clear that the churches are in the middle of a storm of considerable proportions.

That's not all the bad news.

THE MONEY GAME

In the area of financing religious institutions, the picture is mixed but overall no more encouraging than the membership trends. One very positive piece of news is that mainline church members have risen to new levels of generosity. Although there has been a significant decline in membership, the loyal members left are more and more generous to their religious institutions. Per-member giving has risen more rapidly than inflation. In the short term, more dollars are being given by fewer members. As an example, the Episcopal Church, which moved to support tithing at all policy levels, has had a strong response to a concerted national effort.

But in the long term, resources are likely to decline sharply if present membership trends continue.

I will outline some significant problems.

The members who give are older as well as fewer than in previous generations. The givers are not being replaced. The full impact of this will not be known for a decade or two, but it is an ominous bit of news. The younger generation of members, perhaps caught in the tension of lower family incomes and higher costs, does not yet seem to have bought into the level of generosity that marks its elders. Certainly that pressure is acute where single-parent families are involved. Changes in society that have required many families to depend on two pay checks have restricted the availability of funding for church programs.

Of course congregational-institutional expenses are rising at least as fast as income. In many locations costs are rising faster than income. The result? A squeeze in congregational budgets for at least the past two decades, a crunch in the budgets of those dependent on congregational offerings (including regional judicatory budgets), and chronic crisis and periodic emergencies in national budgets.

The prognosis for those who depend on congregational financial support is cloudy, to say the least–schools, colleges, seminaries, benevolent agencies. One can understand the aggressive way those institutions are emphasizing planned giving and endowment.

The closer an agency's or institution's ties to the local church, the more likely it is to find support. Denominational leaders tend to see this as reflective of narrow parochialism; I do not agree. The problem simply is that costs are rising more rapidly than income. I see no evidence that it will get better.

Denomination after denomination has engaged in systematic budget cutting every year for twenty years.[11] We do not seem to notice it until there is a cataclysmic shortfall, as has occurred with Lutheran, Presbyterian, and Episcopal churches in the early nineties with major staff lay-offs. Looking at the statistics and the trends, I wonder, Who will be next year's victim? Remaining denominational staff seem to be saying, with crossed fingers, "Thank heaven it was them and not us. Besides, we fixed the problem when we bottomed out last time."

My statistics do not deal with the emotional toll taken on conscientious staff people in judicatory and denominational offices who face annual cuts in the resources they need to do the jobs they feel called to do and want to do well. Most of the talented staff people I know in national offices have faced year after year of decreasing budgets, with dollar increases less than inflation and with salary increases on hold almost every year. Many of our talented people sit in offices without the funds to mount programs or even call meetings. This has something to do, also, with the adversarial climate that develops between congregations and their regional and national bodies.

A vicious circle exists. Denominational staff people design programs to respond to what they hear congregations needing. They announce the new programs based on what they hope budgets will fund. Then income shortfalls make no new money available to produce the programs already announced and expected by congregations. Nobody takes responsibility for the shortfall. Denominational staff sometimes mutter about "having to make bricks without straw." We have been asking them to do exactly that for more than twenty years, and we have been complaining about the quality of the bricks at least as long. Everybody seems trapped, victimized. The fact is that there is no money and we do not know how to cut back.

The interrelationship of costs and budgets was dramatically presented to me recently by a Presbyterian friend. "Our experience in 1991 was that national mission giving declined exactly in proportion to the increase in medical insurance payments for the clergy." As local costs increase, money is kept "at home," not sent "abroad." When Hartford Seminary and the Alban Institute collaborated on a study comparing 1970-1980 church statistics in New England and the Middle Atlantic States to 1970-1980 census data, we found that income to congregations stayed slightly ahead of inflation for those ten years, but that the congregations' giving to other institutions beyond themselves did not keep up with inflation (although actual dollar amounts did increase.)[12]

In large, "successful" congregations, it might be easy to overlook the grass-roots implications of such budget squeezing. But the local import of this crunch is described by Rev. Gay Jennings in an unpublished report based on her work in the Episcopal Diocese of Ohio. In this report she has a narrow focus, the economic viability of the "standard" model parish structure that so many congregations struggle to support.

> It is no longer possible to assume that a significant majority of congregations have the resources to employ a full-time seminary trained priest as well as support building facilities, program, and outside giving. Chuck Wilson and Wes Frensdorff published a study concluding that the budget threshold for this full complement is between $75,000 and $85,000. In 1992, the Diocese of Ohio has concluded that the bare minimum needed is approximately $80,000. That's the magic number. Forty percent of the one hundred and eleven congregations in the Diocese of Ohio have budgets of less than $80,000. Almost half our congregations are near, at, or below the level of financial viability.[13]

She goes on to put her experience in perspective:

> In 1982, only seven Ohio congregations were served by clergy on a part-time basis. Today (1992) thirty-three of our congregations, or just about thirty percent, are served either by cluster clergy or bi-vocational

clergy. The Diocese of Ohio is not an unusual diocese. We are not a blip on the curve. And we are not a poor diocese either.

What this talented staff person is saying is echoed across the country in difficult local decisions as conditions change, making it impossible for religious institutions to carry the financial responsibilities they have in the past. Let me be clear–I am not upset that we are being forced to face difficult decisions and make changes. At this point I am simply noting that the financial squeeze is having impact in community after community, denomination after denomination, year after year. It is a part of the big picture, and the news is not good. This is all part of the storm we are in.

THE SECULAR-SOCIETY GAME

I have already mentioned the Hoge-Johnson-Luidens research, published as *Vanishing Boundaries*. This empirical study of six hundred Presbyterians raises large questions for those of us who would position the churches as a resource to the coming century. I will summarize some of their work.

Between 1989 and 1991 these researchers located about 500 upper-age baby boomers (people who were just under forty-two at the time of the research) and, for comparison, 125 people from a slightly older group. All were Presbyterians, and all had gone through the Presbyterian system as young people up to and including being confirmed. With a lot of persistence and help from local congregations, the researchers contacted most of those on the target lists for telephone interviews.

The full results of these fascinating conversations can be found in their book. For our purposes it is useful to note that as middle-age adults 52 percent of the 625 were still actively involved in church life; 48 percent were in categories defined as "unchurched," but only 8 percent of the total were defined as "nonreligious."

What had led to people "dropping out" of church life?

Clear, definitive answers did not come out. But researchers made some conclusions contrary to the common wisdom espoused in denominational debates.

First, it is not true that many mainline kids have moved to conservative or fundamentalist churches. At least this is not true of the sample we studied.

Second, it is not true that these young people have left because they were sore at denominational leaders or policies. In reality, few know about these matters and few care. The majority aren't interested in denominational politics or even denominational identity.

Third, it is not true that they have left due to attitudes about congregational church life (as opposed to belief factors).[14]

Most of these drop-outs did not drop out primarily because of something the religious institution was doing or not doing. Rather, it is simply as if the church somehow slipped off their radar screens. It ceased to be important to them.

The researchers hypothesize that the most important factor in the drop-out is not something the churches are doing or not doing, it is the character of the culture surrounding the congregations.

This information is startling and dismaying to church leaders. It suggests that the things we know how to do best have little to do with who stays or who goes. We know how to develop programs. Apparently this population is not interested in programs. It suggests that the very way we organized ourselves to respond to the problem of church drop-outs may have very little ipact on the people who drop out.

The cultural environment may be more determinative to membership losses than the character of what the congregation is and does. That seems to be the lesson of this particular piece of research. It helps us get perspective on the fact that 80 percent of the people in Alabama belong to a church while only 15 to 20 percent of the population does so in California and Oregon. I have a hard time, much as I love my friends in Alabama, believing that they are four or five times "better" than my card-carrying church friends in California. What's *outside* the congregation may be more determinative of continuing membership than what's *inside*. Can this also be true of the attraction of new members? Might it also be shaped more by the environment than by what we do inside the churches?

But if the issue of losing members is so greatly a matter of the social environment, how, then, do we address it?

I am not convinced that the researchers have the final word on this one. Is there more we need to know? Yet their research raises the stakes for us in religious institutions. Our very ways of doing anything about the declines may be in question. What do we always do to fix something that has gone wrong? Analyze it and develop a program to fix it.

What happens if the problem does not respond to program? That is the provocative question raised by this research.

In the area of membership losses, we are not dealing with something that is responsive to a new program—even a very good program. We are engaged in a basic interaction between religious institutions and the nature of social environment. The researchers have lifted the problem to a new level of difficulty and called us to move beyond our narrow answers to address larger issues than we have heretofore had the guts to face.

If I am right, we do not need a new set of programs. We need churches with a new consciousness of themselves and their task. The structures we have inherited have shown little capacity for such radical rethinking of their identity.

That is more bad news for the religious structures we now have. That is another part of the storm we face.

SOME UNEXPLODED BOMBS THAT ARE LYING AROUND

I want to describe a few things that I see lying around the churches or the society with the potential for having enormous impact in the years ahead. My vision is narrow: I am thinking about them in terms of how they may well affect our religious structures. It may actually be good for some of these bombs to go off; the society and the churches might fare better than we are right now. But if any of them were to go off, we would have to make major adjustments in our thinking.

Tax Policy

Religious institutions are supported by many elements of our governmental tax policies. A few obvious examples:

- When filing income taxes, people itemizing deductions can claim 100 percent of their gifts to churches.

- The IRS allows people some deductions for property or services that a church would otherwise have to pay for. (When I bake twelve loaves of bread for my parish bazaar every year, I can deduct the cost of the flour from my taxes.)

- Most real estate owned by religious congregations is exempt from local property taxes.

- Over and above their salaries, many pastors receive tax-exempt income as housing allowances and utility payments.

The case can be and is made that religious institutions provide important, valuable services to the community. But that case can be made only in a society that generally looks with favor on religious institutions. My parents, for example, had no difficulty justifying their paying a little higher property tax each year to make it possible for the churches in our town to have "free" fire and policy protection. They believed those churches were important, even the ones they did not belong to. I am not sure that point is as obvious today to people paying property-tax rates that have "gone through the roof." Times have changed.

In many places these tax-exempt policies are likely to remain intact for another generation or two. Perhaps more. But then what? Only thirty or forty years ago I never would have dreamed that neighborhood organizations would oppose the building of a new church. Today in many communities Sunday morning parking is a more valued resource than another religious institution. In metropolitan Washington, D.C., where I live, churches have serious problems attempting to expand or relocate. Similarly, as local communities and the federal government find it harder and harder to balance budgets, they are sure to reconsider the tax exemptions of church property. Churches will simply have to pay the costs of police and fire services. This will be especially true as property owners who have nothing to do with churches take a jaundiced view of a group that seems to be getting a "free ride" on the backs of their own higher taxes. This may not happen for years in some places, but I think the pressures are inevitable.

My father, a small-town doctor, never charged a cleric of any faith for professional services. That practice was mirrored by drug stores and department stores and many local merchants. Those practices were a way that society's values quietly subsidized religious activity. How quickly those practices change. They seem quaint just one generation later. The only "pastoral discount" I count on is free parking at two local hospitals when I make pastoral calls wearing my clerical collar. Pastors' families have adapted to changes like this, partly by the rapid increase of two-income families in the manse or rectory.

What would happen in your congregation if the pastor's housing allowance became fully taxable? Many congregations would try to find a way to increase the pastor's income by several thousand dollars to compensate for lost purchasing power. Where the congregation simply did not have the resources to do so, the pastor would face a significant effective decrease of income. That has already happened in relationship to Social Security taxes. When clergy became eligible for Social Security several decades ago, they were declared "self-employed" for Social Security purposes. Congregations with the means to do so often give an "allowance" equal to half the Social Security tax (the amount regularly paid by an employer). In congregations that could not provide this payment, the clergy took a significant hit. Some spouses decided to seek employment. Such choices have economic implications for all congregations and for the support of clergy. When money is short, hard choices have to be made.

What would happen if all church property except the worship space were put on the tax rolls of the town? (This is already happening in some places, with argument only over what constitutes "worship space.") What would happen to a congregation's ability to make mission gifts outside the congregation? What would happen to the ability to pay salary increases?

What would happen if charitable deductions were to be limited to 5 percent of taxable income? Or to a maximum amount—say five thousand dollars—to any one institution? Such a "hit" would require pledgers and tithers to do some hard thinking and planning. Some would not maintain their level of giving if the gifts were taxed. What would that do to our ability to keep up building and pay salaries, much less make assessment payments to our denominations? (What will happen even this year to small congregations that have to take on new recording and notification responsibilities to help donors justify gifts of $250 or more reported to the IRS?)

My crystal ball does not tell me that any of these scenarios will happen this year or even in the next decade. But my reading of the society says that these policy changes are likely at some time in a world increasingly divorced from religious roots. If past experience says anything to us, any of these changes could happen very rapidly through legal actions.

In summary, a change in tax policy could have direct and negative impact upon how churches do their work.

Medical Costs

This bomb has already started exploding. Medical costs are escalating out of sight. I previously mentioned the impact these rises seem to be causing in the Presbyterian Church. But the impact is across the board. (This very day, as I write, I have received a letter from the Episcopal diocese that carries my credentials. The letter portends a health cost crisis. Either the benefits will have to be reduced or the premium payments made by the clergy will have to be increased.) Every congregation, every pastor, every judicatory will have a rapidly growing worry about this matter, no matter how it funds its medical insurance. Again, there is little churches can do directly: the problem is societal. If these costs are contained in our lifetime, if national universal health insurance is in place and proves to be workable, the rapid increases may come under control. *May* come under control. Until that happens every congregation will face it every year. Every judicatory will face it every year. Every national pension board will face it every year, and many congregations will have to deal with increases every year at budget time.

Actually, medical expense is just one—currently most obvious—piece of a larger category of potentially exploding commodity costs that could have similar impact. Does any one remember 1972, when oil prices doubled and doubled again in a few months? Do you remember the struggle with church budgets that had been honed and finally balanced—and then blown out of the water? In our high-tech age there is potential for other unexpected bombs of cost to explode.

The medical cost bomb is already going off, and it has potential for continuing impact on the churches. There may be others. They are bad news.

Litigation

My generation grew up in a world in which no one would have dreamed of suing the church for anything. We now inhabit a world in which people who fall off the curb in front of the church think about suing. Many pastors wonder if they should carry malpractice insurance. Judicatories are already swamped by unexpected legal costs. The burst of sexual misconduct cases of the late eighties and the nineties is a long overdue call to accounting for professional behavior, but it brings in its wake unexplored thickets of liability and cost. Even such routine things as extending a call to a new pastor may require expensive private investigations of personal behavior. It does not seem that these costs will diminish, and they could skyrocket.

Theological Education and Unemployed Clergy

We have invented an enormously expensive form of professional theological education, the graduates of which are priced out of the financial reach of more and more congregations. We are not alone in this. Other professions (legal and medical, to name but two) have developed similar overcapacity for training. My crystal ball does not tell me what might happen in this realm, but I note it as an important worry for us all. Whenever there is such an excess of capacity for training in comparison with the market for services, there is cause for concern.

It is difficult to articulate the full problem. Many denominations really do not know how many candidates for ordination are in the pipeline and how many clergy are needed. It is clear the full-time pastor assigned to one place is affordable to fewer and fewer congregations. Gay Jennings states that in one decade 26 of 111 congregations in her Episcopal diocese stopped being able to afford a full-time pastor.

The other side of the issue is equally challenging. The churches have developed a large cadre of people who feel a powerful call from God to be pastors: they have made real sacrifices to be trained but for one reason or another they cannot be placed in pastoral leadership. They have been displaced for many reasons. In the Catholic church marriage disqualifies thousands of trained pastoral leaders. Many highly trained women ready and able to move into pastoral leadership in that communion are blocked by the prohibition on their ordination. In Protestant churches many congregations who want a full-time pastor cannot pay a living wage. In still other cases well-trained, able female clergy are not able to be placed because congregations are not ready to accept their leadership. Thousands of people are trained and would like full-time pastoral positions but are inhibited for one reason or another. One wonders at the hidden costs of disappointment and bitterness that churches may be storing up in some of their most caring people.

I know of one study that may throw light on this issue: Gay Jennings, whom I quoted above, did another study to find out what happened to people who were selected out *before seminary training*. She discovered that whatever high potential those leaders had when they applied for ordination

was effectively lost to the denomination as a result of being "selected out."
A high proportion of those disappointed candidates did not return to their
congregations in roles of lay leadership but left with anger and bitterness.
Speculating from and going far beyond these findings, I worry what will
happen to people who seek ordination, go through the rigorous and expensive training for the necessary years, then find their gifts superfluous to the
institution for which they had been prepared to sacrifice so much. It feels to
me that such a system of stewardship of leaders is fraught with danger. I
would certainly welcome further studies in this area.

If we have developed an expensive institution for training pastors, if
fewer and fewer churches can pay for those pastors, and if this experience
is a negative for trained and unemployed or under-employed people, we
have more bad news about the future of the church.

CONCLUSION

Bad news is never much fun to the bearer or to the receiver. My hunch is
that much of what I've writt en is not a total surprise to my reader. I do not
believe I am exaggerating in saying that we are indeed in the middle of
stormy seas. The situation the churches are in is much worse than we have
been led to think by leaders whistling in the dark, telling us that the troubles
have "bottomed out" or that "we are turning around." As I see it, we will
not get out of these complex issues in the simplistic ways we have used
before. This is not something we can generate a program to fix. A project
to increase church membership will not work. Nor will a new improved
stewardship program. This news is bad news precisely because what we
have done in the past is no longer sufficient. What we know how to do is not
going to still the storm. This is not good news.

And yet, I write this book because of my confidence in the religious
community and its dedication to trying to listen to and follow God. I want
this book to help us end our shallow optimism that everything will turn out all
right. I want this book to help us face God's call to reshape our lives and our
institutions in faithfulness to God's call into the future. This is not an optimistic call for us to "fix it." It is a statement that we are, indeed, in the middle
of a vast storm, the end of which we shall not see.

NOTES

1. C. Kirk Hadaway, *What Can We Do About Church Dropouts?* (Nashville: Abingdon Press, 1990), ch 2-3.

2. Kenneth B. Bedell, ed., *Yearbook of American and Canadian Churches* (Nashville: Abingdon Press, 1993). The data for the illustrations also draws on the figures from many such annual reports as published in David A. Roozen and C. Kirk Hadaway, ed., *Church and Denominational Growth* (Nashville: Abingdon Press, 1993), appen., Table A1.1. This raw data is noted in Appendix B. In the interests of accuracy it must be noted that in several years since 1990 the Episcopal Church has showed a small net gain in numbers, but not percent of population. This encouraging statistic is, however, problematic in that the definition of "member" was slightly changed.

3. Figures 1, 3, and 5 chart denominations categorized as "liberal Protestant." Figures 2 and 4 are for denominations categorized as "moderate Protestant." Any such designations involve difficult judgment calls. These categories are described in William McKinney and W. Clark Roof, *Mainline American Religion* (New York: Pilgrim Press, 1984). The same categories are used in Roozen and Hadaway, *Church and Denominational Growth*.

4. Fellow North Carolinians may remember a classic story about how things have changed in churches when it comes to pointing fingers in blame. Bunny Boyd was an immensely popular professor of religion at the University of North Carolina in the forties and fifties, when the Revised Standard Version was first released. In backwoods Carolina the newfangled language for the familiar stories was a shock, to say the least. One conservative pastor staged a book burning at Rocky Mount. This hit the headlines in newspapers across the state and caused an uproar in Professor Boyd's nine o'clock class. "What about what happened in Rocky Mount?" they asked.

"What happened?" he responded, not having checked the morning's *News and Disturber.*

They told him about the book burning and he replied, "Wonderful!"

When asked to defend his statement, he said, "Book burning is much better. We used to burn the people who translated!"

5. Dean R. Hoge and David A. Roozen, ed., *Understanding Church Growth and Decline* (New York: Pilgrim Press, 1979). See especially ch. 14, "Some Sociological Conclusions about Church Trends," 315-33. See also Andrew Greeley, *Religious Change in America* (Cambridge, Mass.: Harvard University Press, 1989).

6. Dean R. Hoge, Benton Johnson, and Donald Luidens, *Vanishing Boundaries: The Religion of Mainline Baby Boomers* (Louisville: Westminster/John Knox, 1994). Findings are summarized in a number of papers and articles, including "What

Happened to the Youth Who Grew Up in Our Churches," *Congregations*, no. 5 (September-October 1992).

7. In fairness to the authors, I need to say that this is not their main point. They are doing an impressive study of what has happened to baby boomers in one denomination. Even this minor point of theirs is an extremely important new issue for denominational leaders to take into account. How much more impressive is the rest of the book.

8. See Roozen and Hadaway, *Church and Denominational Growth.*

9. Data in these two graphs are derived from data noted in Appendix B. The idea of the graphs is derived from *Vanishing Boundaries*. Two things show dramatically here: the period of anomalous growth between about 1945 and 1965 and the steeper downward slope of recent church membership.

10. Here Hoge, Johnson, and Luidens, *Vanishing Boundaries*, makes its major contributions. See also McKinney and Roof, *Mainline American Religion.*

11. I tell my denominational friends that our budget reductions remind me of a Carolina friend who had a marvelous hunting dog that he took hunting every Saturday. Trouble was, the dog's tail was long and shaggy, and it would pick up cockleburs. By Monday he would have chewed them all out, but he also had a mass of painful sores, yet the dog loved to hunt. . . . So the owner said, "The only thing I can think to do is to make him a bob-tailed dog." He continued, "But I really don't want to hurt him. So I think I'll just cut off an inch of tail at a time!" I rest my case.

12. *Church Membership Statistics: 1970-1980* (Washington, DC: The Alban Institute, 1983).

13. Gay Jennings, unpublished report, Episcopal Diocese of Ohio, 2230 Euclid Ave., Cleveland, OH 44115. Some similar points are made in Dean Hoge, Jackson W. Carroll, and Francis K. Scheets, *Patterns of Parish Leadership* (Kansas City, Mo.: Sheed and Ward, 1988) This book examines the cost of providing professional leadership in congregations of four denominations: Episcopal, Roman Catholic, Evangelical Lutheran Church in American, and United Methodist. The research was carried out on 1984 budgets, so it dealt with one of the Lutheran bodies that later formed the Evangelical Lutheran Church in America.

14. Hoge, Johnson, and Luidens, "What Happened to the Youth Who Grew Up in Our Churches," *Congregations.*

CHAPTER 2

The Heart of the Matter:
The Apostolic Task of the Church

GOING TO THE ROOTS:
THE GOOD NEWS AND ITS PROCLAMATION OF JESUS

If the churches are in the middle of stormy times, facing perhaps unprecedented challenges over the next few generations, it is important that we be clear about what we need our congregations to be. If we are to transform the congregations,we first need to get clear about why we need them and what we need them to be for us. Earlier generations had assumptions about what congregations were. Those assumptions worked for hundreds of years, helping Christian men and women carry out what they understood mission to be in their time. Those assumptions led to the establishment of institutions and structures in addition to congregations, all shaped by the church's concern to build Christendom.[1]

Those assumptions no longer work in our times, leading to increasing trouble in our congregations and in the institutions around them. In addition, the storm we are in has led us into confusion about the way that lies ahead. We often feel lost, and with some desperation we sometimes defend our congregations and our other religious institutions.

But for what purpose? That's the important question. For what? The question pushes us to look to the roots of what we need congregations for.

One can visit congregations that seem to exist to preserve eighteenth- and nineteenth-century music. I love music enough to hope somebody takes on that task, but I'm not sure that's what I want congregations for—or that that is what they have to contribute. Do congregations exist so they can preserve genteel social structures? I'm not opposed to that, if some people want to do it, but I'm not sure that's what we need congregations for.

Are they to preserve an ethnic heritage from the past? Again, I think that's a good thing, but I'm not sure we need congregations to do that. Do we need them to provide meeting places for Alcoholics Anonymous? Do we need them so every community will have a paid pastoral counselor available to those who cannot pay for a therapist? Do we need them to provide a meeting place for people concerned for community betterment? I have no quarrel with any of those as by-products of congregations, but none of them seems big enough, frankly. None of them carries–by itself–the kind of power that comes from connecting with God's purposes and intentions. They are nice enough in themselves, but they hardly provide the kind of energy that turns societies upside down.

What are congregations for? I want to address that issue first. That is what I mean by going to the roots. Once we do that, we can work on how to make congregations move toward fulfilling their purposes.

If the bad news that surrounds us is as pervasive as I suggest, it is all the more imperative that the efforts we make to shape the future focus on the essentials. For me, going back to the roots is to go back to the story that remains normative for me–the biblical record, and within that, the story of Jesus.

The heart of the matter begins in a gospel story in which Jesus goes to his own roots of meaning. He quotes from the Hebrew scriptures, a primary source of his own spiritual nurture, as they are of ours.

Luke's setting is familiar. Jesus has returned to his home town after a series of events that might now be called a vocational crisis. Whatever he had been and known before (and the record is thin) probably after a period in a desert community, this young man, Jesus of Nazareth, has had a life-changing encounter with a prophet at the River Jordan. The impact of his encounter with John the Baptist sent him to a prayerful solitude in the hills–to grapple with God's will for him. What actually took place there in the hills, we will never know; the recorded story of his choices and options is a series of poetic images that probably go back to second- or third-hand interpretations of stories he told some of his friends, perhaps at night by a campfire. From what we later learn of the young man, we can be assured that when he went up to the hills to sort over his life, he did what he did at other moments of crisis: He reflected on the law and the prophets, on the great writing that he knew by heart. He thought and rethought the story of his people in their love-hate relationship with God. He probably hummed the tunes of the psalms or ran through them in his head the way we do with favorite hymns or songs. He prayed. He wrestled with the message of John the Baptist. As he struggled with who he was and was called to be, it is clear that he returned again and again to the words of Isaiah, particularly to what our biblical scholars call Second Isaiah.

When he subsequently went home ot Nazareth, home to his family and friends, to his home synagogue, those words of Isaiah haunted him. He chose the text to read as the welcomed home guest:

> The Spirit of the Lord is upon me becasue he has anointed me;
>> he has sent me to announce good news to the poor,
>> to proclaim release for prisoners and recovery of sight for the blind;
>> to let the broken victims go free,
>> to proclaim the year of the Lord's favour. (Luke 4:18)

The impact was dramatic. In the context, his friend and family and neighbors recognized a proclamation of identity. *This, my friends and neighbors, is what I am all about.* Although they laughed him out of town for his presumption, we know he spoke the truth because the rest of his life testified to this claim. Here in Nazareth he "talked the talk." For the rest of his life he walked the walk. When he left the synagogue that day, he started fulfilling his mision, and he did not stop until he was stopped on Golgotha. What did he do? He announced good news; he acted out good news; he demonstrated good news. The good news of liberation. He showed that God's rule was a present reality within the world, that it had the power to overcome all the bad news of the world, all the bad news of illness, rejection, sin, and oppression. This is what he demonstrated the rest of his life.

When we someday sort ourselves out—we who follow this man, we who follow the tradtion of this people, we who look to the same Lord who spoke to Abraham and Sarah—I think we will discover that this is what we are called to be about. This vocation Jesus claimed in Nazareth points to the vocation to which we are called, the vocation into which our congregations are called to discover their own identity. His identity led him to identify with and speak to the pain of his world. He invites his followers to that same vocation of demonstrating and proclaiming good news.

If we, too, are to have a role in its procalmation, it is critical for us to get a good fix on what he meant by good news, and how he seems to have interpreted Isaiah's message.

We are not called to copy the specifics of what he did in first-century Palestine; we cannot re-create those conditions.[2] But the stories about what he did and how he tried to communicate his liberating message of good news should give us clues for our own lives. With this in mind, let us look at three short gospel stories that tell us how he did it. Let's consider the stories as if they might be recorded by different ones in our community. I'll paraphrase the first story as might a more liberal theological colleague.

Paraphase of Luke 4:31-37: ### *Jesus Heals a Demon-Possessed Man*

Once upon a time Jesus was called to speak at the congregation in Capernaum, a city in his home territory, through which his reputation had spread. The congregants were astonished with the power of his teaching because he minced no words and stated clearly what the scriptures meant. There was no "as Rabbi So-and-So says . . . and on the other hand, Rabbi This-and-That, speaking for the Jerusalem consensus, puts it this way . . ." He did not hem and haw, but he spoke clearly and authoritatively.

Well, there was a well-known troublemaker in the congregation, contentious, bitter, constantly disrupting the community and injecting poison into whatever he was part of. He showed up and began to pull his old tricks. Pretty soon the whole congregation was in an uproar. He interrupted, made personal attacks, questioned each speaker's motives, and was generally disruptive.

Jesus spoke directly to him. "Stop. Be quiet. I command you!" The man was so astonished that he fell silent. He was speechless. No one had ever spoken so directly to him or called him to account for his behavior. He sat down. That very evening he began to reexamine his life. Years later both he and others remembered that moment as a crucial turning point in his life.

If you wish, you may take offense at this almost classically liberal interpretation. Take comfort. I almost went so far as to suggest that Jesus convinced the man to a twelve-step program! I am well aware that this is not the only interpretation possible, and I use other modes with some of the other stories. This telling suggests something of what may have happened in that synagogue in Capernaum. Perhaps it was much more dramatic, perhaps not.

The point about Jesus' encounter with this demon-possessed man is clear, no matter how we interpret the actions. Jesus directly addressed that man's pain, his peculiar issues or demons. This was no matter of mass psychology. He spoke no generalities. If Jesus' task was to bring good tiding, as he had announced in Nazareth, then it was good news highly specific to this man's bad news. This man was in trouble, and Jesus spoke directly to the trouble. Were there actual demons living in that man? If there were, Jesus spoke to them and took power over them. Is my pale liberal version more palatable to our age than the traditional translations? The record indicates that Jesus dealth with whatever the pathology was. The man's life was transformed at the point of his pain. Jesus recognized and addressed whatever was destroying this man's life. The result? The man was liberated from the demon-possessed life he had previously suffered.

The story is a model of how Jesus acted in situation after situation. He looked to the specific pain in front of him, and he responded to that pain with good news related to the pain. That is the essence of his ministry and the heart of the task of congregations and of everyone who would follow him.

Let us look at another story.

Paraphrase of Mark 8:1-9: The Hungry People

As Jesus' reputation spread, large crowds gathered wherever he was expected to teach. One day an enormous crowd–about four thousand–showed up in the countryside. They were still around three days later, and Jesus was concerned that they might not make it home without some sustenance. When his friends asked what in the world he could do about it, he asked what resources they could lay hands on. When they said they had seven loaves and a few fish, he took what they had, blessed the food, broke it, and fed the people. To everyone's astonishment, there was plenty. As a matter of fact, when they collected the fragments left over, they filled seven baskets–after four thousand people had eaten. Then he sent them all home, full.

This story is told in a more conventional style. But in its own way it makes the same point as the former. Jesus paid attention to the specific character of what was in front of him, and he responded. He had good tidings to proclaim, and he did that for three days. But at the end he became aware of an area of need that he had not addressed: physical need for food so people would not get sick on the way home. Prosaic? Yes, but very real

to anyone who was hungry and headed home after three days at a "conference." Jesus tuned in to the specific need—the bad news experienced by
that particular group, and he responded to it.

Those of us who live in sacramental religious cultures can richly em-
bellish the story—images of eucharistic worship, phrases such as bread of
life, meanings of the mystic number seven. But for the purpose of trying to
figure out what it means to be a messenger of good news, it is enough to
note that Jesus had no difficulty understanding "good news" as serving up
bread and fish to hungry people. What seems to matter is identifying a
specific need—and responding to it. When he brought good news, it seemed
to have direct relationship to pain or to bad news. The people were hungry
and he got bread for them.

Let's look at another story, this one from John's gospel.

Paraphrase of John 2:1-11: The Marriage Wine

Early in Jesus' ministry he and his disciples were invited to a wedding, probably of a friend of his mother's because she felt some
responsibility for how the reception went. It was a festive occasion, and the guests rather outdid themselves with the refresh-
ments. Jesus' mother noticed that the wine was giving out, and
she took her concern to her son. Jesus seemed at first reluctant to
respond in such a setting, perhaps thinking, as I am sure I would,
that this is a relatively trivial matter, hardly worth getting hot and
bothered about. But the mother knew the son and told the servants to do whatever he asked. Seeing the enormous pots standing there for ritual purification, Jesus told the servants to fill them
with water. They did. Bucket after bucket they poured until all six
were full. Then Jesus told them to serve the water to the guests.
Incredibly, the water turned out to be wine—the finest kind of wine.
So fine, indeed, that the guest commented on it to the host. I'm
sure Jesus' mother was not surprised.

As a story, this doesn't have high drama. There is nothing of life or
death at stake here. What is the worst that could have happened? Some
embarrassment over a shortage of wine? A dressing-down of the wine-
steward for underestimating the heat of the day or the number of bottles
needed for the crowd? In the scale of things, this is no big deal. Jesus helped

some people have a more enjoyable wedding. Yes, there are other meanings. There is the affirmation of marriage. There are hints of the eucharistic wine and fore shadowing of Jesus' death. There may be ambiguity, also. Is the line about changing the ritual purification water into wine another of the church's anti-Semitic put-downs of Jewish faith and community? (Somehow we should have learned by now that it is not necessary to put others down to affirm what one is!)

For our point—trying to understand the task to which relgous congregations are called by this wandering rabbi—once again the meaning is clear: Jesus responded to the need of the people around him. He did not write out a great check. He did not get another musical group. He did not organize the games for the guests. He did not preach. They were short of wine; he provided wine. He gave them good tidings—wine. No big deal.

Three stories. There are many others like them throughout the gospels. Every one I can think of underlines what I am pulling out these three. Jesus always made good tidings available in terms of three characteristics.

1. For Jesus, good news was always in dialogue with bad news. Good news is profoundly contextual. For a blind man, good news is sight. For a lame person, good news is the ability to leap and dance or even walk. For the guilt-ridden, good news is being forgiven. For the person in prison, good news is getting of prison. For the lonely, good news is community. For the person—or society—crushed by oppression, good news is freedom. For a person possessed by demons, good news is to be released from their power. For hungry travelers, good news is food before they face the journey home. For a marriage running short of wine, good news is a few buckets of good wine.

2. Therefore, good news comes in many forms. It is not one thing or one way of doing things or one concept, even. Good news comes in as many packages as does bad news.

3. These stories lead me to think about Jesus; respect for boundaries. Each person is allowed freedom. The demon-possessed comes to Jesus and begs to have his torment ended. The hungry look up to be fed. The mother asks Jesus for help. Jesus' interventions are not coercive but responsive. He responds to openness; he does not come with his bag of tricks to do this thing in spite of those around him. In one case, he even checks with a lame man before trying to heal him. "Do you want to get well?" he asks. He listens, and where people will open up their bad news, his good news is ready. He does not force or push his good news, but he never holds it back.

These are important clues for the purpose of our congregations if we would try to build congregations that generate good news for our world: communities that are good news to be part of; communities that are deeply responsive to all kinds of needs, that are able to recognize the infinite kinds of hurt and pain that we are called to address; communities that respect and honor the personal and group boundaries by which we secure our identities. Our congregations are called to be communities that follow Jesus in bringing good news to the pain of the world.

No small task.

Let me be clear that I know I am walking on slippery ground. These words and phrases—good tidings, good news, and even *gospel*—have all been translated into the word *evangelism* from the Greek *eu angelion*. Good news. What I am talking about here is a far cry from what denominations and churches talk about as evangelism. Indeed, I find much of what churches do in that name singularly wrong-headed and misleading. The biblical concept to which I am trying to be true is a word of reaching out, not of gathering in.

I may be arguing for a reinvention of evangelism. I am arguing that this business of communicating good tidings is at the heart of what our congregations must be about, and it is what our congregations need to be helping each one of us do.

Let us explore how we might better rethink this central task of every congregation.

PROCLAIMING GOOD NEWS IN OUR TIME

Two Models

Growing up as a Christian in the South, I experienced a world that thought of itself as Christendom, even though its actual life was far, far less than that. But in that world I was exposed to two giants of faith.

Although most people around me had an aversion to at least one of the two, from my earliest exposure to them I understood that both were evangelists and both were giants. I met only one of them, and he is now dead. Although I see the other on television occasionally, we have never met. Both were southerners and Protestants like me, so I felt regional kinship with them. One was black; the other is white. Both were Baptists, the predominant faith of the world I knew, far distant from my own low-church Episcopal traditions.

Over the years I watched them, learned from them, and admired them, but I kept wondering how they could be so different, have such different messages, and yet still represent to me what evangelism was all about.

Martin Luther King, Jr., represented the prophetic strand of our heritage, standing strong against oppression. Many people in the white culture in which I grew up, people I cared about, thought he was the tool of the devil. Others thought the sun rose and fell on him. As a child of my culture, I started out with the former group and had to do some growing to discover that he was a true prophet for me. One of the treasures of my life is the worn copy of the *Letter from the Birmingham Jail* I found in my father's effects after his death. I did not know what my father thought of Martin Luther King, Jr., until I found that letter filled with my father's appreciative marginal notes.

Billy Graham is the other giant. The people with whom I normally consort—generally leaning liberal in politics and theology—have such low regard for him that I rarely bring up his name in their company. With those folks I keep Billy Graham as my private closet saint! Early in his ministry I sometimes wondered about his seeming blindness to the prophetic dimensions of faith, but I was willing to leave it to God to sort out the flaws of either of my giants.

I simply knew that personal friends and acquaintances had heard and had their lives changed by the good news one or the other of these two men had spoken. I saw evidence that they had brought good news to situations in which I had previously seen the bad news. That fit my understanding of evangelism. Their words and actions carried the presence of God's kingdom into some lives and situations with which I had personal knowledge.

For years I accepted the fact that my admiration of the two defied rationality; what they were was more important than whether or not they fit into my categories. Struggling with their different gifts as evangelists, however, led me beyond traditional ways of thinking.

If both of them were evangelists, if both of them were bearers of good tidings, then our definitions are simply inadequate. Evangelists are not just one thing and always the same. The truth is more complex than is comfortable. My first clue came when I recognized that King and Graham were speaking from the same gospel, but that each had a different target. They saw the bad news differently. Jesus saw good news as contextual, and that good news differed in relationship to the bad news being experienced at any time. What I was facing was two people, each of whom was committed to the gospel, but each of whom saw a different kind of bad news.

Billy Graham speaks to the bad news he sees as he looks at the human condition. He sees that human beings turn away from God, separate themselves by their actions or their values, and build barriers against God's presence in their lives. He sees such self-centered life as leading to separation from one another and from God; indeed it leads to moral and spiritual death. Although Graham has a place for the community of faith in his message, it is not central because he sees the bad news as so focused in the individual's choice of turning from God. The issues of life and death involve a profoundly individualistic encounter between each person and the grace of God in Jesus. Graham understands that the sicknesses of society come from the profound separation that begins as one woman or one man turns against the grain of the universe, choosing to turn away from God's ever-ready love.

That is the bad news that Billy Graham addresses with his good news. He proclaims that human beings do not have to be condemned to separation and death. He speaks the message that Christ through his cross and resurrection has broken down the walls of separation, making possible true community with one's fellows and with God. All one must do is place trust in Christ. Graham witnesses to the God-given power to turn from the death of self-centeredness to real life centered in God.

If you live with that bad news, if that way of living burdens your heart and life, Billy Graham articulates incredibly good news for you. People I know and love have had their lives transformed by this message. If that is not where you are, the message will likely leave you cold.

Martin Luther King, Jr., knew and preached that same doctrine in most of his sermons to his congregations in Montgomery and Atlanta, but that is not the message for which he is best known, nor was it the good news that made me know him as an evangeilst. King saw a very different dimension of bad news. He saw corporate systems whereby one group takes oppressive power over another, destroyng the humanity of both the oppressor and the oppressed. He spoke in the context of the issues between the black and white people of the nation, but he saw the larger issues of class and power and wealth as equally oppressive. He saw more than one form of slavery, and he recognized all of them as bad news. He saw the spiritual power of our corporate demons—nationalism, racism, classim—and he saw the pain they brought, binding up Americans and Vietnamese, blacks and whites, rich and poor.

To that specific bad news King preached good news that was quite different from that preached by Graham. He saw and proclaimed that God's love means liberation not only of the soul, but also of human society. King demonstrated that both the oppressed and the oppressor can enter into liberation, and that indeed one part cannot be freed without the other. He saw this liberation as dependent upon the power of God's love. He helped us see that through love the power of nonviolence could overcome the bad news of fear, hate, oppression, and violence within the structures of society.

For those suffering from oppression and social discrimination, and for those who oppress and discriminate, Martin Luther King, Jr., spoke good news. His vision of the bad news and his articulation of the gospel has transformed many lives and has changed the shape of history.

Again, King's way of stating the good news is very differnt from Graham's, yet both are grounded in the story of Jesus. They speak different messages out of the same gospel because they address different situations. The difference is in how they see the bad news.

So the good news is not some monumental single unity. In this illustration of Billy Graham and Martin Luther King, Jr., we see a continuum of bad news. At one end is the lone individual, lost in self-centeredness and separated from God. At the other end is the social system that destroys through oppression and enforced subjugation.

But I suggest more. A call is involved. Graham and King are drawn to their bad news "targets" by their inner visions and are pulled, almost as if by gravitational pull, toward particular bad news. There is a sense of inner call to match the observed pain with the message perceived in the Jesus story.

This is how I graph two versions of the continuum:

The Pain		Corporate
of Individual	- - - - - - - - -	Oppression;
Separation		"Society's
from God		Sins"

Graham's		King's
Vision of	- - - - - - - - - - -	Vision of
Good News		Good News

On this continuum, Graham's vision tends to focus on the left. King's vision tends to the right. Neither man can be captured by a single "location," yet it makes sense to talk about each having a characteristic focus.

I see each of us as having a role as a responder to God's world and the bad news that floods across its face. At this point in your life, where would you place yourself on this continuum? We see and respond to different types of pain. One of us is concerned about the welfare system; another wants to help a particular man at the subway stop. It is not that what others see is less or more important, but just that we see some hurts and not others. Some things grab us; others do not.

I suggest we each may have a giftedness in what we perceive the critical bad news to be. We are drawn to grapple with it, worry about it, and seek to understand the good news that specifically addresses it. Why the attraction? I have no idea. Perhaps our own experience of life or of the power of God opens us up to that particular dimension more than to any other. Perhaps or own weakness focuses our eyes and attention upon one dimension of the good news that most gives life to us. Perhaps we discovered good news as we lived through catastrophic bad news and were forever sensitized to that pain.

A basic theme of this book is that the ability to "see" bad news relates to our discipleship. The willingness to "do something" about it relates to our apostleship.

I suggest that the inner pull to respond is much more than a pull or an attention grabber. It is no less than our perception of call. It is our open door to the good news we have to share. (See the Appendix A for an educational design I use to help people work with these ideas to locate different perceptions of bad news in their lives.)

Jesus' good-news proclamation had three characteristics: It is related to specific bad news; it appeared in contexually appropriate forms; and it was respectful of individuality and personal boundaries.

Is it really a surprise that each of us is called to our own vision of the pain of the world, that each of us has a voice to speak something unique to a special reality of the world?

I believe that this individual sensitivity is a clue to where our call to service may lie. Among all the possible things out there in the world that cause pain and hurt, there are some—perhaps only a few—that claim us, that call us to bring good news. I sometimes say that every pain in the world has a special kind of Velcro on it, and that each of us has grown a patch of our own special brand, also. We can bump into all sorts of pain out there, but we do not respond until there is a match. Then we have no option. We are seized by the pain that matches our call, and we must act.

There is no magic in this understanding of vocation. Nevertheless, I think this pull, this sense of being seized, is God-given and helps us sort out what we will do with our lives, what jobs we try to take, and what causes we sign up for.

Congregations have a stake in this dynamic because their task is to help us become carriers of good news. Training in discipleship involves increasing the sensitivity we have to the pain of the world at the same time that we are more deeply engaged in the good news of the Jesus story lived out in our congregations. More about that later.

A More Wholistic Model of Proclaiming Good News: A Map of Evangelism

Another dimension to this simple continuum broadens our understanding of what it means to be a proclaimer of good tidings.

As I thought about the differences between Billy Graham and Martin Luther King, I realized that the continuum described above identifies only one of several dimensions. It targets the bad news but ignores the framework within which one is called to serve.

Graham understands the response to the bad news of estrangement from God to be articulated and acted out in a "religious" context and with "religious" language. Consequently he speaks of sin and salvation; his calls to action are to make "a decision for Christ"; the movement he urges is into religious community and sustenance.

King, from a very similar religious tradition, came to represent a response in the "secular" context with "secular" language. Where he perceived systems oppressing the human spirit, he called for action mostly in the social arena outside religious institutions. Consequently he spoke language of oppression and freedom; his calls to action were to meet violence with nonviolence on city streets; the movement he urged was within the secular social structures, the judicial systems—the political and economic realms.

This brings me to a very broad map of what is called for if we are to be a community proclaiming good tidings. Instead of a linear continuum, I see a map that includes great diversity of vocations, not just one way to proclaim good tidings. I see a map that encompasses a larger vision for the religious task of congregations than I generally see. Here I outline that map as a grid that includes a vertical continuum suggesting the different styles with which one might respond–from a religious style to a secular style.

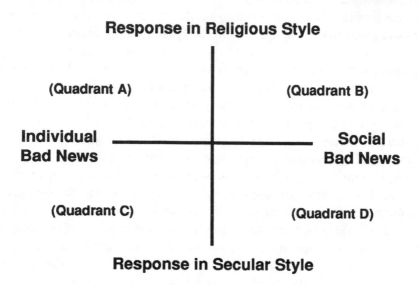

Response in Religious Style

(Quadrant A)   **(Quadrant B)**

Individual   **Social**
Bad News   **Bad News**

(Quadrant C)   **(Quadrant D)**

Response in Secular Style

I share this schematic as a pointer to truth, not as truth itself. Like all schematics, it oversimplifies and exaggerates. But it is a useful tool to point to the kinds of work I think congregations are called to enhance. This picture can help us enlarge our vision of the field of evangelism, the arena in which we are called to be bearers of good news.

Again, can you place yourself on this map? What bad news most frequently grabs your attention? And how do you usually respond? I am sure one's point of sensitivity and response changes from time to time. So location is simply an approximation of where one is right now.

As on the continuum, there is no "bad" place on this grid, nor is one quadrant "better" than the others. Billy Graham's call to evangelism is not better than Martin Luther King's. Nor is King's better than Graham's. They are different perceptions, different callings. Indeed, as I pointed out in the case of King's preaching as opposed to his "public" ministry, it is possible for one person to respond in more than one way to the hurts of the world. At different life seasons we may locate ourselves more in one area than another, only to discover ourselves pulled or called to another way at another time. As I have already suggested, King ministered in his congregations in a style one might identify with quadrant A. Within his leadership of the Southern Christian Leadership Conference, his location on the map was more toward quadrant D.

Each of the quadrants points to a different set of sensitivities to vocation and evangelism. Let us look at them briefly, one by one.

Quadrant A. People whose life and faith stories make them particularly sensitive to an individual's needs and who have a internal compass set within religious categories would likely find themselves in quadrant A. Such people, one might speculate, would bring strength to one-on-one teaching and care minstries. They might be at the heart of a congregatoin's ministry of intercessory prayer, but even more so of contemplative prayer. These people are sensitive to spiritual lostness and yearning and generally unafraid to speak directly from a wellspring of faith-language and faith-experience. Such people would be frustrated and useless in most committees and would flee social projects like the plague. Some might make gifted spiritual directors. I locate much of Billy Graham's ministry in this quadrant.

Quadrant B. These people are aware of how people need each other. They are tireless in supporting denominational programs and institutions, such as colleges and seminaries, and counseling centers and care programs established by the congregation or denomination. They are generally good members of worship task forces and heavy supporters of study programs—the more biblical the better. Pastors and rabbis in charge of congregations need to "spend some time" in this quadrant, whether or not it is the center of their lives. Much of my own life—some forty years of workin in, with, and for congregations—tells me that this is home territory for me, although I have periods in which I have focused elsewhere.

Quadrant C. What I call the anonymous saints dwell in this quadrant. I think of people who go through life doing what needs to be done, some of them in quite humble circumstances and some in prominent roles, but who never say much about it. I know a garbage collector in Washington who runs an evening tutoring program for black junior-high kids. I think Dag Hammarskjold may have belonged here—his life and work as an international statesman undergirded by a remarkable but unspoken spiritual life. I think of my father's life-long ministry as a doctor and community leader who rarely said much about his faith. These may be the people who show up at early morning services but never serve on the board. They are known in the community by how they treat people and make a difference, but they are embarrassed to be asked much about their congregation. Most people they work with may not even know they belong to a congregation.

Quadrant D. These I call secular saints. They see the primary focus of their lives to be service to the hurts of society. Some are articulate with prophetic power, while others are foot-soldiers in one revolution or another. Such people often get irritated at the slow pace of the congregation in being able to "get on with it," and they can be servere critics of the values incorporated in a denominational budget. Their center of gravity is not the congregation or the denomination, but their compulsion to respond to social needs. More than a few of them become religious "alumni," actually leaving religious structures and life to try to change the character of the world without a continuing link to a congregation. I suspect that many who populate environmental associations would find themselves here. Such peole often leave the religious community because of the values they learned in that very community; they are unable to "wait" for the congregation or church leaders to respond to the pressing needs they see in the world.

Use your imagination, for a moment. Look at that grid–all quadrants–and you will be looking at the whole realm of bad news. You can differentiate, as we have, among different kinds of bad news and different needs for good news in the lives of people and the structures of society. It is a map of–or a window on–the needs for God's good news, for evangelism. Looking out that window, we see the fields white with harvest–as near as our imagination, as varied as our callings. The variety of needs out there represents our need to send an apostolate as varied as the needs.[3]

In terms of the qualities represented by these quadrants, congregations need to be as comprehensive as possible, not because diversity is a modern fixation, but because the needs we face are across the board. A congregation that lacks people from any one of these quadrants will lack something the ministry needs for its health. A congregation that overbalances itself or its program in one quadrant does so at the cost of missing important areas of need.

I believe the task of congregations is to do two things at once: (1) to help more and more people look through that window to the world to identify what needs call out to them, and (2) to nurture and strengthen each person and send each out to use unique gifts to respond as only he or she can. As members identify their calls and are nurtured and sent, we will see the development of the apostolate of the future church.

Congregations of the future need to be congregations that nurture varieties of sensitivities to the bad news of the world and respond to those many forms of pain. These will be congregations open to more than one point of view.

Every member of the church stands before an imaginary window, facing all the need and hurt of the world. Most, but not all, of us feel a pull to engage with some of that pain, whether it is physical pain or homelessness, ignorance or spitefulness, hunger or illness, guilt, a sense of lostness, hopelessness, or despair.

A congregations's task is to help us to know and claim the power we have, commit ourselves to engage the pain of the world, and then to manage the process by which we are transformed from passive onlookers to sent people—apostles. Our congregations are there to help each of us grasp and be grasped by the good news that God has uniquely for each of us, and then to empower us to go out as sent people—apostles—to the pain of the world as bearers of our own special version of the good news.

The story of Jesus leads us to become disciples and apostles carrying forth the kind of good news that Jesus modeled—a good news that is profoundly contextual, touching the different kinds of pain present at any place; a good news that comes in many shapes and sizes; a good news that always leaves the recipient free to accept or reject it. Congregations, then, are about helping us all become disciples and apostles.

The root of it all is transformation. The transformation of each of us into a disciple whose life has been touched and shaped by Jesus' good news. The transformation of each of us into a special part of the apostolate Jesus is calling into being to proclaim his reign over all.

NOTES

1. Loren B. Mead, *The Once and Future Church* (Washington, DC: The Alban Institute, 1991), 20-22.
2. It is interesting to note that some of Jesus' ways of proclaiming the gospel

are no longer open to us because other of his followers beat us to it. Jesus healed many lepers in his day, and those who follow him have come close to eliminating leprosy around the world.

3. The truth is probably much more complex than I stated here. See David Roozen, William McKinney, and Jackson Carroll, *Varieties of Religious Presence* (New York: Pilgrim Press, 1984), a provocative book based on important studies of churches in the Hartford, Connecticut area. It describes four types of congregations in terms of how each understands its relationship to its environment. Their four categories of group identities are quite close to the quadrants I have noted here for individual relationship to the world: quadrant A being analogous to their "sanctuary church"; quadrant B corresponding to "evangelistic church"; quadrant C to "civic church"; and quadrant D to "activist church." Carl Dudley's research in the Midwest suggests an even more complex set of categories than these. One wonders about the possibility that congregations may, in their own cultures, preserve important and different sensitivities to good news. This may be an unexplored frontier for thinkers about ecumenism.

CHAPTER 3

The Task of the Congregation: Transformation — Preparing Disciples and Apostles

In the last chapter we stood before an imaginary window that looked out over the world, and we speculated about all the needs out there for committed action and caring. That window looks out across the landscape of the world in which the variety of human and social bad news calls for those sent to bring *eu angelion*, good news. That is the field for the action of the apostolate.

Looking out that window onto the world one can see a vast cacophony of hurts and pain, inhumanity and injustice. The ability to see the world's pain as a field for engagement comes only to those impelled by a religious vision. Having such a vision is what it takes to become an apostle. Helping transform ordinary people into apostles involves first helping them discover their discipleship.

In this chapter we will start by reversing the window perspective. Having stood behind the window looking out into the world, now we step outside and look back through the same window. Now we focus on the inner life of the congregation itself. What needs to happen there to support and send apostles into the world? Having looked at the critical functions that build up disciples, we can then address the process by which disciples are transformed to enter the apostolate.

As we looked out the window, our focus was on the apostolate—the work of church members in the world, bearing witness to the kingdom of God and seeking to bring it to reality in the midst of the world's pain. As we turn around and look back through the same window from the world into the congregation, our focus is on those processes that call out discipleship and nurture each person in ever deeper discipleship.

In the New Testament, building on the traditions of the Hebrew scriptures, particularly the prophetic literature, Jesus announced the beginning of a new kind of human community. He called it the kingdom or reign of God. Within that realm he described what Isaiah and Jeremiah dreamed of–a place where the poor were cared for, the sick healed, where the blind received sight and widows were supported. A place where those who were lame could come to leap with joy and where those who were in prison or oppressed would break free of their prisons.[1]

Jesus announced that this kingdom had already begun, and his actions were based on the reality of the kingdom. In his announcement of the new society and in his actions, there was power. The new society began as he acted. The Word led to the actions. More than that, he invited his fellows and followers to act in the power of that kingdom

They did. I think of the remarkable story in Acts 3. Peter and John, going up to the temple, run into a lame beggar at the Beautiful Gate. The story picks up drama. Their purses are empty, and they have nothing visible with which they can respond to his need. Is the beggar out of luck? No. Peter acts in the power of the new kingdom. He says, "I have no money, but I can give you something else. Get up and walk." You know the story. The lame man got up and walked. I'm convinced that the lame man was stupefied to find himself cured. I think Peter was, too. The good news seized him *as he acted* for the new world. He had the power to engage the demons of the world before he knew he had the power. He was a potential apostle until he acted as an apostle. It was his stepping out to act for healing that made his apostolate real.

Had Peter not acted on the presumption of the kingdom, the lame man would not have walked, the power to cure would not have appeared, and Peter would not have become an apostle. What made Peter act beyond his knowledge? What made him go beyond his previous faith? I have no answers to this set of questions because I think we are on the edge of the relationship between one's faith and that in which one has faith; it is not fully a matter of Peter or of God, but of a life-dialogue between them. We can use pale language–*vocation, faith-response, leap of faith*–but I am not sure we will ever capture the mystery. God offered Peter the option, and Peter took it. The kingdom appeared when Peter acted in its power.

I think the task of the local congregation is to help ordinary people become engaged in that mystery, people willing to make the leap from the known to the unknown as Peter did; people who act on the basis of the new society, who claim the power of that kingdom, who then act for peace and justice and love and healing. The congregation's task to call the faith forth in us and send us to act with no positive assurance that anything at all will happen.

In all the complexities of history, in all the encounters with organizational realities, in all the theological debates and philosophical analyses, I think we have lost sight of that simple focus of faith. I have no idea if congregations will grow or decline if they act on that focus, and frankly I don't give a damn. But I know they will lose their soul if they don't. That part is simple.

How to do it is not.

I want to make it clear that there is much mystery in what I want to talk about. I will describe established ways by which we have developed disciples and processes of transformation. I will begin a conversation about how we may go further in our congregations. But I confess that I do not have final answers. This may be like reading a dialogue but having a script that includes only one character's lines. There is another actor who speaks and moves in ways we do not control or always understand, but of course that party is key to the dialogue. (In Jesus, my tradition teaches and I believe, the two sides of the dialogue spoke with one voice and acted with one will.)

As we think about this mysterious process of transformation by which people begin to act as citizens of the new society, I want to explore four functions, traditional to congregational life: (1) the community within the larger society—what the early church called *koinonia*; (2) the life-giving process summarized as proclamation—what the early church called *kerygma*; (3) the lore, the tradition, the stories, and their transmission with power—what the early church called *didache*; (4) the role of serving—what the early church called *diakonia*. Each of these functions is a means for the transformation of ordinary people into disciples and a necessary support for a life of discipleship. The stronger these functions, the more likely the congregation is to be an active apostolate reaching out to the bad news of the world.

Koinonia: The Congregation as Community

The regular oscillation of the church person between the outward life of the public and the inner life of the congregation is the stage for much transformation. Facing outward, congregations open up to a public world in which their members engage, are influenced, and exert influence. Facing inside, congregations are an environment for growth and support. In *koinonia* a member of a congregation lives in the tension of religious heritage and public arena.

The outward engagement of the congregation with the public is a critical issue for today's world. Parker Palmer has opened up for us a vision of what that public world is or should be:

> The word "public" means all the people in a society, without distinction or qualification. A public school is a place where no child is barred from entering, a place where the common culture of a people can be passed along to the next generation. A person in public life is one whose career involves accountability to the people as a whole, one who carries a public trust. Even the weaker phrase, a public figure, means a person whose life is visible to all who care to watch it. When information appears in the public press it is available to everyone, and a public library collects and stores such information so that it will be available to persons yet unborn. And the word is used in less grandiose ways, as in the English "pub" or public house, which is a gathering place for the whole community.[2]

One reads this description with nostalgia because *public* has many negative connotations today. Palmer explores why this rich concept of a deep bond that can bring a diverse people together has degenerated into a term that makes us think of interest groups competing with one another for a place at the "public trough." He suggests that the rich potential of the word *public* has been eroded by our willingness to give away the care and maintenance of our common life to external, impersonal, often political structures. He argues (as do Robert Bellah and his colleagues in *Habits of the Heart*[3]) that the public realm becomes a sea of competitive forces and society becomes a conglomeration of aggressive and defensive organizations and people locked into competition for resources.

With a public vision of life limited by what the law allows, we create a self-fulfilling prophecy. Palmer continues: "fewer and fewer people venture into public without being well-armed (figuratively and literally!) Small wonder that more and more people retreat from the public arena . . . into the sanctuary of private life." Society and government cannot generate a vision of a "public life of variety and breadth, a life in which the human impulse toward community is drawn out and encouraged." Government can and does help competing groups balance their different interests; it can protect those who cannot protect themselves; it can punish those who offend the public order; but it cannot produce a vision of what it means to live in community. It cannot generate community.

Palmer's insights echo biblical language in Paul's convoluted discussions of law and grace. Society can define itself and set limits, but we all yearn for a community in which we know that we are cared for and valued in ourselves. Society can help us defend our prerogatives, but it cannot help us reach out to others (or others reach out to us.) Society can define what is fair and legal, but it cannot make our hearts care for others, particularly those who are different from ourselves. Law is essential for life together, but it is incomplete in itself. We want and need more than society by itself has to give.

On the most mundane level, public law can define gross misconduct as felonies, but law cannot eliminate the patterns that lead to felonies. It can lock up people who commit felonies, but it cannot produce people who love to do good and who love mercy and care about their neighbors. Some believe the problem of crime in our society can be solved by stiffer sentences and better law enforcement. In this conversation about public life we can say quite clearly that you cannot hire enough police and you cannot build enough jails to produce a public life of meaning and value. That is a dead end. Though perhaps necessary, it will not lead to a vision, a hope, and action for a realm that is governed by self-giving rather than self-aggrandizement.

The larger society *needs* the community graces that are vital to church-congregational *koinonia*. As citizens become disciples within the congregation, they build the potential to be carriers of grace within the public realm. Congregations are laboratories that can prepare us for public living and service. In congregations citizens can be generated as provocateurs of grace within a society shaped by law.

Ten Features Characteristic of a Good Congregation

Palmer lays out ten features that he says are characteristic of public life—as it should be. How can each open up to us the opportunity to move creatively back and forth between our two worlds?

These ten characteristics of the public and my reflections on them suggest the wealth of the gifts that congregations bring to a nation (or a

world) that seeks to become *community*. Indeed these congregational gifts
may be essential to the building of a viable public life. At the same time, this
is no one-way street. A dialogue with these characteristics of the public
world may provide new depth to the life of congregations.

The word *dialogue* is critical in this discussion of *koinonia*. This calls
for engagement–engagement that brings strength to each world.
In Palmer's public:

1. *Strangers meet on common ground.* Dare we assume that strangers bring gifts, not threats? In today's outside world we are taught to steer
clear of the stranger. "Don't make eye-contact!" But it hasn't always been
this way. In our congregations we have a laboratory for reaching out beyond ourselves and our families. Can congregations open us up to at least
civility to those beyond our community of family or friends? Dare we think
of the possibility of a public world ruled by the values of hospitality? Can our
congregations demonstrate that possibility to each of us personally and train
us for that kind of public life? Can congregations raise up disciples who live
apostolically in the public world?

2. *Fear of the stranger is faced and dealt with.* We do have fears
about people who are not "like us." We have all sorts of stereotypes and
prejudices, all kinds of unexplored myths about "others." Such paranoia
cripples the social order and sets discriminatory processes in stone. All
congregations, even the most seemingly homogeneous, have within them a
mixture of ages and sexes, points of view and backgrounds. Can our congregations be seen as safe places where we can reach across boundaries,
where we can support experimentation? Indeed, many congregations have
a history of sending groups of members into other communities to work and
socialize with others–pounding nails, digging ditches, or stitching layettes.
Within the safety of a congregational work-group, the individual disciple can
more easily join the stranger-community in common work. Can our congregations become intentional laboratories for exposing us to people outside
our groups.

3. *Scarce resources are shared and abundance is generated.* In
our society this essential characteristic of public life may be as threatened
as any. We seem to be a social order in which the rich get richer and the
poor get poorer. Who is there to speak for and act on another vision? Who
will speak if not the children of the scriptures, the Book in which poets and
prophets made it crystal clear that God has a special concern for the poor
among us? In the last decade I do not think I have seen a congregation of

any sort, big or small, rich or poor, that does not take a regular offering or other action to get food to people who do not have enough. In our larger cities a very high percentage of hungry people who receive a free meal get that meal at a local congregation. It is so much a part of our life that we don't realize how unusual our actions are. Sharing resources is just what life is "supposed to be." There is no big deal, no brass bands. It is just who we are and who we are trying to become. As we act on our vision, we are saying something to our society about what public life ought to be. We are acting in the power of the new society. In the public realm our social order speaks with fear of diminishing resources: If you get yours, there is less for me. Our biblical heritage speaks of abundance, not scarcity: The more you have, the better I will be. Can we bring this consciousness to the world we inhabit? Can we nurture it in our congregations, or are we, too, going to become locked into scarcity thinking? In the years immediately ahead, as resources are more and more limited in our religious institutional life, as everyone around us in churches and in the public realm is talking of cutting budgets, we may have a more and more difficult time witnessing to abundance as disciples. There will be tests of our discipleship?

4. *Conflict occurs and is resolved.* Our congregations, whatever else they are, are seething pools of conflict. We have different way of decorating altars, and we fight about it. We have different ideas about who the pastor should be, and we fight about it. Sometimes our fights are donnybrooks, but more often they are the tight-lipped, controlled, hard-to-finish type. The grudge-generating kind. Some fights turn into feuds that last generations. Sometimes those outside congregations are more comfortable than we in dealing with differences. We "religious" folk have a way of calling God in to the fight to help us destroy the opposition.

But times are changing. We are trying to learn how to reach consensus, how to rebuild when fights fracture our communities. Our tradition brings perspectives about forgiveness and reconciliation that help us reach out to one another for community, not just cessation of hostility. As we deal with our differences, we learn about reaching beyond hostility in the public world toward a different vision of society. Can we learn to use our own spiritual resources of forgiveness and reconciliation within our own communities, learning to bear witness to the same power in the world outside our congregations?

5. *Life is given color, texture, drama, a festive air.* Every act of worship should be a laboratory in celebration of community. It is interesting

to note that religious communities invented drama and music and probably public festivals—all pointing to the rich possibilities of community beyond fear and conflict. These dimensions in our congregations and in our communities give us opportunities to dramatize a oneness and commonality with others. A church on Easter, a town park on the Fourth of July—both speak to what *community* means, and our presence involves us in that community. Congregations need to help their members engage in celebrations of community and engage the public in its celebrations that pursue a vision of what the larger community is called to be.

6. *People are drawn out of themselves.* The locked doors and barred windows of city living, the residential sections protected by armed guards and attack dogs—these realities speak vividly of the isolation toward which our society pushes us. Congregations cannot leave this as the last word: We have a mandate to reach out and to bring in. We bear a high tradition of hospitality. In that sense congregations are counter-cultural—or at least counter to the way the culture is drifting. As congregations reach out to the isolated, they become places where the isolated can engage with others. In a society with strong pressures toward privacy, the public realm needs congregations to have vision to root people out of their hidden aloneness and train them for community. Members of congregations need to become neighborhood leaders helping citizens enter the lives of their neighbors.

7. *Mutual responsibility becomes evident and mutual aid possible.* I have already noted the matter-of-factness with which congregations assume they are supposed to do something about the hungry. Many congregations have a list of people to pray for—the sick, the shut-ins, the grieving. And many have cadres deployed weekly to take flowers to the sick, to take elements of the Eucharist to those who cannot get to church, to call on people in the hospital. The church I walk by on the way to my office has a whole set of parking places reserved for three hours daily for those who come to take Meals-on-Wheels to shut-ins. Taking responsibility for one another is taken for granted in our congregations but not in our public arenas. In this area can our ordinary community life be a beacon to our society at the same time that it prepares us to offer these gifts of service outside our congregational bounds? And should not congregational members be among those who lead and carry out efforts to rebuild neighborhoods and encourage citizens to care for one another's safety and security?

8. *Opinions become audible and accountable.* In this "characteristic feature of public life" I must admit that congregations have as much or

more to gain from as to give to the public. The modest political systems within congregations need to be opened up to the candor with which public figures articulate and defend positions. Congregations would be strengthened by more such accountability. Having said that I also note that congregations and their members do have much to contribute. They generally have a feel for the legitimacy of opposition, for the ultimate value of those who oppose one another. Congregations bring a dimension of civility to public contention.

9. *Vision is projected and projects are attempted.* People in congregations are regularly exposed to transcendent visions of what life is supposed to be. They seem indefatigable in trying to address hurts and pains they see. If they are to be faulted it is because of the quixotic nature of some of their projects—going up against human evil (or city hall) with water pistols. Yet an invaluable gift congregations bring to public life may be the way their hope is grounded theologically in this conception of God. Congregations bring persistence to the table. Because their visions are grounded in an understanding of God and God's purposes, congregations are not as likely as the general public to drift away from important visions—such as caring for each person. Congregations are grounded in a sense of God's purpose and movement through history—something that does not fade after a few defeats, as does political optimism. There is a big difference between optimism and hope. Congregations bring the latter. In a gun-flooded society, congregations know about a world in which swords are turned into plowshares. In a society of gangs and drugs, congregations witness to a world in which the lamb and the lion can dwell together. We bring visions. That is part of what we are.

10. *People are empowered and protected against power.* The checks and balances of governing structures should provide a framework that protects the citizen against unwarranted assumptions of power. At the same time, these structures give space and scope for a citizen's gifts to be shared. Congregations, in their life of worship, act out and celebrate the importance of freely given gifts shaped and conformed by structures of authority and custom. They also understand the limits of human integrity, the presence of sinfulness, and the necessity for larger frames of values.

Koinonia and a Congregation's Critical Distinctive Identity

Congregational community life has always been understood as the locus of the ordinary church member's growth and development. This is true despite the fact that for a thousand years or more it has been assumed that one "picked up" and absorbed *from the society* one's knowledge of faith and grounding in one's heritage. The whole world of Christendom–rather than the life of the congregation itself–was the "teacher" of the faith. It was something that happened without having to pay attention to it, as one might "pick up" decay-proof teeth by drinking fluoridated water. That was basically the Christendom assumption. Community religious festivals, the legal codification of a value system, and the character of life in the society was understood to ground and root one adequately for spiritual growth. During this period the faith-community suffered a loss–its ability to distinguish itself from its environment. As the faith-community was swallowed up in the cultural environment, it lost its sense of "distance" by which it could understand its distinctive identity and the distinctive nature of what it had to offer to and receive from the environment. Social scientists describe this as the loss of a sense of boundary. A community will have little to offer a larger society it if cannot distinguish itself from that society, and it will not long maintain its distinctive heritage if it cannot train new members in what is special about the community itself.

If our congregations are to nurture their members, empowering them to be disciples and apostles, we must take a hard look at a surprising gap between the experiences ordinary people have of God and the experience they have of their local congregations. Over the past two decades a number of researchers have been surprised to discover a very large number of people who have had what they identify as direct experiences with God or transcendence.[4] Of course, there is ambiguity in the reports, but the surprise has been in the widespread nature of the phenomenon.

Several of us discovered–and Jean Haldane later discovered independently–that people do not connect those experiences with the religious congregations to which they belong. Haldane pointed out that ordinary people who have extraordinary spiritual experiences often do not think that their congregations or clergy would be interested in or able to help interpret such experiences. It is as if people have separated deep personal religious experience from congregational life. They feel that the congregation expects their support and attendance at worship and activities, but that the congregation has no interest in their religious experience.

I know that seems absurd. But it is a sign of how much we must do to rethink the character of community within our congregations. Congregations must let go of their preoccupation with programs and activities if they cannot also be a home in which religious experience and religious yearning is welcomed and nurtured. We need congregations with a sense of community in which each person's experience of God is affirmed—or at least brought into the open.

Congregations need to provide space for intimate storytelling that encourages members to share those deep experiences with one another. We need to develop spiritual directors in every congregation—the ministry seen as a matter of course, not only and always as a function of "professionals." We need congregations that take the experience of God as the norm. We need congregations that expect healing to be part of one's faith-life, whether or not one uses the ordinary medical arts. Healing may be as life changing with the help of Blue Cross/Blue Shield as it can be with the help of laying on of hands. Our congregations need to be the places where all of these experiences are seen as related to a life of faith.

Left outside the worshipping community, such experiences can lead to all kinds of psychic pathology. Paul was obviously both drawn to and nervous about such experience in the early church. He wrote appreciatively of the power of speaking in tongues, but he was also eager that such gifts be brought under the discipline of the community. The congregation-community has little chance of influencing such practices toward health if it refuses to pay attention to the lack of this necessary part of *koinonia*.

At this point I simply note a continuing congregational weakness—their inability to identify and communicate to members their distinct nature. This inability handicaps our congregations in fulfilling their purpose and mission to their members and to the outside world.

Koininia Wrap-Up

Congregational members live in the tension of their two worlds. They move back and forth as citizens of two realms—the public and the religious—potentially enriching each. Within the congregation, they inhabit a community that celebrates and tries to understand God's realm of shalom. Within their own bounds, congregations are communities of growth and support. This makes them a key resource for the transformation of each member. In this area we have much work to do if congregations are to fulfill their function of making disciples. When disciples move into the public realm, as apostles they bear with them the marks of God's realm.

As one looks from the congregation outward to the world, one can see the "good news" of the very presence of the congregation as it relates to and in that larger world. In the midst of a public community that is increasingly divided and antagonistic, where contention is the rule, it is good news to see islands of community that live by a different set of values. Congregations can assist in the transformation of society simply by being places where a different kind of community life is experienced and witnessed to. This ability to incarnate community is far more important as good news in the world than congregational "outreach programs." In this sense, congregations are communities that can be transforming influences in and examples for the world outside.

Congregations remain one of the key places where self-centered citizens may be transformed into disciples ready and eager to become bearers of good news to the needs of the world. And from these places the power of God's community can begin transforming a society into a community.

Koinonia, long a key characteristic of the congregation, remains a key to the congregation's ability to be a transforming reality for members and for society.

Kerygma: THE PROCLAMATION OF GOOD NEWS

Congregations have traditionally been the places where as a people we have been grounded in our story and in its meaning. Story came first, literally. Both the Hebrew scriptures and the New Testament existed as stories recited in community long before anything was written down. Congregations gave birth to scriptures. In congregations the storyteller was asked to tell the stories, and those congregations passed the stories along, sometimes bending them a bit in the passing. There is no way to go deeper into our heritage than through the stories faithful people passed on through their congregations to future generations.

The stories have always had transforming power. Nathan told a story to King David, a simple story of a rich man with many flocks and a shepherd with one precious lamb. When Nathan described how the rich man took the shepherd's one ewe lamb, David was outraged at the character's aggression. When Nathan, referring to David's sin against Uriah and God, said, "Thou art the man," David heard. The story carried power to convict and to transform.

Jesus told stories that have been retold generation after generation, and the stories have new power in each generation. The story of the Good Samaritan has spoken to prisoners of war and their captors. It spoke to Florence Nightingale. It spoke to me as a young man about racial injustice. In these days, it speaks to men and women who bear responsibility for policy about ethnic strife in the former Yugoslavia. That simple story leads to sleepless nights for policy makers two thousand years after Jesus told it to his followers. I will have more to say about story below, but first I turn to a special way in which congregations have come to encounter the transforming power of stories.

Churches speak of the power of the Word to transform life. They understand "the power of the Word" to mean scripture, yes, but also profound reflection upon it. They have experienced its transformative power in the act of preaching. In response to that strange, familiar activity of preaching, for generation after generation, gathered congregations have been transformed by the spoken word.

Who knows what all happens in preaching? Phillips Brooks, perhaps the best Episcopal preacher[6] since John Donne, spoke of it as "truth communicated through personality." William Dols, executive director of the Education Center, speaks of "Maieutic preaching," likening the task of the preacher to that of a midwife: A preacher assists the hearer to bring forth new meaning from the story.

Clearly there is more than rationality involved when a congregation responds to good preaching. The relationship between the preacher and the preached-to is an essential component of what happens. More involved than meets the eye or strikes the ear.

Where preaching has transforming effect, there is a giving and a taking of power. The one who listens holds power that can be given or withheld. The hearer can give or withhold that power. When it is given, the preacher is freed to go beyond recitation to proclaim truth with authority. In such a case the seed falls on the fertile ground. If the hearer chooses to withhold power, holding back from the experience, building walls to close out any communication, the Word will be held back. The seed will fall on barren ground and will fail to bring fruit.

In my experience more hearers are ready to give that power than preachers are to claim it. There is a moment early in the preaching event in which some deep parts of the listener are opened up to the preacher as one is not routinely opened up to a neighbor or a friend or even a spouse. That moment is an invitation to transformation and an opportunity for a dialogue from depth to depth.

If the preacher reaches from authentic depths and touches those open places with real stories of faith, something happens. Transformation can—and does—happen.

All too often we preachers, so insecure in ourselves, are busy explaining why we are there or ingratiating ourselves with a joke or bon mot. Where we succeed, we alleviate our own anxiety; a few people will remember our brilliant repartee, but the moment for transformation may disappear. Preaching is a dramatic engagement, not public speaking. The business of preaching is transformation, not transmission of information.

In that dialogue between preacher and listener, the preacher's role as an identified religious leader generally helps the process of transformation, but it is not essential. The fact that the preacher is usually a clergyperson sets this activity apart from ordinary conversation. That religious role sets this piece of communication within a framework of memory, relationship, and expectation that often predisposes the listener to open the inner door, but does not guarantee that the door will stay open for long. Any memory of religious leaders we have known or even heard about affects our openness. Our present and past relationships with pastors, rabbis, and priests perhaps not even of our own faith community will affect our openness. Expectations about what we want and hope for in relationship to God affect how we listen and approach this moment. Our own memory, relationships, and expectations are held there in the preaching moment in the community that surrounds us, where each other listener is bringing those same dimensions of experience to the spoken word.

The result is a moment, perhaps more, of credibility—credibility that has been earned by generations of faithful pastors whose influence continues to lead many listeners to be open to the Word of God, trusting that they will not intentionally be exploited by this particular preacher. That credibility remains, in spite of negative experiences many of us have had with scoundrels masquerading as clergy. That credibility is a precious commodity in every congregation and for every pastor. Where there has been personal exploitation of the congregation or its members by clergy in the past (I am including the sensational material that gets in the papers and also the many less dramatic ways in which clergy may misuse relationships or their position of trust), the new pastor and the people have a major job of rebuilding trust, even for so simple a thing as bringing back power to the preaching ministry. Clergy do more than private damage to themselves and the particular person or people with whom they break this kind of trust; they violate the framework within which gospel can be preached and believed; they fracture the trust that makes it possible for one to speak and another to hear. Where liability can be proved, the worst punishments the courts can mete out are minor compared to the damage to the heart of religious community.

The preaching we know in congregations is ordinarily an activity within the context of worship. But traditionally, preaching has existed as a much larger engagement. Amos preached by using a plumb line to demonstrate God's desire for justice. Jeremiah walked the streets of Jerusalem carrying a yoke on his shoulders to illustrate the fate of the nation if it did not turn from its ways. People of faith have also demonstrated the Word in their actions. The demonstrations organized by Martin Luther King and the SCLC were proclamations of the Word, as are Billy Graham's crusades.

Congregations I know demonstrated the Word by going to South Florida after hurricane Andrew and repairing houses. My own parish sent a group of young people to Honduras to build screen doors and install them—this in a place where there were disease-carrying insects and it was too hot to sleep with a closed door. Many people I know participate in a "grate patrol," handing out sandwiches to homeless people who sleep on the subway ventilation grates in cold weather.

Although different in many ways from traditional preaching, all these activities become dialogical. Those who go as the proclaimers of the Word always are changed by those to whom they "speak." These who carry a message discover that they are changed by those who receive it, that power and good news flow both ways.

Yet the ordinary task of preaching belongs in the heart of the congregation. It is one of the givens. It is there, week after week. In the congregation you must be able to count on this transforming activity being regularly practiced, regularly available. In God's good time, this ordinary gift becomes extraordinary.

The effectiveness of the preaching will always have elements of mystery because of the three parties involved—the listener, the preacher, and God. Each party has its own personal history and unique relationship to other parties. And of course, the mystery is magnified by the character of the life of community in the congregation itself.

Mystery is also key to the other primary kerygmatic action of congregations—the act of remembrance, the act of thanksgiving in which Christians relive the Last Supper. Here also three actors—the participant, the celebrant, and God—make this a moment of transformation unlike other transactions. With wide variations in specific theological interpretations of this dramatic action, Christians through the generations have found that this act places them within the history of salvation in an unique way, nurturing a life of faith and a commitment to action within the believer and the believing community. Things happen there that simply do not happen in other places. Hearts are touched, intentions formed, commitments made, restorations experienced, foundations rediscovered, relationships reborn.

In *kerygma* the faith that grounds the church is recounted, spoken, and re-enacted in such a way that faith comes alive within the congregation.

As *koinonia* is two things at once—a power to support the development of disciples and a sign to society of God's intent that we live in community—so *kerygma* is both a source of transforming power to those in the congregation and an impelling force in their encounters with the outside world.

Didache: The Teaching

Koinonia, *kerygma*, and now *didache* describe key functions of the congregation as a disciple-making system.[7] None of these functions is fully separable from the others. Teaching occurs in community and its content is the proclamation and stories of the heritage.

In today's churches ministries of teaching inside the congregation stand in urgent need of repair and renovation. Educational ministries may be the most routine deficiency found in congregations. The generations that grew up in the paradigm of Christendom could make assumptions that "everyone" knew what it meant to be a member of the congregation. Today, with even the illusion of Christendom long gone, our educational ministries still assume a population of religious literacy. The level of information about, much less comprehension of, the religious heritage has grown appallingly low. With each generation the level decreases.

The story is told of a relatively recent examination of candidates for ordination. The first candidate was asked, "Who is the patriarch Abraham?" The candidate scratched his head, hesitated, then said, "Wasn't he the first president of the United States who won the Revolution and freed the slaves?" The committee turned warily to the second candidate: "What is the religious meaning of Christmas?" She spoke up quickly, "That's when all the angels make toys for Santa to deliver in the chimneys!" The third candidate was ushered in to a depressed committee. "What happened on Good Friday?" they asked, "Oh yes," the candidate said thoughtfully, "that's when Jesus died on the cross." "Wonderful!" the committee chair said. The candidate warmed to the subject. "And they buried him in a tomb and rolled in a stone for a door." Committee members glowed. "And on the third day they roll away the stone and he comes out. If he sees his shadow, he goes back in and there are six more weeks of winter."

A widespread lack of a grasp of the faith makes it almost impossible for the congregation to establish a set of standards for its teaching ministries or make demands upon its leaders. Without knowledge of the story that sets the religious congregation apart, there is no basis for calling for a different standard by which members are to act. A boundary of knowledge helps members of the community distinguish themselves from the pagan society around them. The establishment of such a boundary is necessary for congregational members to differentiate between the moral and ethical standards of their faith and the customs of the pagan society in which those members live. Equally problematic, this lack of knowledge makes it impossible for parents to nurture their children in their heritage.

We simply must invest major energy across the board to build adult education to bring this generation of adults on board the biblical story and the heritage of faith. We need to expand the network of capable teachers in every congregation. This may be the most important task of the clergy for the next generation.

One area of education is getting some attention—the education for the newcomer or the nonmember. Denominations as well as congregations have recognized that the entry point is a critical opportunity for the new member to be brought into what it really means to belong to this faith-family. The mainline denominations are generally weak in dealing with one particular kind of newcomer—the complete stranger to faith, one not nurtured in a different denominational family. These clergy and congregations tend to have educational systems geared toward nurturing people toward maturity, but they are not very competent at leading people through conversion experiences. This deficit must be filled.

Pastoral care during life-crises has long been a strong suit of congregations and the training of pastoral leaders. Congregations today need to look, however, to the gaps in their sensitivity and caring. Why have people turned outside the church to programs such as AA, Parents without Partners, and the many twelve-step programs? These programs address human needs for care and support that are basically not included in the congregation's menu. In the short run congregations can be grateful for these caring ministries and work to support them and provide them meeting spaces. Doing so will extend the ministries of the congregation, using people who generally know something about the subject. In the long run we need to send our pastoral theologians to school with developmental psychologists, students of social trends, and futurists to analyze the new tensions of modern life and to begin inventing the pastoral care systems that fit the changing needs as congregational members face the crises of new patterns of life.

In all of this, the work of *didache* is to help open up the scriptures, the stories, the lore of the faith so that they are alive and known. When Jesus' life was turned upside down in his encounter with John the Baptist, his mind held the words of the psalms—memorized from weekly and daily recitation. He had heard stories of the Maccabes from the old people of his village. His mother had taught him strange stories of her own encounters with God. He knew the words of Isaiah and had struggled with their meanings. He had heard other stories from his rabbis. So when his moment of transformation and call occurred, he had at his disposal the words and images to define his vocation and shape his work. He had the raw material ready at hand.

Without such raw material from the rich dialogue of people with the stories of the faith, there really is no community of faith. Without continuous grounding in the story that is the Story, there is no good news for us to pass along. Without continuous grounding in the story, there is no purpose for the congregation, no way to inspire each person to reach out to the bad news that calls each to be a proclaimer of good news. We need congregations in which the word of the psalms and the stories of Jesus are in the ordinary current of life, available as people face daily opportunities, and also when crises occur.

Every congregation must be a center of teaching in an era in which the stories of the faith have slipped away from the consciousness of the wider community. Every adult should be seriously engaged with the scriptures on a week-by-week basis. And each congregation needs to be calling out the teaching skills of more of its leaders so that the story of faith is compellingly presented to the new and the long-term member, the young and the old.

It is the business of the congregation to order its life so that each of us is prepared for our side of the dialogue with the outside world, equipped as

Jesus was at the River Jordan—knowing the songs and stories of the faith and ready to respond.

Diakonia: THE SERVING ROLE

Few images are more dramatic than that of Jesus washing the feet of the disciples. Few fit so poorly our image of leadership and authority. Most of us have real sympathy for Peter's drawing back from a Jesus who would wash his feet. We are more comfortable with a leader who is more authoritative and overtly powerful, even though culturally we now feel more rebellious against such authority than former generations. We may feel that independent spirit and yet we like to know where we stand, which means we take some comfort in having an authority who calls the shots. Peter was right to feel threatened. We, too, are more at ease with the kind of leader whose feet we must wash than with a leader who washes ours.

But it is just this image of the servant as leader that we bring as a gift to our world and as a vocation for ourselves. In Christendom we had our flirtation with power, sensing that our call was to build empires and kingdoms shaped by our perception of God's will. We have organized crusades, waged battles, and built networks of power. We have driven ourselves and our society to establish the controls of power and law. We have rarely tried the way of powerlessness, the leadership of servanthood—in spite of Jesus' clear and often-repeated injunctions. His followers, he tells us, will become as little children, will serve one another, will wash one another's feet, will not lord it over one another. Like James and John, we are more comfortable jostling one another to see who gets the seats of privilege. Not many of our elections of church leaders fail for lack of candidates.

How else will they serve? As Jesus demonstrated, by going to the places of hurt and bringing healing, by going wherever there is bad news to proclaim good news.

In our time the shape of servant leadership seems to call less for great crusades of masses of people than the committed actions of disciples, one by one. Crusades were for a time when empires were being built, when we believed in empires of faith. The message of discipleship and service today is closer to Jesus' message that the kingdom of God is within and among you. The task of service is for one transformed heart to search out the feet that one set of hands is called to wash. One by one.

For congregations this means fewer great campaigns of social change and more opportunities for each member to discover gifts of serving and calls for service. My argument is based on the assumption that each of us is, indeed, gifted for serving and called to specific service.

The task of servant leadership is primarily outside the congregation—in the community that surrounds the congregation. This apostolic ministry presents special needs for training in the congregation. Within our congregations, we need more and better understanding of the community. If we intend to serve well, we need the skills of community analysis and the ability to understand the economic and demographic trends affecting the world outside the congregation. The servant leader outside the congregation needs all the skills available to serve in the ambiguous community world.

In coming years, effective servant leaders will need to draw together to learn from one another after engagement with the structures of the society. In time this may become so customary that our ordinary Bible classes and adult study groups will routinely engage in community analysis and reflection on work in the community. For now, we probably need to develop some new educational resources to help servant leaders find their way in this strange and changing world.

Koinonia, *kerygma*, *didache*, and *diakonia*—these, then, are the key functions that congregations are called to provide for the church of the future as they have been for congregations of the past.

THE DYNAMICS OF TRANSFORMATION: FROM DISCIPLESHIP TO APOSTOLATE AND BACK

These four functions are needed to bring persons to the fullness of discipleship. We see them as we look inside the church through our imaginary window. If, as I suggested above, we look out of our imaginary window, we see the whole world as quadrants of need, four places in which people of faith are called to give themselves to the world. The flow back and forth between discipleship and apostleship continues throughout one's life, with ever deeper grounding in the life of discipleship.

I diagram the model in this way:

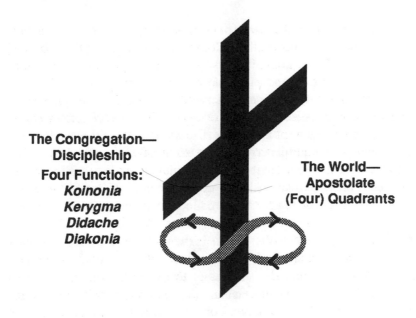

The Congregation—
Discipleship
Four Functions:
Koinonia
Kerygma
Didache
Diakonia

The World—
Apostolate
(Four) Quadrants

All conceptual models violate truth in the attempt to be clear. Certainly this one does, too. But perhaps it can help us see the interrelationship of discipleship and apostleship, the way there is a functional system binding each member to complementary growth as disciple and as apostle.

My assumption here is that every member of the congregation is called to function on both sides of the window, not just one. One "side" is not the prerogative of the clergy or of the laity. Both must interact in such a way that the entire system produces disciples and apostles and continuously reinforces them in faithful serving.

But that is not all. In my diagram, what about the window itself? I want to suggest that for this model the heart of the operation is its dynamic character. It is not enough that the apostolate is built. It is not enough that the discipleship is built. Each depends on interaction with the other; each needs to flow to the other to remain alive. There is a continuous flow from one side of the window to the other. And the heart of the model is the critical transaction as both discipleship and apostleship move through the "window" to enter the other side.

One of the most provocative descriptions of how this congregational dynamic results in transformation comes from Bruce Reed, president of the Grubb Institute of London.[8]

Reed calls his theory the theory of oscillation, building on research and theories in psychodynamics, anthropology, and theology. He describes the process of human living as a continuous cycling back and forth (oscillation) between two poles of dependence. One pole, in which human beings engage the world and its forces, make interventions, and carry out plans, represents life with internalized resources of competence and direction. This is analogous to my category of apostolate, the world outside the window, the world into which the faithful person is sent to respond to pain and need. The other pole represents life when it becomes depleted by the engagement and needs to reestablish its relationship of dependence on its ground of existence. That pole is related to what I have called the inside of the window—the arena of discipleship.

The oscillation between these poles is the story of life, Reed contends. The effectiveness of engaged life grows only out of the ability to depend on strength from beyond oneself. To attempt to live always in the engaged mode is to invite burnout and increasingly ineffective action. To live always in receptivity and dependence leaves one withdrawn from service in the world.

The rhythm of engagement and withdrawal, each leading to the other, is itself the congregation's structure of transformation. The congregation receives its people as they return from a week's engagement with the powers of the world, wherever each has served. Taking those people into the corporate activity of worship gives them back their citizenship in the realm of God and their dependence on God and on each other. The activity of worship once again places them in ordered relationship to the dependability of God and readies them for renewed engagement with the world.

Looking at this model, I see two critical areas for congregational initiative. The congregation needs to see that each member returning from the apostolate is greeted by many opportunities to experience *koinonia*, *kerygma*, *didache*, and *diakonia*. The congregation needs to manage the transitions from apostolate to discipleship and from discipleship to the apostolate.

The congregation's responsibility for the apostolate, contrary to modern church discussion, is severely limited. It has a role in helping members analyze the needs of the world and it has a role in helping members reflect on their ministries, but it has little role, corporately, in engaging the world. The temptation to do just that is a major temptation to build religious empire in the model of Christendom. Bruce Reed suggests that such efforts are actually the temptation to secularism—using the tools of the kingdom of this world and rejecting the spiritual tools of the kingdom Jesus proclaimed.[9]

Let me be even more explicit, using an illustration from Chapter 2, where I described a map or grid that explores the breadth of ways and styles for being a conveyor of good news. At this point I will illustrate on the grid the "locations" of individual people in a mythical congregation. Each # is the self-selected position chosen by one congregational member. I have used this grid with a number of groups, and although this placement is fictional, it is not unlike the pattern I find typical of many mainline congregations. I discover that congregations with a different orientation often give a quite different profile. Remember, this is attempting to graph one's self-perception of what kind of bad news tends to grab one's attention, and whether one is drawn to act on that bad news through religious or secular structures.[10]

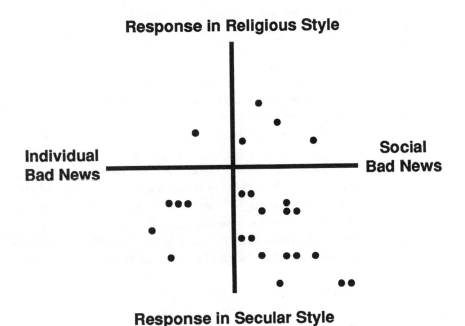

I've found that tracking a congregation on such a grid is valuable for exploring possibilities and relationships, but hardly provides accuracy or predictability. It is a teaching and reflection tool, not a planning tool. Having said that, I find that it helps to discuss how congregations are transformative communities and how that transformation happens. (See the Appendix A for instructions for using this grid to "map" a congregation.)

Where does the mythical congregation I've graphed concentrate? What kinds of bad news would catch attention there and what kinds of programs would such a congregation probably be good at mounting? Conversely, what are the blind spots of that congregation? Where would it be slow to perceive and inadequate in responding to need?

With the majority of people concentrated on the right side of the grid, this congregation will be "at home" in group activities and will understand the need to develop "programs." If this group concentrated heavily on the left side, the question of "programs" would be moot. They would not naturally think about working that way.

This congregation has few members in the upper left-hand quadrant; the largest cluster is in the lower right-hand quadrant, representing those who are grasped by social concerns and tend to seek to deal with them in the secular style.

In such a congregation leaders would probably have natural passion to engage with others to address community concerns—perhaps homelessness or hunger. They would see such engagement as obvious. Necessary. They might have a hard time understanding why everyone did not share the same passion.

In this congregation there is also an obvious low concentration in the upper left-hand quadrant. Those who located themselves there would not be greatly taken with the "majority" passion for programs to alleviate social pain.

Suppose *that* is the quadrant the pastor is attracted to. The pastor's sermons would probably reflect the good news she feels so keenly; the life of prayer and contemplation is the critical good news needed by the community. Many on the board might think of them as "pious" sermons. The pastor might be confused by there being little response to her conviction to feed the life of prayer and contemplation in the midst of the busyness of the community. The board might be more concerned about the need for a solid interchurch council to encourage more low-cost housing and soup kitchens.

The point is that each point on the diagram represents a legitimate but very different understanding of what good news needs to be addressed to what bad news.[11]

The task of the congregation, and consequently the concern of congregational leadership, looks very interesting against this backdrop. Managing the transformation process involves a sensitivity to the diversity of vocations that members feel called to. Unlike models of leadership from an earlier time, the task is not to get all the energy of the congregation focused in one missional thrust but to build as diverse a support system and sending system as possible. In the congregation noted above, leadership should be concerned about what needs to be done to nurture the few in the upper left-hand quadrant. Perhaps leaders should be wondering what such underrepresentation means in the congregation's life. Someone needs to consider how to bring strength to that undeveloped area of congregational life. Does that lack, for example, suggest an area of spiritual blindness?

Managing the moment of transformation from apostleship to discipleship and back again is important if we are to be strengthened to engage the world's bad news. Religious leaders and congregations have no more important task than to help each of us in the movement from discipleship to apostleship and back, continually deepening our awareness of our gifts and of our call. The better that flow, the better each of us will be in proclaiming good news.

All too often we do not have adequate tools to diagnose what we feel called to address or to identify our own personal resources, the gifts and tools available to us through our heritage and faith. Instead of purposeful action, we end up in embarrassed silence or confusion, wishing we could turn the whole thing over to somebody—a pastor—who can deal with it for us.

If our congregations are to help members be transformed from passive onlookers to active participants in communicating God's good tidings, they have large responsibilities in all these areas.

Our congregations have the task of helping members perceive what is going on around them. Being true to the map I have laid out, the need is not only the one liberals have been describing for the past decade—a social analysis of society—but also the one the conservatives have paid lip service to but have not addressed in depth—the spiritual vacuum of humans living in a one-story world. The social analysis of society that our liberals call for sounds like the thinking of sixties radicals dressed up in politically correct language, chasing after the newest trends willy-nilly, paying more attention to *The New Republic* and *Rolling Stone* than to Jeremiah. It has a thin and Godless taste. Similarly, I think the personal analysis of need offered by conservatives is simplistic and narrow, owing more to nineteenth-century morality and piety than to biblical faith.

We need more from each of these families in the churches. Our congregations need to provide much more and deeper engagement in both directions—toward society's transformation and toward personal transformation.

That is their business—helping people find their place in the dynamic of good news, being transformed from passive observers of mission to active participants in it.

This is not a call to activism and it is not a call to contemplation. It is a statement that each of us is called to an engaged ministry in which faithfulness of some will lead to social activity, from do-goodism to advocacy and political action, grounded in our religious heritage. For others it will mean a contemplative or personal involvement with God's purposes for individuals, one at a time. Congregations need to be able to help us find our place in the kind of engagement to which we are called.

Consider again the map of mission above: The point representing each person is best understood as being in orbit around the center, representing the fullness of ministry, with all quadrants active and strong, each part balanced and related to the whole.

There is more. In the map I have shown and the mythical congregation I used to illustrate my point, each person is symbolized by a particular point on the map. In my experience that is inadequate. That spacial location may hold true at the time, but people change. One's call and response to the call differs from time to time. From our own stories we know that we have grown and changed in how we see and engage in our ministries. So it is for all who seek to proclaim good tidings.

A primary task of the congregation is to be a reliable center around which the variety of its members can orbit, as it were. The stronger the center, the stronger each individual can be in holding true to that moment's sense of call and mission. The stronger and more reliable the center, the more secure the individual can be in exploring new aspects of call and mission. I say even more: The stronger the center, the further out to the extremes in ministry can individual members be encouraged and supported. Perhaps the strongest mission congregations of the future will not be those with the greatest, most visible projects or services, but the ones that can sustain their people in the most diverse and extreme ministries of service and caring one can imagine.

This is a different understanding than most people have of the role of the congregation, but I think it is what is called for in the emerging age. The common understanding, and the source of much congregational strife, is that the task of the congregation is to affirm one place or quadrant on a map as the right place, and to program things to encourage everyone to see mission as defined by that position. Clergy tend to think that their conception of the mission is the correct one; they see their job as getting the congregation's program to reflect that sense of mission.

I do not believe the clergy's role has to do with that at all. The clergy have a right to claim a special place within the map of mission, but no right to try to bring the congregation to that place. The clergy's role is to help the congregation establish and hold its center, which is the normative center of the religious tradition in its fullness, not the normative center of that clergyperson's particular vision. The congregation needs so to center its life in its religious grounding that it provides a secure place, able to affirm and strengthen members' various ministries, even those that vary wildly from one another. In this view, a congregation might well be suspicious if it became too uniform in its understanding of mission, if too many began to agree that real mission involved perceiving and acting primarily in any one of the quadrants of the map. A pastor's task might well be to try to initiate strength in a quadrant where the congregation is lacking strength, even when it is a quadrant different from where the pastor locates mission.

Holding the center, then, is the task of the congregation. It is a task not of doing but of being. It means exploring and reflecting on the deepest parts of the heritage, experiencing the presence of God, centering in worship, living and breathing the scriptures. It means building an interpersonal community within which each person can be nurtured and strengthened as well as challenged and sent. It means taking very seriously the diversity of God's call to mission, a call that is direct, different, and evolving for each individual. It means taking seriously the complexity and diversity of the good tidings called for by the needs of the world. It means taking seriously the unique set of gifts each person has to mediate between the needs of the world and the good news of God.

I believe that to be a challenging mission for the congregation. Is it, however, a pearl of such great price that we can risk changing the operating structures of our congregations for it? I believe we must.

NOTES

1. I once saw this prophetic message acted out. I was in Washington at the time of Helen Keller's death, and I attended her funeral at the National Cathedral. The blind, the deaf, and the lame were there, celebrating her life. A choir from a school for the bind sang like angels. Sen. Lister Hill of Alabama read the lesson with a powerful voice trained in southern oratory. For the first time in my life I watched as the lesson was signed. As he spoke of the deaf hearing, the blind seeing, the lame leaping for joy, we saw the good news acted out even as we also experienced God's power in the life of Helen Keller.

2. Parker Palmer, *Going Public* (Washington, DC: The Alban Institute, 1980).

3. Robert Bellah, et al., *Habits of the Heart* (Berkeley: University of California Press, 1985).

4. In 1972 Tilden Edwards, Parker Palmer, James Simmons, and I talked to a group of twenty laypeople about their experiences of spiritual growth. The paper we wrote, *Spiritual Growth* is out of print (Project Test Pattern, 1973). Jean Haldane made similar discoveries, reported in *Religious Pilgrimage* (Washington, DC: The Alban Institute, 1975). In more recent times Gallup polls have found among interviewees a high number of personal experiences with God.

5. Keith Russell argues that Koinonia *was* the primary thing the early church had to offer society. People were drawn to the church because its living community spoke to the bad news of their society. See *In Search of the Church* (Washington, DC: The Alban Institute, 1994).

6. As an Episcopalian myself, I am well aware that many of my non-Episcopal friends understand "Episcopal preacher" to be an oxymoron!

7. For more details see Loren B. Mead, *More Than Numbers* (Washington, DC: The Alban Institute, 1993), ch. 3.

8. For a fuller exploration of the theories, see Bruce Reed, *The Dynamics of Faith* (London: Darton, Longman, and Todd, 1978). For a shorter version, see Bruce Reed and Barry Palmer, *The Task of the Church and the Role of Its Members* (Washington, DC: The Alban Institute, 1975). Reed's work in group relations and the dynamics of organizations has been critically important to many in this country. I am particularly indebted to him.

9. I have never fully understood the fascination certain denominations have exhibited in the use of the New Testament role of the deacon as a special agent and representative of the church in the world (what I have characterized as the apostolate). My own understanding is that the baptized person operating as an apostle is the church's representative to the world.

10. The placements I note here are the sort that one gets when using the design in the appendix.

11. David Roozen, William McKinney, and Jackson Carroll, *Varieties of Religious Presence* (New York: Pilgrim Press, 1984), suggests that congregations "hold

the center" as I have described in this grid. That book also suggests, helpfully, that individual congregations may have different "centers." A congregation may have a central understanding of its message that could make the community itself focus in one of the quadrants. If so, the congregation's task would be to hold that center and provide a dependable reference point to which members could return for renewal of their special calling.

CHAPTER 4

The Role of the Judicatory

Every congregation is surrounded by denominational structures designed to support and strengthen the total mission of the church.[1] As the storm described in chapter 1 has gathered, and as clarity about what "total mission" actually means, judicatories, like congregations, have found their role confused and uncertain.

In the previous two chapters I have attempted to go to the roots of what congregations need to be about as a first step to our reinventing them for our time. What is true for congregations is also true for the judicatory structures around them. In this chapter I want to begin the conversation about what judicatories need to be for us as we try to weather the storm and reconstruct a church for the next century.[2]

OUR JUDICATORIES

Our different denominational groupings and ecclesiological backgrounds give us a hundred ways for congregations to be connected to and communicate with one another. Often we have become so enamored by our own system that we spend our time arguing its superiority or trying to find evidence in scripture that what we inherited through our convoluted history is really what God intended in the beginning.[3]

Some of the connectional systems—such as the Catholic and the United Methodist—have clear, sharp delineations of relationship, role, and authority. You can easily find out who makes what decisions and when. When you ask questions, people respond by quoting the book of order. Others—such as the Presbyterian and Episcopal systems—have clear definitions but live with them more casually until there is a fight. Presbyterians will sometimes quote their book of order, but Episcopalians tend to get pretty vague and say, "It must be in the canons somewhere." Still others, such as Baptists and congregationalists, take pride in their independent ways but still find models of community and interrelationship that are mutually supportive. Their habits of relationship and common heritage provide the structure that meets their needs.

Some people are concerned with the collapse of national structures in American mainline denominations. Although I am aware of the difficulties on the national level, I see those problems as being a minor concern when compared to the weakening in the structures of the middle judicatories. Those structures simply are not working well in any of the denominations I'm familiar with. Though less visible than the problem of the national structures, the middle judicatory woes have more pervasive long-term implications. Most of the essential work of the churches—the making and deploying of apostles—goes on without much regard to national policies and directions and could probably survive the demise of those structures without much trouble. That is not so of the regional structures.

Regional middle judicatories are the closest resource to congregations and usually have a responsibility for the care of those congregations. Depending on the denominations, judicatories are given varying amounts of power to intervene in the congregation, but the denominational differences are less than the ecclesiologists claim. Catholic and Methodist systems have clear authority to step into the congregation, where they can do pretty drastic things—remove a pastor or a board or take other disciplinary action. On the other hand, congregationalist denominations give the judicatory very little power for intervention. In fact, for both of these systems, "reality" is somewhere in between the connectional and congregational rhetoric. The quality of the relationship between the judicatory and the congregation speaks volumes about how far the judicatory intervenes. Where little trust exists between judicatory and congregation, Catholic and Methodist bishops know they have been in a fight when they have simply set out to do what they have the legal authority to do. On the other hand, where the trust is high and built on experience, an executive of the United Church of Christ or a Baptist convention can move with more authority than the book allows to help a troubled congregation sort itself out. The in-between denominations, such as the Episcopal and Presbyterian churches, work hard at the trust issue but can get into hot water by making assumptions that the office of the bishop or the authority of the presbytery carries more weight than it does.

The judicatories' accessibility to the congregation is the functional issue I want to focus on. Judicatory offices are relatively close to the congregations. (I see the bishop of Montana and the presbytery executive of Alaska rolling in the aisles at this point. And one judicatory executive in Canada tells me it is nine hours by car from one end of his region to the other!) The judicatory is generally the first office called when there is a crisis of some sort. Judicatories are the first back-up system for congregations.[4]

In choosing to start this discussion by focusing on reconstructing the function of the judicatory, I am obviously excluding two other possible starting points: denominational tradition and organizational precedent. Why do I exclude denominational tradition? Because too often the theological or ecclesiological definition of the judicatory's role has become a religious justification for current organization. If not that, then the language of the heritage has been bent to support structures clearly not envisioned by those who first worked out the meaning of the polity. Why do I exclude organizational precedent? I find that starting there makes it impossible to question the sacred cows of the system. Starting in either of those two places makes it too easy to rationalize what we already do and makes it virtually impossible to initiate change at a base level.

There may be an even more important reason to work at reconstructing our denominational links: This relationship between congregation and judicatory is where the loss of trust most urgently handicaps our religious institutions.

What Congregations Need from Judicatories

Over the past decade I have observed judicatories of many sorts as they tried to provide support to congregations. Each year at the Bishop and Executive Leadership Institute,[5] I have a chance to learn from three or four dozen working executives or bishops. I am deeply indebted to some three hundred of our "alumni" who have shared their wisdom and their questions. Out of those experiences I have developed a list of what congregations need from judicatories. Rephrased, these functions would answer this question: What does a judicatory executive need to be good at? In the spring of 1993 I revised and reworked that list with the help of a group of Presbyterian executives at a conference at Ghost Ranch.[6] Here I share this list with you.

Congregations Need Help When They Get in Trouble

Anyone who has worked closely with congregations knows that from time to time even the best of them get in some kind of trouble.

At the Alban Institute we are particularly conscious of the explosive fights that break out from time to time in all kinds of congregations for all kinds of reasons; at this juncture congregations or judicatories often call on us for help.[7] Church fights break out at unpredictable moments and can range from minor tiffs to major shoot-outs. We have discovered that church fights often erupt as a surprise. The people in the congregation may not recognize the conflict for what it is. The pastor may be away or, worse, may have flipped into panic. Nobody is prepared to deal with it helpfully. A first symptom of the conflict is often the signing of a petition about something, followed by a carefully worded ultimatum from the pastor. Within a brief day or two, the first visible symptom may have led to all-out war. A judicatory that is alert can often do damage control and bring the conflict to a constructive outcome.

Church fights are just one of dozens of troubles a congregation might face. Often enough the denomination's book of order or canon has procedures for the more common problems, but once again the people of the congregation often do not know about those procedures. What are you supposed to do when somebody misappropriates funds? What are you supposed to do if a major program of the church collapses on you? What do you do if somebody says you are going to receive a bequest? What do you do if the highway department wants to build a road through your church building? What do you do if someone threatens a law suit? What do you do if the pastor has misbehaved and the board knows it? What do you do if the pastor has misbehaved and the local paper knows it? What are you supposed to do if the board cannot get a quorum to do its work? What are you supposed to do if you suspect the pastor has become an alcoholic? What are you supposed to do if nobody can find the official records of the congregation? What are you supposed to do if a congregation takes a nose-dive in financial receipts?

Others who work with or in congregations will have other items on their lists. You can be sure of one thing: The list is long. Congregations can have the same difficulties as any other organization, but the problems can be exacerbated by two scenarios: (1) a habit of speaking about plain things in theological double-talk (a screw-up in committee assignments can become "a violation of my vocational commitments"), and (2) the likelihood of an appeal to a higher court—God—in a way that escalates a difficulty into a confrontation of Good and Evil (when you thought you were just working on the budget!)

Judicatories need to develop a capacity to help congregations clarify what's at the bottom of the trouble and work out a strategy for dealing with it. I do not think the judicatory needs to be able to solve the problems. Not at all. But the judicatory needs to have a relationship with the congregation in which the congregation respects the judicatory and its advice. In some cases judicatories will have direct answers, but in most cases they can help most in diagnosing the problem and in advising the congregation as it deals with the problem or secures other help in doing so.

Congregations need the judicatory to be clear about what kinds of situations it can provide help for and what kinds should be referred to outsiders. Let's be honest. That call is hard for a judicatory to make if it thinks it must solve everything that comes along or if it has an unrealistic idea of what its limits of energy and skill are. If a judicatory executive is insecure or anxious, he may be unable to permit outsiders to help. He is likely to attempt an in-depth intervention in a two-hour meeting because that is all the time he can spare. We have found that some kinds of interventions—a "hot fight," for example—can take six to ten full days of careful work to move to resolution. In such a case the judicatory executive does not help the congregation by trying to force a quick fix—which usually exacerbates the problem.

A United Methodist congregation I know asked its district superintendent to help it design a long-range planning process. As he worked with leaders of the congregation, the DS picked up their anxiety about mixed signals they were getting from their pastor about his leaving or staying. The DS was able to help them make a better diagnosis of their problem so that they could clarify their relationship with the pastor. Then the long-range planning started to get off the ground. That congregation was strengthened by a judicatory executive who dug below the surface issue and helped them deal with a deeper issue.

A Disciples congregation in an urban setting struggled with keeping up a soup kitchen with increasingly burned-out volunteers. When they discussed it with their judicatory executive, she helped them go to other congregations of other denominations and ask for help. The executive also pointed the pastor toward a course in which he could learn more about the care and feeding of volunteers.

These illustrations are deliberately undramatic. But they illustrate the kinds of questions a judicatory has got to recognize as important and be prepared to help a congregation with.

I predict that the stormier the future gets, the more judicatories will have their hands full. Two trouble spots are likely to increase exponentially over the next decade—calls for help in conflict management and with financial short-fall. Judicatories will do well to increase their skills and locate trustworthy allies in these two areas—people who can be called in to add to the available resources. They need to have a large adjunct staff—people whose salaries they do not pay, but whom they can call in for "piece work." That is one of the most productive roles the Alban Institute plays, backing up the energies and skills of judicatory leaders.

From time to time, congregations need help. Judicatories need to be ready to provide counsel and/or resources.

Congregations Need to Be Left Alone

For the most part, when congregations are not actively asking for help, judicatories need to leave them alone. Most congregations have programs in place and energy harnessed to their tasks. Most congregations have a pretty good working relationship with their pastors.

If such is the case, congregations ought to be left alone most of the time to get on with their work. I state this inelegantly as my *bias toward neglect*. Perhaps I would not have such a bias in other generations, but now is the time....

Judicatories often operate as if they were being remiss if they are not calling a lot of meetings, working with a lot of task forces, and sponsoring many judicatory activities for laity and clergy to be engaged in. Most congregations do not need it.

I get nervous around judicatories that are toolling up to develop mission statements and long-range strategic plans. Maybe it is a good idea sometimes, but maybe it is organizing to do something nobody needs to have done. The person being served in much judicatory activity is the judicatory itself or its staff members who need to exercise their creativity.

My point here is to encourage a judicatory to operate strategically in terms of its primary task—strengthening the congregations within its bounds. That means not treating all congregations alike, but differentiating among them—being prepared to make strong interventions where needed, and to leave others alone.

Congregations Need to Be Jacked Up When They Are Off Base

Congregations need somebody who cares enough about them to tell them when they are genuinely off base. When poverty abounds in their neighborhoods, somebody needs to raise questions if they plan opulent new buildings. When children and families are at risk, congregations need to be brought up short if they drop day-care centers on which their communities have come to rely or pull out of coalitions for family aid or support for the public school systems. Congregations need to be called to account if they neglect opportunities to support mission efforts outside their own local programs. Congregations need to be jacked up when they are irresponsible in their rebellion against their own denominational structures. Congregations need to be called to account when they misuse their staffs or pay subminimum wages. Congregations with significant financial resources need help learning to be good stewards. Warning: They probably will not accept help from the judicatory itself. (They probably do not trust the judicatory, often for good reason.) This means the judicatory needs to be sure they have access to resources the congregations will trust.

When I say congregations need somebody to hold them accountable, I do not mean that the judicatory should see itself as calling the shots in all the areas described here. The point is that somebody needs to get involved, ask questions, if necessary put congregations on the defensive and make them think through what they are doing. If they take time to reflect, check their status and direction of their mission, and then go ahead, I think the judicatory has done the job called for. I do not believe the judicatory has the responsibility of always being right or even obeyed.

Congregations Need Pastoral Care

I speak here about the corporate pastoral care that congregations need in their life together. Of course the pastor has a task here, but some things need another dimension of care.

Congregations need grief-care when facing the loss of a pastor or a key lay leader. Congregations need care when the building burns down or is flooded. Congregations need care when a big local business goes belly-up or a local catastrophe strikes—a hotel burns down or a plan crashes. The congregation needs pastoral care after a fierce congregational battle. Congregations need lots of care when they have been betrayed by the misbehavior of a clergyperson. They may even need care when there is prominent misbehavior by a clergyperson of another congregation, even in another denomination.

Good pastoral caregivers often see needs those needing care do not see. Pastors recognize grief and need to be aggressive in "moving in," even though the grieving person may not "want" attention. Pastors know that sometimes withdrawal is a sign of depression. Similarly, judicatory executives need to be willing to be a bit pushy when they know help is needed—such as when a pastor leaves and grief hits the congregations. This is one place (there are others) where congregations cover over their feelings with all sorts of self-important verbiage-like the child who tells the parent, "I can do it myself." Parents need to be on the lookout for the child who is involved in something he really cannot handle by himself and be willing to step in. So, too, with judicatory executives and bishops and their staffs.

My focus on the negative experiences that trigger a need for care should not negate the need for the judicatory to be there for the moments of celebration and the marking of milestones. There are times and communities that need a message of congratulations when the high-school team wins—or comes in second—in the state basketball tournament. Or even when a fund drives goes over the top.

Congregations Need Pastoral Care for Their Pastors

No one needs to underline the pressure pastors are under today. As paradigms of ministry change, clergy are also buffeted by financial pressures, insecurity regarding their professional futures, and a diminished public image of their role in society.

The multiplicity of changes that have simultaneously hit clergy leave them stressed and feeling burned out as they try harder to accomplish their work with reduced resources. All too often I find clergy almost imobilized—they are so aware of their pain and need. When in that state, they forget what they have learned in pastoral care—that pastoral care does not equal pats on the back and hand-holding.

The pastoral care clergy need from their judicatories is the kind that gets them to be the first-class professional leaders they intend to be. I have worked with clergy for decades, and I find them happiest tackling their work, solving problems, making their bricks whether or not anybody gets them the straw. Judicatories need to avoid infantilizing their clergy, thinking of them as "poor sweet babies" needing constant care. Clergy, like everyone else, can become bottomless pits of needs if their leaders pander to those needs.[8]

Judicatories do need to be aware of the heavy stresses and try to see that resources are available for the clergyperson temporarily overwhelmed, seriously depressed, or ill. But I would urge a *bias toward health*, giving clergy additional challenges and resources, not sympathy. Even where there are difficulties, clergy need to be encouraged to take action for their own health. Having a good list of opportunities for professional education and a solid scholarship fund is more important than planning a clergy development program that is fully funded by the judicatory.[9]

We do need to recognize the extraordinary pressure on clergy. The older they are, the more revolutions they have lived through. What is expected of them has changed 180 degrees. Once the front-line troops of a crusade, they have become the mess sergeants in an army they do not control. Their role as community leader often has been eroded. The clarity about their work has disappeared. They catch more cirticism than previous generations of clergy. Most of them were trained for another role, another institution, another history, another world.

Judicatories exercise pastoral care by helping these dedicated people pull up their socks and stockings and pitch in as the competent learners they can be.

Congregations Need Help with Leadership Development

Many congregations do not adequately train new leaders and see to effective leadership transitions—for laity or clergy. The most serious gap is in the adequate training support judicatories give when clergy and lay leaders are starting up a new leadership team. Every judicatory needs to give priority to ensuring that every pastor moving into a new position has training or consultative assistance to put together a new working team of clergy and laity. I see this as the most strategic opportunity to raise the level of effective leadership in a congregation. Every judicatory needs to have such a program in place every year. It should be a built-in expectation. At the Alban Institute we have helped Episcopalians and Lutherans begin such programs.

A lesser opportunity is available every year when new board members are selected for the congregation; every such change is an opportunity for new team building for the congregation leadership.[10] Most congregations are left to fend for themselves at these transitional times, with the result that few congregational boards operate very effectively. Large congregations need team building and training for their staffs. Even though they have resources at hand, they often forget to do it. Judicatory executives need to push them to act on this need. If there are several such congregations in the judicatory, annual or biannual staff-building conferences can be very helpful.

Small congregations may have limited ability to train leaders. Some fail to see the community benefits of such training. In many smaller communities, the church-based leadership training is virtually the only leadership development available in the whole community. The Alban Institute has found that when we work with a small-town church to resolve conflict, the whole community gains resources for dealing with other conflicts. Leadership training in communication skills, in how to manage small groups, in how to design effective meetings, in how to put together an educational design—all are needed in every congregation. Yet only the largest megachurches have the resources to do it for themselves.

Some judicatories have been able to broker the training resources available in larger congregations for use in smaller ones. Large congregations often have more staff resources than does the judicatory.

Congregations Need Technical Assistance

Many congregations have limited resources of technical know-how in managing their own lives or interacting with the outside community.

Basic planning skills and knowledge about how institutions work are important for congregations in changing times. For instance, techniques for fund raising and fund management can help congregations order their lives, but someone has to see that those resources are available. Some of the issues addressed earlier in this chapter have to do with technical assistance—knowledge about conflict management, for example, or understanding the impact of grief on corporate groups.

Congregations often also need help from outside to understand what is going on in the world in which they minister. Few of them have skills in reading demographic or economic trends in their town or county. Information and interpretation is often available, but they do not know how to access it. Someone "outside" may have to help congregations connect with this knowledge if it is to help them with their ministries. A judicatory office that has a list of phone numbers of county planning agencies in each county can really help its congregations that want to plan for the future.

Most congregations also need a great deal of help in professional techniques for fund raising. Few congregations are able to give members adequate help in planned giving, but judicatories can locate such resources and make them available.

Congregations Need a Sense of Their Place in a Larger Mission

Too many congregations get locked into the local sense of mission with such enthusiasm that they turn their backs on needs beyond their boundaries. This is both good and bad: good in that it often is a new and important commitment of direct, hands-on, grassroots action that proceeds from their faith; bad in that it disengages them from mission concerns that genuinely belong to them and have a claim on them.

The judicatory has a special responsibility to help the congregation widen the horizon of its concern for mission. The judicatory has a difficult, slippery path to follow—pushing congregations to respond to more distant mission responsibilities, while not using that simply to justify the judicatory budget. Much of the suspicion of congregations toward their denominational structures comes from a discomfort that all the talk about "mission" is just a ploy to garner money to pay bureaucrats. Or, what may be more destructive of trust, that the judicatory is just interested in its own pet project, most of which do not look like mission to the people in the pew. This has dug us into a hole in which even the most high-minded pleas of church leaders are likely to find considerable suspicion among many generous contributors who care for mission and care for the church. In such a climate, judicatories dig even deeper holes when they hold ever bigger and more frequent "extra mission giving" campaigns in which they disguise the fact that they are raising money to continue doing what people have decided they are not enthusiastic about doing.

Even though past practices have damaged trust and credibility, judicatories have a responsibility to work at widening the vision of the local church. So they have to rebuild trust. That's not a bad thing to be working on. If the judicatory does not help the congregation look beyond its bounds, it will be damaging the congregation. Yes, the task is difficult and there are patterns from the past that will haunt us. No matter. I do not suggest a bias toward inaction.

Congregations Need Someone Who Listens and Listens and Listens

The most important thing a congregation needs may be somebody outside who just listens and pays attention. Someone who reads its weekly bulletin and picks up signals. Someone who knows the group well enough to recognize when it needs some kind of intervention. Someone who is not afraid to follow up on hunches that things are not going well or—perhaps—when things need celebrating.

I have, then, good news and bad news for those who work in judicatories offices, whether they be bishops, executives, regional/area ministers, superintendents, moderators, or . . . some name I haven't yet heard.

The bad news is what most of you already know in your bones. The old system is not working. It is based on organizational assumptions and functions designed for another age and another way of thinking. It is based on sets of loyalties and understandings of authority that do not hold today. What may be worse, the financial underpinnings of the judicatory are threatened almost everywhere, and that threat will not be dealt with adequately by working harder at the no-longer-working system.

I hope I am being very clear that the bad news is very bad and very urgent. The effectiveness of every regional judicatory I know is in serious trouble and it is not getting better. I dramatize my point by asking judicatory executives how they will do their jobs in five years when they have half the staff they have now. I ask them where their successors will get salaries from.

The good news is good news indeed. The need for what a judicatory can provide is sharp and real, even if it may be different from the functions called for in past generations. It is also true that the functions are needed by the part of the system that has the resources to pay the costs—if convinced that the functions are focused on helping mission happen. The connection between congregations and judicatories is of enormous self-interest to each—not simple selfish self-interest, but a self-interest in seeking to carry out their call of faith, to make a difference in the world and for the kingdom of God.

William McKinney, widely known teacher, leader, researcher, and consultant who works at Hartford Seminary, was recently asked to analyze the role played by people who worked regionally in a project (run by the Center for Congregations in Community Ministry at McCormick Seminary in

Chicago) to support local congregations as they got involved in social ministry projects in the Midwest. These support people were not acting as judicatory executives, but I see McKinney's findings as being useful to our
judicatory discussion: McKinney described their role as that of "persistent
friends." These people worked for the project but were external to the
congregations, bringing skills and challenges to them. They prodded the
congregations, advised the congregations, "held hands" with the congregations, helped the congregations find resources, found ways for them to overcome divisions and conflicts, showed them how to plan, and also stood by
and watched. They did not give up on the congregations when they got in
self-defeating patterns. They kept coming back and coming back, calling
the congregations to higher expectations.

Yesterday's models, in which executives acted as if lording it over
congregations was the best way to help them work in fewer and fewer
places. They no longer generate loyalty or produce results as they did in a
different world. Similarly, the models in which the executives stood back
only to come in—with apology—when blood was on the walls do not do
justice to the critical developmental needs congregations have today.

We can clarify the executive role only as we understand the life of
congregations and the functions needed if congregations are to be engaged in their work of reaching out into human lives and communities.
This chapter has been an attempt to begin looking at those functions "from
the ground up."

McKinney's phrase "persistent friend" is a good place to start. The
model of those Chicago project leaders is instructive. As long as there are
congregations that seek to make disciples and send them into the community as bearers of good news, those congregations will need persistent friends
who challenge and support them in their task.

NOTES

1. Nomenclature is always a problem here. Each denomination has a different
name for the structure that provides this organizational environment for individual
congregations. I will use the awkward word that has become used by consensus:
judicatory. I do so even as I harbor a few unkind thoughts of my Presbyterian
colleagues who apparently coined the word and foisted it off upon us. The
word is actually used for any level of the church structure outside the congregation, but I will use it almost exclusively for the regional organization of the church,

not the national. Even the word regional is awkward. Some denominations have two levels of judicatory between congregations and national structures. Presbyterians have regionally small presbyteries and larger synods. Episcopalians have regionally close diocese and vestigial provinces for larger areas. In this discussion I am talking about the close-by judicatory–the one in direct and regular contact with congregations.

2. See Loren B. Mead, *The Once and Future Church* (Washington, DC: The Alban Institute, 1991).

3. As a life-long Episcopalian who grew up with doctrines of apostolic succession as the basis for having bishops, I remember hearing the story of the early efforts of the Protestant Episcopal Church to send mission workers to Japan. In the story the early missionaries were perplexed at why the Japanese had a hard time understanding the denomination, until they had translated back to them the Japanese name for the church; The Society of Contradicting Overseers. Frankly, that's not a bad name for the way the house of Bishops operates, but I'll defend them to the death!

4. A hot spot that has come to life in the nineties has been the role of the judicatory and the congregation in cases of sexual misbehavior on the part of the male pastor. The more "connectional" systems generally have more power to act to discipline the pastor than the denominations in which pastoral discipline is more heavily congregational. A pastor who has misbehaved, even misbehaved flagrantly, sometimes is able to maintain the fervent support of the congregation. Pastoral loyalty sometimes combines with blame-the-victim thinking to give some such pastors immunity.

5. This is a five-day educational event for those in the role of bishop or executive. Sponsored by the Alban Institute, this event is held for three dozen or so people. Information is available the Alban Institute.

6. Ghost Ranch in New Mexico is more familiarly known to northern Presbyterians as "heaven." Southern Presbyterians reserve that term for Montreat, North Carolina.

7. My staff colleague Speed Leas is one of the pioneers among church leaders in developing ways to work with and through conflicts. His writing, teaching, and wise counsel have helped dozens of conflicts turn to growth for the people involved. The potential for escalation always hits me humorously when I read the prayer found in many evening liturgies. How many churches have prayed this prayer? "O God, make Speed to save us!"

8. See Edwin Friedman, *Generation to Generation: Family Process in Church and Synagogue* (New York: Guilford Press, 1985), a prime resource for judicatory executives and bishops.

9. See Roy Oswald, *Clergy Self-Care.* (Washington, DC: The Alban Institute, 1991) and any other books by Oswald.

10. Two programs, both initially begun by the Lilly Endowment, Inc., try to

address some of this. Operating out of Trinity Episcopal Church, 3242 N. Meridian St., Indianapolis, IN 46208, a nationwide effort (Trustee Leadership Program) is helping to develop congregational boards using models form nonprofit organizations and educational institutions. Chuck Olsen, a Presbyterian pastor, is also completing the Set Apart Lay Leader project to discover models and methods to help church-board leadership. Contact: Dr. Charles Olsen, 15003 NW Seventy-second St., Kansas City, MO 64512.

Chapter 5

Roadblocks and Directions for the Journey

Those of us who seek to reinvent our religious structures for the next generation are aware of the complex and resistant forces we face.[1] It often seems that when we take one step ahead, we slip back two. Our "new project" ends up putting us in more trouble than we were in before. How many important attempts have been made in how many creative ways? And yet the winds of the storm are unabated. We sometimes wonder if our sheer stubbornness keeps our hopes alive.

I cannot number the wise and committed colleagues I have seen charge up the hill, year after year, all with conviction, most with great plans, all absolutely certain that this time, this time, they would succeed. I hear that conviction in the voices of those who phone me to tell of the great plan they have developed—and I remember how excited someone was thirty years ago who tried that very plan in Chicago or in the Bay Area. I have a memory bank full of failed efforts. None failed because of stupidity. Nonc failed because of lack of faith.

Perhaps we underestimated the problems that stood in the way. Per- haps we underestimated the power of the Opposition. Perhaps we were naïve. I have a feeling that one of our most powerful idols is "My New Idea," "The New Program," or even "The New System." Martin Marty once told me that my work with congregations had reminded him "that there are no big deals any more."

Some of us have no choice but to charge up that hill again. As Luther put it in a more overtly theological sense, we "can do no other." And what can we begin to do that is different? We can more consistently try to learn from our experience and map out those forces that consistently get in our way. In this chapter I want to name some of the major impediments ahead of us and the clues I have for moving ahead. I am aware that many of the obstacles are connected to the others. We are unlikely to be able to solve them one by one; we will have to deal with the whole system at once.[2]

WE HAVE DUG OURSELVES INTO A FINANCIAL HOLE

One of the major prophets of the twentieth century is a shadowy figure described by Woodward and Bernstein in their story of Watergate. Deep Throat, as they named the man who spoke from the shadows of the parking garage, said, "Follow the money!" They did, and they brought down a president.

Deep Throat's advice to the reporters is a guideline for looking at problems and directions in any institution; it has great relevance for the difficulty we have in dealing with congregations and in trying to change them. Let's discuss several areas in which our relationship to money is crippling our ability to do what we say we want to do to renew our institutional life. Leaders of churches, especially clergy, use language all the time, often to obscure rather than clarify. But here I will use unvarnished language, saying things more directly than in our churchy style. Forgive me if I offend.

We Have Consistently Misappropriated Funds

I probably have your attention. The point is that churches consistently use large amounts of money in ways the donors do not understand or approve of.

There is no criminal intent. This is what happens: Those who give to their congregations do so for a variety of motives and in a variety of styles—from those who "pay their dues" to those who want to "make an impression" to those who give in simple gratitude to God. But there is an implicit contract in all cases that the resources will be used to support the purposes and concerns of the religious community. People who give to churches expect that the money will be used for the purposes—the mission—of that church. Not many people who give do so stating narrow restrictions, although some do. Most people are prepared to trust their leaders and give some latitude in how the funds are spent. They know that it may be important to support some things they are not enthusiastic about. They expect that their money will be used to make a difference in something important.

But in the past few generations a gap has grown between what "mission" means to the spenders of the money and the givers of the money.[3]

I first saw this misappropriation in action some years ago as a parish pastor in North Carolina in a judicatory that prided itself on the forward-looking and extensive ministry it supported in the regional universities and colleges. We had clear plans to place a full-time college chaplain in as many key places as possible. The area had many fine institutions of higher learning, parents of college students were in all the congregations, and few parishes had any questions about support for this vital work. What happened? Over a relatively short period of time, the function of the college chaplains changed. At first college chaplaincy was basically a one-on-one pastoral ministry not unlike youth ministry in a congregation. Then, responding to pressures and needs they discovered on campus, chaplains began to work at ministry to educational, institutional structures and then at ministry to structures of society. In many ways this was a requirement of the time—the sixties—when to be in touch with student life one had to be concerned for the issues that engaged students. College chaplains, if they were to be in touch with the students, felt they had to be counseling groups that were planning demonstrations and getting out "were the action was," not planning church suppers and liturgies and visiting dorm rooms.

The hindsight of a few decades makes it easy to argue for or against that change of "job description." Some things were gained, others lost. That is not the point. This is: The supporters of college ministries thought that they were supporting the older model of ministry. At annual convention after annual convention, support for college ministry was called for by denominational leaders *who themselves knew that the work had changed, but those leaders did not mention the changes to the laity.* Many of the donors did not know the change had occurred.

Often the donors discovered the change by reading a newspaper account of a college chaplain making a speech in the middle of a controversial meeting or demonstration. More than one chaplain got fired. Many donors felt betrayed. Other donors—probably the majority—recognized the change and came to accept it but lost a little trust in the system. The people who had the power to set the policy did not work at helping the donor understand how the mission had changed.

What I have described here in one small story about college ministry has been happening for a generation in many other areas of mission work. Denominational and regional leaders have genuinely struggled to find more effective ways to do the work of ministry, developing imaginative and important new directions of mission. But they have allowed terrible gaps to develop between what they are doing and what the donors think they are doing. To the donor, such a gap can feel like betrayal of a trust.

The point is not whether their programs were right. (My bias is that most of the efforts have been well motivated and on target.) The point is that we have allowed gaps to develop that have eroded trust.

The public media occasionally step into this gap to the dismay of religious leaders. Every decade or so *Reader's Digest* publishes an article about what the World Council of Churches or the National Council of Churches or one or another of the denominations is *really* doing with the donations it receives. "The people in the pew" give a loud cry because they have not known that their church leaders have changed programs. The church leaders get equally upset, thinking that important mission concerns are being undercut. Both have a point. But again, my point lies in the fact that our religious leaders have not felt accountable for their choices. In their enthusiasm for important mission initiatives, they have acted like intellectual elites. At their worst, some of them have actually felt contempt for the narrow vision of some of the donors, and they have felt justified in using the funds in ways those donors would never support.

The prophetic task of the church often requires some to step out beyond the common denominator of understanding. But prophets understand that there is cost to that stepping out, and they have to expect to pay it. Many people expect denominational leaders to exert prophetic leadership, but no one seems to understand that prophets rarely have been known to lead institutions. Samson is rightly honored as prophetic judge, but look what happened to him when the walls fell down on him. I sometimes call this pattern of denominational use of funds the Samson syndrome of leadership. It may do some damage to the Philistines, but it's hard on the prophet, too.

Our problem? Our way of operating has led to significant loss of trust in our systems.

We Refuse to Pay Attention to the Disaster That Is Approaching

Congregations and their religious systems have their heads in the sand in terms of their future support. I see a brick wall thirty years down the pike. I don't hear anybody else talking about it.

All of the evidence we have points in one direction: Younger generations do not contribute to religious institutions as generously as did their elders. Published studies of the philanthropic giving of baby boomers are not encouraging, although a few optimists hope that their behavior will change when the mortgage is paid up and tuition payments have come to an end.

I see little evidence that the denominations are exercised about this problem or being aggressive in trying to overcome it. With all the professed desire for expanding the diversity of the churches, denominations are avoiding the problem of research and development of ways to increase giving among a more diverse range of groups and givers.

More than that, the donor base of the mainline denominations continues its dependence upon a monochrome constituency—white, middle-aged or older church members. The donor base is aging and is not expanding in numbers, diversity, or age. This alone shakes my confidence in our denominational leadership. It is one thing to try to change things and fail; it is another not to try.

In the foreseeable future, demand for financial resources is likely to continue to outstrip "supply." Indeed, I believe financial resources will continue to diminish. In times of diminishing resources, any project, program, or ministry that is not self-supporting will be in trouble. Subsidies of any kind will be hard to come by. Church leadership will increasingly be concerned with staff and program cuts. Inevitable cutbacks will always engender conflict between those whose priorities differ. We already see this being worked out in hundreds of judicatory budget debates and in all the national denominational debates.

There is some good news and some bad news in the reliance of our institutions on their proven donor base.

The good news is the growth of strong pledged annual giving over the past generation. Mainline church members now talk about proportional giving and even tithing. An increasing number practice one or the other. Some mainline denominations, like mine, the Episcopal Church, have experienced remarkable growth of pledged giving with strong leadership from the top down and from the bottom up.

Some of the bad news is related to that. Most of our denominations are so dependent on this single source of funding that they put all their fundraising energy into it. They seem to pay little attention to the fact that the pool of givers is declining, making this a short-term strategy. Their success keeps them from developing other approaches. The denominations seem to have forgotten that pledging itself is a relatively recent practice. All the eggs seem to be in that one basket. Other baskets are needed.

The most perplexing neglect is of planned giving.[4] Denominations and congregations that are strong in support of tithing blanch when the word *endowment* comes up. I wonder why it is so salutary to give 10 percent of one's salary to one's congregation and at the same time so dangerous to give 10 percent of one's estate to the congregation. There seems to be a theological position of some sort staked out on the old saw, "The only way to kill a church is to give it an endowment." Clergy, almost to a person, are energetically suspicious of endowments. Few clergy are open to their parishioners who want to leave substantial sums to their congregations. Few of us seem to realize that for most of its history most of the church was financed primarily through resources gained by bequest. A few judicatories and congregations have appointed planned-giving officers, but lack of interest in their work tends to marginalize them and decrease their effectiveness.

While I have never heard of a seminary, a college, a hospital, or even symphony orchestra saying, "We would be unfaithful to our traditions if we accepted resources for the future! (the only healthy hospital is one whose patients bear the full load of the costs)," I hear that regularly from congregations and from clergy. The situation may be worse. I know of seminaries (with aggressive development programs) that teach students that endowments are bad for congregations. The same seminaries have aggressive planned giving programs for their own support.

Congregations (or judicatories) with significant endowments do have some special challenges.[5] Managing the endowment itself takes energy. There are big–and different–problems of priorities. Stewardship education is difficult in such congregations. More than a decade of working with endowed congregations has helped me see that the problems they face are formidable. I cannot understand why this so frightens most church leaders. It is as if church leaders, particularly clergy, assume that money itself is evil–a strange theological position for those whose scriptures include the story Jesus told about the talents. I can understand anxiety about a difficult task; I cannot excuse the cop outs I see in this area.

The fact is that *all* congregations are endowed already. Some of them are heavily endowed even though they do not admit it. They have buildings given them by past generations. (Often the current users of the building are noted only for the fact that they are inadequately maintaining that endowment.) They have forms of organization and a heritage of faith that is an endowment from past generations. They have a story of ministry that they did not invent. Even most with treasurers and boards who plead "poor mouth" have a certificate of deposit or two stored away somewhere or a sizable "reserve fund."

Their fear of "admitting" their endowment is instructive. It suggests how threatening it is to admit one's gifts. It also suggests that one can avoid responsibility and accountability if one denies the giftedness.

Neglecting planned giving is bad enough, but we have more on our heads.

This generation of church members has spent up the endowments of previous generations. Former generations, loving their churches and acting in good faith out of the best insight they had, built an infrastructure for that church's mission.[6] The infrastructure includes great buildings for worship. Former generations recognized the need for church-affiliated seminaries, colleges, and schools. They built great national commissions and boards to shape mission effort. None of it was easy. And they built them for us.

Our generation is using up those gifts, spending them prodigally. Of course those who went before made mistakes in what they thought we might need. They did not know that we would have a hard time paying the heat bills for some of the stone monsters they built. But what gifts they tried to set aside for us! They built for the future they thought we had in store. Our generation seems intent upon complaining about their mistakes and dismantling the infrastructure they built. We have built very few institutions for the next generation. In former generations, some would have torn down the inappropriate buildings and built better ones. We sit around and complain.

Instead of making provision for the church for future generations, this generation of church leaders is being prodigal with the gifts of the past. It is only in the church's institutions of education that I see signs of awareness that funds for the future must be generated. (In those institutions I suspect that energy for seeking endowments comes from their roots in the financial quagmires of higher education rather than their heritage in the churches.)

We do not have much time to do a turnabout. In 1993 Larry Carr, president of the Presbyterian Foundation, said that within the next seventeen years $6 *trillion* will change hands, as one generation's resources are passed along to the next. This will be the largest transfer of resources in history. That means that in those seventeen years the most generous supporters the church has ever had will be among those whose resources will pass to other hands. Within the next two decades, the current generation of tithers will be replaced by a generation that has not yet been convinced that tithing is a good idea.

Unless we change our behavior radically, our current generation of generous supporters of the church will be told to take their gifts elsewhere.

If the churches ever had an opportunity to develop resources for the future, the time is now. The time is not likely to return. The clock is ticking.

I see almost no one in the churches paying any attention. We are not suffering from some inevitable decline of resources; we are committing institutional suicide. It is what Elisabeth Kubler-Ross called denial.

Continuing this head-in-the-sand approach will be disastrous financially. It is even worse when we realize that our avoidance of this issue also represents our avoidance of every American Christian's primary spiritual problem—being wealthy. Here I am making the case for the institutional problem we have. There is a deeper problem more directly related to our mission. Our avoidance of this issue is part of a larger avoidance at the heart of our spiritual task as churches. Almost all Americans are rich. Even our poorest are infinitely better off than the poor elsewhere in the world. A primary spiritual task of churches is to help Americans deal with the dilemmas of wealth. Our avoidance of the issue of endowments is a symptom of our avoidance of that larger spiritual task. A church that cannot face the sin and grace involved in endowments is crippled in dealing with the sin and grace with which every one of its members has to live daily. Here I am not arguing that great issue. I am speaking of the narrow institutional concern: We are committing institutional suicide.

WE HAVE FAILED TO ENFRANCHISE THE LAITY

The laity has never had institutional power in the churches.[7]

Let me defend that overstatement. Most people in Protestant denominations point to significant areas in which the laity does, indeed, have great power within the institution. Some of those denominations can point to historical moments or even legal entitlement today that support assertion of power by the laity, sometimes at the most critical points of the institution's life. I do not deny those arguments. I do not deny that laypeople do frequently shift the balance and affect the outcome around issues under debate. But churches are institutions the ordinary operations and decisions of which are guided by clergy. Churches are clergy-run organizations.

It is a situation comparable to this: The justice system in this country is a lawyer-run operation. Or this: The medical system is run by doctors. In neither case am I saying that the system is necessarily bad—just that each is run by the professional group that has the most at stake in the arrangements of the system.

Most of us know extraordinary lawyers who live sacrificial lives to build a just society in which everyone is treated well under the law. Most of us know doctors who have given their lives and health to bring healing to others. That's not the point. The legal system, the justice system, is run by lawyers who make a living from the law. Over time the rest of us have begun to wonder if that system, as it is played out in American life, really is a system that we can trust to operate for the benefit of those who are not lawyers. Similarly more and more people are wondering if our medical system is working to the benefit of the public and if the decision making should continue to be ruled by those who stand most to benefit from it.

Large questions are being raised across our society about both of these areas. The laity has never had power in the legal system. Perhaps the legal system is too important to too many people to be left in the hands of lawyers. The laity has never had power in the health system. Perhaps the health system is too important to too many people to be left in the hands of doctors.

Our society has not yet come clear about either of these questions, but there is a growing awareness that the decisions made in the past in both systems have not turned out to be as good for society as they have been for lawyers and for doctors.

I could point to an even more dramatic illustration. As a nation we have begun to wonder if it is wise to let those who are organized to promote the use of guns make national policy about guns in the hands of the public. Years ago when our government was being formed, we became clear that war and defense was too important to allow policy to be made by the generals; we mandated political leadership for our war efforts.

The churches' power system has grown into what we now call clericalism. It is a power system that has grown up because it made religious institutions strong and effective over the centuries. But it has become a system that is so busy protecting the past that it no longer serves the future. It is a power system in which the primary decisions about the churches' futures are made by the professional class that has the most at stake in those decisions professionally, personally, and financially. In other situations we call this conflict of interest. The self-interest skews the institution toward the concerns of the clergy. We need to know that some people look suspiciously at our rules about minimum salaries for clergy, our subsidy of clergy training, and our definition that the minimal congregational framework include one paid clergyperson. I have heard it said that the church sometimes operates primarily as an employment system for clergy.

I am saying this as bluntly as I can. I do not for a moment deny the quality of the clergy I know. Of course there are bums and charlatans in the crowd, but I know more, thousands more (I mean that literally!) who are self-giving and live out a dedication that inspires me. I admire no professional class more for its contributions to building community and touching human lives. I claim that professional class as my own, and I am proud of it.

But some part of me knows a more complex reality. The decision-making processes of religious institutions are mostly controlled by clergy. I am not talking about the specific voting processes or the genuinely democratic intent of church leaders and clergy. I am talking about the arrangements around the voting—the way clergy are paid to go to the denominational meetings year after year, gaining expertise and power in the system. I am talking about the way clergy are leaned on and trusted for advice by lay delegates. I am talking about the systems of rotating membership on congregational boards, a system that effectively destroys lay power in favor of the clergy. I am talking about the "old boy" systems from seminary into which women clergy are only beginning to find their way and which shape so many appointments to decision-making roles. I am talking about the way the professional class systematically draws key lay leaders into itself, sending them off to seminary to be co-opted into the power class. I am talking about the way clergy can afford to be there at the midweek meetings when the decisions are made. The arrangements multiply their power.

Few of the clergy I know, and probably none of the extraordinary clergy I know, believe in or want the kind of power I have described in the last paragraph. Most of them abhor such self-serving interpretations of what the system does.

Which is my point. This is a power system that is larger and more powerful than the people in it. It is a set of customs and arrangements grown up through the years that one person has little power to change. It is the kind of demonic power that Saint Paul warns against when he talks about "principalities and powers" (Eph. 6:12 KJV). There is a key truth about such powers when they are uncontrolled. All of them draw their power from the good in them, but good becomes demonic. Lucifer, we must remember from our mythology, was the most beautiful of the angels, which made him the most poweful when he fell to become the Adversary.

The development of clergy over the centuries has been one of the greatest achievements of the churches. Clergy have been at the heart of the growth of theologies and schools and sacrificial living of all kinds. Each of us has been nurtured by our relationship with great clergy.

That is precisely why clericalism is so powerful. When clergy become a power system, the system is clericalism. It takes power and authority unto itself, away from the church it is intended to serve. That makes it demonic.

The same can be said for any *ism*. Our usual problem with understanding this simple spiritual truth is that we generally *like* some of these demons. In our common parlance, we disapprove of bad demons such as racism, sexism, ageism, and we excoriate those who act in their power. But not the demons we like! All the "political correctness" talk is about how we choose certain demons to attack, while harboring our own demons as personal pets.

The church of the future must break the power of clericalism. The continuation of decision making based on the welfare of one professional group will be financially and organizationally disastrous. More than that, it will increasingly focus clergy as functionaries in a dysfunctional institution, when we need clergy who can lead us with religious authority.

The church of the future needs clergy who can lead us into deep places, who can teach us the enduring story of the people of God. We do not need them to be managers of an institution.

Clergy by themselves cannot and will not relinquish their power. There will be no change until the laity takes the lead. The church is too important to be left in the hands of the clergy.

WE HAVE BUILT UNHEALTHY DEPENDENCY SYSTEMS

Over the generations institutions and groups within the churches have become stratified into levels of power. As in most historic institutions, those stratifications became hierarchical, with those considered most important at the top and those less important at the bottom. Who knows how it got started? Some read the development as part of a conspiracy of males to dominate females. They may be right. Some read it as a dialectic of history. They may be right. Some read it as a simple functional development of society. They may be right.

Wherever it came from, it leaves some obvious problems for those who want religious institutions to weather the storms of change we have described. There are emotional overtones to the hierarchical structures that developed in the churches, overtones that complicate our concern to make the structures more responsive to today's needs.

One of the simplest and most helpful insights into this structural problem was given by Thomas Harris, in his book *I'm O.K.–You're O.K.*, a popular self-help book of several years back.[8] In that book, Harris used our familial experiences as children and parents to describe patterns of reaction in dependency systems. I want to use this model to point to similar patterns in the hierarchical structures of churches.

Harris reminds us of the characteristic messages we received from parents—commands or exhortations to do something we usually did not want to do. He describes those messages, collectively, as a set of tapes we record in memory. The tapes say things such as: "Clean your plate. Put on your galoshes. Don't ever do that again! Stop that ! Behave yourself. Sit still and listen. Do what you are told." Most of us can add to the list from our experience.

Those collective experiences are recorded in our memory, Harris suggests, as our own memory-cassette of "parent tapes." He suggests that they become the emotional framework we use in dealing with our own children. When push comes to shove in our relationship with those dependent upon us, we usually flip back to use those remembered tapes.

Hold on. There's more. In response to the parent tape, the child develops a set of emotional—and verbal—answers: "I don't want to. I won't. Make me. It's not fair. Jimmy doesn't have to, why should I? You can't make me."

Those become our "child" tapes. Harris says these tapes go underground in our consciousness and pop out an unexpected places. We may be secure professional adults but when a fellow worker says, "You better get that report in on time," a dormant child tape is triggered to feel *says who?* We actually respond with something like "You don't have authority to give me that assignment!" Acting out of remembered emotions, we give a rational version of a childish response, probably triggering our fellow worker to even more parental patterns: *I'll make you do it,* transmuted into "Well, I'll see it gets on your performance report!"

Most of us can recognize the dynamic. Often we deplore our own behavior and know we are complicating things when we respond that way, but we almost cannot help it. In some situations or relationships we just feel driven by those tapes. They take over. I have worked with some people who have just set me off. When they walk in the room, I'm ready to tell them why I won't do what they want me to, even before I know what they want. Then there are others I know are not going to do what I want, so in my anxiety I approach them very parentally.

Harris says that one of the few ways to break out ot these unproductive exchanges is for someone to intervene with the "adult tape," which states facts or asks for data and tries to solve problems.[9] It attempts to focus attention on the issue at hand and it seeks collegiality in dealing with it. In the exchange I noted above about getting a report in on time, it might help if another fellow worker said, "Wait a minute. Who needs the report, and when do we have to have it ready? What do you need to get it done?" Harris says, and experience supports him, that just as a parent tape can trigger a child tape (and a child tape can trigger a parent tape) an adult tape can nudge people who are behaving parentally or childishly to get back into functional behavior.

What does all this have to do with churches and our need to transform them? Quite a bit.

The hierarchical structures that churches developed over the years have been overlaid by emotional interactions that closely fit the Harris model. The people, the offices, the structures at the "higher" levels often communicate with the "lower" levels using parent tapes. "You must do this, or we will report you to the annual conference. Get your contributions in on time. Where is your annual report?" Pastors relate to lay people too frequently out of their parent tapes: "Get to church on time. Not enough of you have increased your pledges. It is your responsibility to visit the sick."[10]

We should not be surprised by the childish responses: ignoring the messages; resenting the message and criticizing the messenger, dragging feet; being late; not carrying through on promises.

Then we compound the problem. We reward the congregations that do what they are asked, as if they were the "good children." They're the ones that don't get known around the judicatory office as being "problems"–the recalcitrant children you never can count on. On the congregational level, the obedient laypeople become the model leaders. The ones who ask difficult questions at parish meetings are soon seen as "troublemakers." Some congregations and some people become adolescent children who act out; they run away from denominational responsibility; they stay home and pout; they take their marbles and go home.

The connections I describe here are impressionistic, but they are real. Relationships in our organizational structures are overlaid by emotional baggage from past personal and organizational experience. Often congregations are responding emotionally to the way a bishop or a pastor or a national board acted years ago.

There is nothing "bad" in our acting this way. It is only bad if we do not recognize the patterns when we can and try to minimize unhelpful responses. It is bad only if our emotional baggage blocks us from examining the real issues we need to discuss and settle.

Specifically, we need to be aware of how pervasive these emotional triggers are, and we need to be alert to when our colleagues are moving into inappropriate behavior. We need to help one another relate as adult-to-adult so we can deal with what is really going on. As long as we are trapped in parental or childish tapes, we are being emotionally reactive to others; we are not making conscious choices or exploring what needs to be done.

There are structural things that can help. Elsewhere[11] I have pointed out that we need more accountability in our relationships in religious organizations. Pressing for clarity about expectations tends to move one toward adult relationships where what is to be done is thought through, defined, and spelled out. Parent-child agreements are often overlaid with unwritten expectations and undefined emotional contracts. Volunteers within a congregation need to get some clarity about what is expected of them and what resources they can count on to do their jobs. Otherwise they are pushed into the childish position of having to fantasize what is expected against the backdrop that one can never do enough. It is no wonder that volunteers burn out and grow resentful of how they have been treated.

The continuation of unhealthy forms of dependence is a barrier to the kinds of religious institutions we need. Being aware of this simple analysis of relational patterns may help us get out of emotional reactions when our parent tapes or our child tapes are triggered. And even if the awareness does not help us control our own reactions, the concept can be a resource to help us recognize these patterns in others.

WE HAVE BECOME "FUNDAMENTALISTS" IN THE WAY WE VIEW OUR STRUCTURES[12]

In churches, perhaps more than any other place, we make idols out of our structures. We become fundamentalists about the forms by which we do what we do. We are fundamentalistic about what a pastor is, about how a congregation should be organized, about what a bishop or an executive is, about how one educates religious leaders. The *forms* become holy, and anyone who suggests changes in those structures is seen as a heretic.

I see parallel patterns in how we view the insides of the buildings we use for religious purposes. After a generation or two of use, the *furniture* takes on new meaning. What was bought as a chair for the pastor to sit on when waiting to preach becomes *the pastor's chair*, and woe betide anyone who suggests that it be replaced.[13] Or even moved. Where it is becomes important. You can tell when the process is well along because things like pastors' chairs start having brass plaques attached and they become memorials to somebody. By then you are dead if you try to move it.

Different traditions have different areas of rigidity. Ask those in Catholic hierarchical roles about the authority of the priest or bishop, and you are likely to hear a response based on morphological fundamentalism, as this phenomenon has been called. Ask an Episcopalian why the laity should not celebrate the Eucharist, and you discover "the beast." Ask a Presbyterian why the presbytery executive cannot intervene in a clergy-lay congregational dispute, and you will see what I am talking about. Ask a United Methodist bishop about itinerancy or a Baptist or Congregationalist why their congregations cannot agree on a common policy.... You get the picture.

Despite these differences, we share a terrible difficulty in being able to accept change in how we are structured, even when we become aware that the structures are not working well.[14] We are comfortable with the old ways. We've "grown accustomed to her face." That happens everywhere. Businesses and corporations have trouble changing things people have gotten used to. But religious institutions may have it more difficult than others.

Another paragraph about furniture may be instructive. When I got a new office chair. I felt a momentary pang. I loved the old one. Ted Eastman sold it to me eighteen years ago. My bottom was comfortable in it, and I knew which of the casters would fall off if you picked the chair up. But after one day in the new chair, which really did feel better and worked better, I lost my loyalty. But if you were to remove the bishop's chair from my parish church and replace it, I think I'd remember the old one Sunday after Sunday for years. They changed the altar rail (I really did not like the old one; it was dark; the brass fittings kept falling off; it threatened to collapse; and its color did not fit the other altar furniture), and after six months I still resent the new one.

Our current church structures are strangling us, but we love them. More than that, they feel holy to us. To change them *feels* like disloyalty to

God—even though we know it's just a chair, just an organizational arrangement, just a leadership position.

We Have Not Recognized
the Complexity of the Change Process

I trust we agree: We must renew our churches for the future. In doing so, perhaps our most difficult obstacle is our very complex relationship to change itself. Here I want to describe one strategic framework for approaching change and two ways of understanding reactions that block many change efforts. But I want to begin by putting the issue of change into perspective.

My Perspective on Change

Frankly, when it comes to change, I'd rather not deal with it. But I have to. The world I live in simply will not sit still. To maintain some kind of equilibrium and have some control over what's going on, I have to make fairly frequent adaptations if I want to stay in touch with my world.

If I were in a row boat in the middle of a lake, I could lie back and enjoy the sun and the motion of the ripples. Frankly, I'd like that...most of the time.

If, however, I were in a canoe in the middle of the rapids, my life would have to be very different. I would have to be alert for rocks under the surface. I would have to paddle to avert disaster or steer to safer water.

In the first scenario, I could go a long time not worrying about change—unless a storm came up. In the second, change is a matter of course. One kind of behavior works on the lake. The same behavior is disastrous if used in the rapids.

In today's world the churches are in the rapids. They are not the only ones. Actually, all our institutions are experiencing similar turbulence. Business corporations that try to maintain the practices that brought them to the top in the sixties or seventies see upstart companies cutting into their markets. Many such corporations will fall apart in the nineties. Some have begun to.

From my perspective, over the next few decades the religious structures that fail to change and learn to adapt will be like the buggy-whip manufacturers of the nineteenth century.

The changes needed in religious institutions may be even more urgent and fundamental than those needed in business. On the whole, businesses are required to maintain some flexibility to respond to the customers. But religious leaders have not been sensitive even to that organizational imperative. This neglect has put us in the position of having severe dislocations in the credibility and effectiveness of our institutions at the national, regional and local levels. The further the ordinary lay member of the congregation is from an institutional structure, the more likely there will be a lack of credibility.

Let me be clear. I hold no brief for changing our basic message. I am a bit fundamentalistic at this point. I do not believe the basic message of the churches can or should change. But if our congregations are to be faithful to the revelation, they have to work regularly at how that unchanging truth needs to be presented in a changing time. They need to work at rethinking the structures and patterns that preserved those truths in the past to see what structures and patterns can do the same in our time.

In the language of my tradition, I do not believe the gospel itself changes. But to be faithful to that unchanging gospel in a changing world, I have to pay a lot of attention to (1) what is changing around me and (2) how I need to adapt in response. Religious leaders who agree with me on this point must be sure of two things: (1) that they are seen to be proclaimers of the gospel, not of change; and (2) that they keep their focus on that gospel; there is no other way to distinguish between that which can and should be changed and that which bears the stamp of the truth. In less elegant language, if you are bathing a baby it helps to be very clear about who the baby is when you need to throw out the bath water!

Although I refer here to the organizational necessity of dealing with change, my perspective is grounded much more deeply in what I understand to be God's will and God's call. I believe that the turmoil around us is at least partly God's invitation to join in the New Creation. Indeed, I understand what is going on as a working out of God's hope. As such, we are involved, as we deal with change, with eschatology. I sometimes describe my work with congregations and church bodies as "operational eschatology."

A Strategic Approach to Change

One of the multipurpose theories of change I have used over the years is the simple and universally applicable framework laid down by behavioral scientist Kurt Lewin.[15] Lewin suggests that organizations are rarely, if ever, at a point of total consensus about what they are and how they should operate. Instead, organizations are in a state of organized compromise, where the forces for change and the forces against change are in equilibrium. This equilibrium is dynamic, not stable. Within a certain range, the whole system can adapt to minor shifts and changes. But there is a sense of mutual–often unspoken–agreement that the equilibrium will not be changed in a basic way. (Although everyone in the congregation knows that the order of the service is likely to have some changes from time to time, everybody *knows* you better not mess with the eleven o'clock hour!) That unspoken agreement is a powerful force to keep change within limits. It makes for the status quo being a kind of homeostasis. If changes are introduced that violate that unspoken agreement, after a period of time things will probably revert to the original homeostasis.

Here in a diagram of a system in homeostasis:

Over time this status quo becomes comfortable, and the different concerns are accommodated fairly well. The wide margins of the homeostatic system indicate some space for making adjustments in one direction or another without triggering anxious responses. Neither the people who push for change nor those who oppose it get all they want, but they have enough; and the system rests.

This understanding of an organization's equilibrium led Lewin to identify three stages one must go through to bring change into an organization.

One must "unfreeze" the equilibrium. Then one must install the change (with all the adaptations of practice and training of organizational members.) Then one must "refreeze" into a new homeostasis that includes the change.

Most attempts to install planned change in religious systems fail because the old systems are never unfrozen. A denomination or judicatory will announce a great new idea or program that is bound to make a big difference. The announced program is then implemented to unanimous lack of enthusiasm by congregations that already have enough on their plates and want another new program the way they want a new mortgage. Year after year this goes on to the increasing frustration of the program designers—most of whom are pretty good at design. The homeostasis never gets broken open.[16]

The process of installing a change is generally done with little respect for the preexisting homeostasis—a homeostasis that includes a healthy respect for compromise. Most religious institutions install changes by strong advocacy of a particular point by the people who have power and want that change installed.

The homeostasis is upset by a strong intervention—often by the new pastor—pushing the system in the desired direction. Here is what generally happens when change is introduced this way:

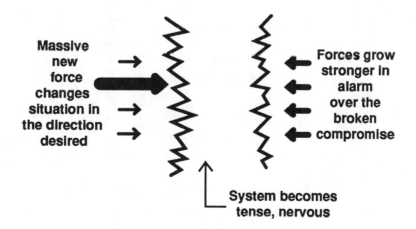

Yes, there is change. The strong input pushes the system in the desired direction. But look at the unintended by-products of this kind of change effort. First, those opposed to the change are startled and wake up to the fact that the truce has been broken. Their energy multiplies as they defend their territory, requiring greater and greater pressure from the pastor or another new intervener just to keep things in place. Not infrequently some of the people on the "change" side desert the ship; they do not want to get involved in a war! The change agent is more and more alone, working harder and harder to keep the gains made in the first push. But there is more. Look at the boundaries of the system. They have become constricted. The room for maneuvering and easy compromise is gone. Probably anything that gets proposed now will be the subject of suspicious nit-picking. Trust has been disrupted and opposition to change mobilized. The late stages of such a change effort are rarely comfortable. Indeed, when the pastor finally gives up or has a heart attack from the pressure, the homeostasis will probably be reestablished pretty much where it was before, except that trust levels will be lower when the next pastor arrives.

Lewin suggests that there is a better way to consider change, a way that is less confrontative and more collaborative and gives more promise of developing sustainable change without loss of trust. Here is a diagram of his suggestion:

1. Analyze forces on *both* sides.

2. Develop strategies on *both* sides to maintain trust and to effect change using already present energy.

Lewin encourages change agents instead to do careful diagnosis of the equilibrium, identifying proponents of change and opponents to change, analyzing the forces involved. Both sides of the homeostasis are included in the planning and thinking about what is needed. By doing so the effort is broadened, and the legitimate concerns of potential opponents to the change are brought into the conversation early enough to make significant impact on what is actually planned. The entire system, not just those hell-bent for a change, works on plans and strategies. Those who use this approach (it is called "force field analysis") find that the resulting change efforts have a high survival rate. The trust in the system can actually expand when this is done well. And the new homeostasis has a chance of being as stable as the last.

What Lewin calls refreezing is universally ignored in change efforts in religious institutions. The institutions act as if once a change is set in place, opposition no longer exists. Refreezing a changed system involves training people in the behaviors needed, making periodic evaluations to take into account what has gone wrong, and listening to opposition, ever seeking to improve the quality of the new homeostasis. Again, collaborative planning and strategizing are helpful, making for a healthier aftermath to change.

The Personal Dimension of Response to Change—Grief

Elisabeth Kubler-Ross' book *On Death and Dying*[17] is a wonderful guide to how personal responses to loss can influence a person's or a group's ability to deal with change.

Because every change involves loss, every change triggers grief. The more one is attached to that which is changed, the more intense one's sense of loss and need to grieve. Almost anything that touches religious memories or meanings touches very strong and deep feeling. That is why perfectly rational people will roar with anger when someone moves something as simple as a chair in the sanctuary of a church. That is why strong, able people can become frantic and panic-stricken when they hear that their pastor has been called to another job—even people who did not particularly like the pastor. It is as if the religious factor acts as a magnifying glass for losses. The responses are often multiplied out of proportion to "reality."

Kubler-Ross notes several characteristic responses to loss—denial, bargaining, anger/guilt, depression, acceptance. Individual responses are not sequential and may recur in cycles. Having reached some level of acceptance of a loss, one may still revert to seasons of anger or depression. She teaches us that grieving takes time; in time one can move beyond grief.

Religious leaders who deal in change need to be aware of the need to minister to all those responses. Change, and responding to it, must be understood to be very time-consuming and deeply emotional. Change is not simply "fixing something." It requires real pastoral care and spiritual discernment.

Pastors often see their work so exclusively as managing the change process that they do not recognize how critical it is to minister to the spiritual needs that block people from being able to accept change. Actually, there is more than enough change—and grief—in anyone's life *even if the pastor institutes no changes whatsoever.*

If I note a characteristic fault of religious leaders it is that they respond to the symptom and consequently miss the opportunity to deal with the larger religious issue—whether it be the fear of the unknown, threat of death, or the question of ultimate meaning. Religious leaders respond as if the expressed anger or depression were the issue, when the issues are deeper.

Also, many pastors worry about this or that angry parishioner, the poor, depressed people who have given up on life, or the "church rats" who are constantly underfoot, trying to do anything and everything to please the pastor. They overlook the needs of the grim-faced stoic who avoids thinking about change by becoming the rock-ribbed bulwark of the status quo. Pastors I know see these characteristic types in terms of how they affect the congregation's program, not in terms of their substantial spiritual need as they face the loss of familiar and valued parts of their lives.

Pastors and church leaders who understand the changes needed in their systems and have worked hard to get them installed have done less than half the job. The more important part is the religious, pastoral, and spiritual task of nurturing, pushing, and supporting people as they see their world change. In the long run, one of the most important functions of a religious organization is as a laboratory in which people are given an opportunity to discover God in the process of living change and loss. Too tight a focus on the change itself short-circuits that deeper pastoral task.

Many church members carry substantial loads of unresolved grief. It comes from a variety of places—disappointments over lost opportunities, remembrances of lost loved ones, bitterness about real or imagined unfairness, alienation or a sense of having been left out or left behind. Everyone has a personal version of this sense of loss, and everyone carries it alongside his or her personal strengths and weaknesses. Similarly, as a society we bear a sense of loss as a people—loss of the memory of a kinder, gentler nation than we see today, loss of our dreams of what the nation might become, loss of certain hopes.

In that context, what goes on in congregations as we learn to deal with change, is, in fact, a doorway for Grace to enter into hidden griefs in personal lives, touching those unhealed places each of us has. Dealing with change and the emotions it raises in our congregations can potentially connect us (as healing conduits) to the pain and grief that wracks our society.

Understanding change as opportunity for spiritual ministry in this way—depth ministry to individual memory and life, and breadth ministry to society's pain—should put a new dimension on the hassles of moving church furniture, winning or losing parish elections, and approaching difficult planning issues.

Organizational Dimensions of Change—Shock and Adaptation

Another important theory about the organizational dimension of change gives us clues to what is going on in religious institutions and may suggest directions for the future.

Writing in a recessionary time some years ago, Fink, Beak, and Taddeo[18] described how organizations they worked with faced crises. The response pattern they discovered in those organizations is congruent with what Kubler-Ross discovered in people—with one difference. Kubler-Ross said that the emotional responses she found in those facing death did not follow a clear sequence. One stage did not lead to the next in a sequential or fully predictable way. Fink, Beak, and Taddeo seem to suggest that the four stages of the response pattern they identified in organizations follow one another sequentially. The organizations that do not move on from one stage to the next may simply not survive to tell the story. Organizations may not have adequate identity to recycle through stages that have not been completed.

Fink, Beak, and Taddeo describe four sequential stages for the organizations that surmount crises: shock, defensive retreat, acknowledgment, and growth and adaptation.

In most organizations shock is the immediate response to crisis. Many of the people in the organization share a visceral understanding that something is seriously wrong. During shock the organization's members fragment, and almost everyone moves into a stance of taking care of himself, distancing self from others. People or groups are blamed, and anger is bitter, often focused on specific actors in the drama. Communications get muddled and trust disappears. Fights break out among groups and individuals. No one has energy to think about the future. If the leaders panic along with everyone else, the others can be particularly demoralized. One of the hopeful organizational dynamics is that different groups hit shock at different times. For example, if the leaders see the crisis early enough and deal with their own shock, they are better able to help when shock hits the troops! Throughout the process, it is best if leaders can deal with their own issues early and mobilize other levels of their group to move on to the next stage.

Defensive retreat is a difficult stage. It is marked by imposition of tight controls, a "clamping down." Budgets may be slashed. People get fired.[19] Although this period rarely solves any basic problems, it can keep the group from total disintegration. Sometimes the budget cuts and staff terminations bring costs temporarily under control and preserve enough financial viability to allow the company to survive. But a prolonged period of shock and denial may have led to such a depletion of financial reserves that even this short-term strategy is too late. The better the leaders have been in processing their own shock, the more likely they will be able to hold things together. When defensive retreat hits the organization's leaders, many others may be experiencing the initial shock of hearing "the news." This is not a time that really faces the future; at this point the survivors begin to find new patterns of working together. You can expect an "in group" and an "out group" with continuing suspicion between them. Flow of information is often rigidly controlled. Anything the organization started right before the crisis—a new program, a new management system, a new bookkeeping system—may be the first thing thrown out, even though it has much promise. The group may revert to previous behavior and previous structures. Leaders are tempted to demand loyalty to the system and to impose authoritarian leadership styles.

Fink, Beak, and Taddeo say that acknowledgment comes to many who survive shock and defensive retreat. (Some do not survive either.)

This marks a turn toward the future. Acknowledgment represents the organization's turning the corner from anger and blame to a search for answers. Here we try to find out what we must not do. Instead of "who's to blame?" the question is "what went wrong?" and it is asked to figure out how to avoid the same mistakes in the future. Acknowledgment often includes a new look at the environment and the organization's "customers" to determine what signals had been missed. This stage questions how things have been done in the past and thinks about new paths. Leadership often relaxes a bit from its tight need to control everything and everybody. Personal relationships among colleagues become less anxious and suspicious. People begin to want to work together on common tasks.

Institutions that make it through the acknowledgment stage can move into the fourth stage—*growth and adaptation.* This is when the organization's coping mechanisms kick back in. The focus is the future, not the past. The purposes and vision of the organization are reexamined and people set out to build for the future. Often new myths build up about "the time we nearly went under."

These theories, based in business organizations, are not totally descriptive of what goes on in religious organizations facing crisis. But I see many parallels. My own diagnosis is that most of the national structures of the mainline churches are in shock, with a few giving signs of having moved to defensive retreat. Of the more conservative Protestant churches and the Roman Catholic Church, I see signs of some people and groups moving into shock, but overall little response to the environmental changes around them.

In the mainline churches, a prolonged shock and denial stage among leaders has seriously eroded the financial base for moving ahead into defensive retreat. Regional structures of the churches seem even more threatened, but all too few leaders at that level have begun to face the crisis.

CONCLUSION

In earlier chapters I have noted the key tasks congregations must address to fulfill their purpose and the functions congregations need from denominational systems if they are to fulfill that purpose in the midst of the serious storm we face. Of course responding to these challenges will set churches on a new course of rethinking and reconstructing things that are very basic to their lives.

In this chapter I have laid out the more difficult organizational issues that block our moving ahead. Right now we can begin to address any one—or all—of these obstacles, and I have given some clues as to how and where to start.

I wrap this section up with one final sobering challenge: The question of reinventing the church—on our side—may come to *will.*

Notes

1. See Loren B. Mead, *New Hope for Congregations* (New York: Seabury Press, 1972). This was my first attempt at "learning from our experience" in working with congregations. At that time most religious studies were ideas, but some remarkable sociologists were trying to understand empirical dimensions of religious organizations. The story of the shift of energy in religious studies from deductive to inductive has only begun and has not yet been told.

2. I have more to say about a systems approach, but that will have to wait for my next book.

3. For details of this shift of consciousness, see Loren B. Mean, *The Once and Future Church* (Washington, DC: The Alban Institute, 1991).

4. If I had my wish, no student would graduate from seminary without having made three or four planned-giving visits to a prospective seminary donor.

5. I speak about my work with founders of the Consortium of Endowed Episcopal Churches and the Presbyterian Network of Endowed Congregations. Each of these groups meets annually to share discoveries about how to minister effectively as congregations with sizable endowments. Attempts to develop similar networks in Unitarian-Universalist, United Methodist, and United Church of God denominations did not result in continuing dialogue. My work with all except the Episcopal group was supported by grants from the Lilly Endowment. See Loren Mead, *Endowed Congregations: Pros and Cons* (Washington, DC: The Alban Institute, 1990).

6. In building the Alban Institute, Inc., we have been conscious that we were working on this frontier. The characteristics of that institute—its focus on building accountability in relationships, searching for an alternate way to fund the delivery of skilled services within the religious world, the effort to develop a network of skilled people who live off the sale of their skills, and its monomaniacal focus on the life of the congregation—represent our reading of some of the characteristics needed in other institutions we need to be building for the future of the churches.

7. Verna Dozier's personal influence, preaching, and teaching lie behind my thinking.

8. Thomas Harris, *I'm O.K.–You're O.K.* (New York: Harper & Row, 1969.) Although I will deal here with the unhealthy side of what Harris describes, note that his book also deals with the positive memories that childhood and parenting can bring.

9. One very practical application of this knowledge has been worked out by my colleague Speed Leas, a conflict-management consultant. In a conflict situation, the most parental and childish responses are frequently in command. Speed finds that one of the most helpful interventions is to "trigger the adult." He gives assignments that force the combatants to get out of childish or parental behavior: "Let us try to agree on a set of rules for how to carry out this conflict." Or, "Here are the six

steps I plan to carry out in working on this conflict with you. Can you suggest anything I have left out?" Frequently he gives combatants team assignments to gather data together—with people who oppose one another having to collaborate on a task that all agree needs to be done. We have found that the very presence of an outside consultant brings potential to increase adult-adult communication and checks the use of parent-child transactions.

10. To this day I am ashamed of the childish resentment I used to feel against one clergyman who exhorted me every Sunday to do this or do that when I was doing all I knew how to do; he never gave me direction about how to do what he wanted. I sat there, emotionally sucking my thumb and thinking "You can't make me!" And I was no kid at the time.

11. See Mead, *The Once and Future Church*, ch. 5.

12. Several decades ago this was known as "morphological fundamentalism." The phrase is so absurd that I've loved it since I first saw it in the Western European working paper of the World Council of Churches' great study in the sixties: "The Missionary Structure of the Congregation." See *The Church for Others: Two Reports on the Missionary Structure of the Congregation* (Geneva: World Council of Churches, 1967).

13. Someone who will read this book remembers the time he asked me, "Is there anything that always causes conflict in a church?" I replied, "Yes. Try moving any of the furniture around." Three years later he phoned me, somewhat sheepishly, and said "You were right. I wish we had listened. We need help with a fight that's broken out about moving the altar." They did a great job of working with the conflict. The altar was moved, but not as was first proposed, and they all lived happily every after. Or at least for a decade or so. He first asked me that question nearly twenty years ago. I would still give the same answer.

14. That was a simple statement when I first made it. But during the period of rewriting this manuscript, we installed voice-mail at the office. I was astonished by my own rage at this new system that I knew was an improvement, that I helped decide was the right one for us, that I even helped raise the money to pay for. How terribly difficult it is to change. For anybody.

15. Kurt Lewin's wide influence as a theoretician about change, about human interaction, and about the nature of groups arose from a life of teaching more than from systematic writing. I got most of my knowledge of these theories from those to whom he had taught them in seminars and small group interactions. Some of his basic thinking is found in the following books: *A Dynamic Theory of Personality* (New York and London: McGraw Hill, 1935) and *Resolving Social Conflicts* (New York: Harper, 1948).

16. See Mead, *The Once and Future Church*, ch. 5. There I dealt with some of these dynamics in terms of "learning points" and "accountability." I think the old joke about the guy slamming the mule with a two-by-four "just to get his attention" is making the same point. If you attempt to change something without getting their attention, forget it. You are wasting time.

17. Elisabeth Kubler-Ross, *On Death and Dying* (New York: Macmillan, 1969).

18. Stephen L. Fink, Joel Beak, and Kenneth Taddeo, "Organizational Crisis and Change," *Journal of Applied Behavioral Sciences* 7, no. 1:15-37. We first became aware of this theory in 1975-76 when, with a group of colleagues, Roy Oswald initiated studies about how institutions and congregations could deal constructively with the financial crises and down-sizing that was prevalent in those recessionary years. The theories have become even more important as it has become clear that down-sizing of religious institutional structures is not a matter of immediate crisis but of a long-range change that has made crisis an intrinsic element of the religious world.

19. An extremely valuable addition to our knowledge has come from the research of David M. Noer, *Healing the Wounds: Overcoming the Trauma of Layoffs and Revitalizing Downsized Organizations* (San Francisco: Jossey-Bass, 1993). Noer's work explores how firings affect the survivors and makes a good case for the critical importance of attention to this neglected area of organizational development. Noer suggests a four-level model of intervention to help reorganization survivors overcome their wounds and build constructive new work lives. Anyone in a judicatory or national church office should have access to this helpful book.

Chapter 6

Transformation and Congregations

Twenty-five hundred years ago Jerusalem was laid waste by an enemy from Babylon. The conquerors destroyed the city that had nurtured rebellion and resistance once too many times. The temple that dated back to David's son was destroyed, with the stones of its foundation left like the ruins of Coventry Cathedral after the Second World War. The gates of the great city of Jerusalem were pulled down as were the walls that had protected the citizens. A great dream of a nation held together as a political state within a framework of religious vocation seemed to be gone forever.

Jeremiah lived as a community leader and a prophet during the last days before that city fell. At times viewed as a national wise man and hero, at other times vilified as a traitor and fool, Jeremiah read the signs of the times against his understanding of God's will, and he called for repentance and change. As the people continued in a suicidal course, Jeremiah read their fate and spoke of the inevitable destruction to come.

Then, with the enemy at the gate, with the destruction he had foreseen immediately present, Jeremiah changed his message and course of action, this also based on this faith and his understanding of God. As everyone else looked at destruction, Jeremiah announced that God would bring new life to the city and to the fields that surrounded it. He predicted that the vineyards and orchards would again be fruitful and that the city would flourish.

With his known world obviously coming to an end, Jeremiah purchased a field in the village of Anathoth as a demonstration of his confidence in the future and in God's promises.

We can understand Jeremiah's time. Although there is no army currently at the gate, much of our civilization seems to be under threat, if not actually in collapse. Our society, like Jeremiah's, is emerging from a sense of religious and political unity and clarity into a cacophony of voices and powers. Called to serve God's world, we have lost the clarity of our vocation and of our direction. The structures of our society and faith have failed to keep us focused on that vocation of service, and often those structures of service and mission have become self-serving. Rather than being servants of God's purposes in the world, we have too often become servants of the structures themselves.

My first message about transforming congregations is that we must do as Jeremiah did: In spite of the wisdom of the world, we are called to commit ourselves unreservedly to the future of God's promises. In Jeremiah's case, that commitment took the prosaic form of making an investment in real estate. In our time, it may be just as prosaic. We are the generation whose gift to the future may not be a complete vision of the new society or even the new church, but the example of holding steady and faithful as the landmarks of the world we have known disintegrate. Our task is to go on holding on, studying and teaching the story of the faith, acting in service to the world, trusting God in the middle of ambiguity, refusing to back away from God's claim upon us. If we hold steady, God will provide the vision when the time is right.

As for the new society and the new church, we will see only the beginnings of transformation. Jeremiah's actions spoke then to his contemporaries, and they have spoken to people of faith for these twenty-five hundred years. He may have bought that field as a specific witness to us. A king named Cyrus was to open the door for the return to Jerusalem. Jeremiah bought the field long before Cyrus was born. Jeremiah died long before that field had its first crop.

The first step in transformation has to do with attitude. (We'll get to tasks in a minute.) We need a simple commitment to the future, obedience to God's promise. There is a difference between the commitment I propose and what the churches seem to be doing. Jeremiah's commitment was not a denial of the destruction of Jerusalem and the exile of the people. Our commitment must be large enough to acknowledge the winds of the storm we are in and go through the storm, not pretend it is unreal. The life of God's people was fundamentally reshaped by the years in exile. As we move into a historical arena in which the church is no longer the center, in which Christendom and Crusades are terms of the past, we have new pages to write about what church is and how we can serve. We will know it only by going ahead.

Two or three generations after the fall of Jerusalem, the exiles in Babylon were startled to learn that a new king had opened the door for them to return to rebuild their beloved city and their temple. The book of Ezra, Nehemiah, Haggai, and Zechariah preserve some of the story of that time and the flavor of a people struggling to rebuild a nation.

The story can be instructive to us, particularly if their task is analogous to that which we face in our time. Perhaps the clearest message is that not everyone in that day was enthusiastic about the task of transformation. Historical records suggest that the first exiles to return with enthusiasm to restore the kingdom and the temple waited nearly twenty years before they started to build. In the press of other things—getting crops planted and harvested, getting families started, worrying about trade and defense—they forgot what they went back to do.

The faith reasons for returning home took back seat to the details of making a living. And even that did not work. Their crops failed, their vineyards did not produce. The people grumbled and fought as they lost direction.

The prophetic voices of Haggai and Zechariah called the people back to their real task of faithfulness. Two tasks were laid out and, in time, accomplished: The city's walls were rebuilt with its gates restored, and in the center of the city a new temple was raised up from the ruins of the old.

Those two tasks are central for us today: rebuilding the city wall and restoring the temple.

REBUILDING THE WALL

The first *task* in our transformation is the rebuilding of the city wall. The city wall of Jerusalem distinguished what was inside the city from what was outside. It helped the city establish its identity. So for us in our congregational life. We must clarify what makes us different, so that we can undertake our vocation as apostles. This requires us to establish the authenticity and distinctiveness of our congregation so that we live visibly in our faith, shaped by the biblical heritage, not by the least common denominator of local values and morality. We must build congregations where people know and follow Jesus, not the latest polls.

Those congregations must become centers that can provide space for genuine encounter, where one may be confronted and supported in the deep experiences of life. These congregations must be communities that can help each of us discover our gifts and our special vocation to serve our society. Rebuilding the wall means clarifying the boundary of the community and continuing to maintain it. It involves getting clearer and clearer about what is inside and what is not inside the community. In our tradition it means actively welcoming those who come to the congregation, but carefully training them in the stories of the faith.

Within our tradition, the wall, the boundary, is not for the purpose of separation but of service. The function of the boundary is not to exclude but to help the community strengthen its identity and its commitment to serving. The purpose of the community is to increase its ability for each to reach out beyond the boundary. The integrity of the wall is to help the community in its continuing effort to discern its mission and that of each member.

Congregations, following the example of those who returned from exile in Babylon, have first the task of rebuilding the city wall so that the people can once again grasp their identity in this alien and confusing world. The wall defines the community that is a training ground for disciples. It establishes the community that sends its members out in service and receives them back for healing and nurture. The wall is to help the community intensify its thrust out beyond the wall.

We are called to reestablish the boundary between our congregations and the society around them, getting clear about the cultural distance between followers of the values of this world and followers of the gospel. We are powerless to change ourselves and the world if we are confused about what our community stands for.

RESTORING THE TEMPLE

The other task the exiles postponed but eventually took on was the restoration of the temple. One can sympathize. Surely it must have seemed more important to clear the stones from the fields and get the crops in before focusing on the temple. It was more important to get roofs over the heads of the children than to rebuild the altars and restore the worship.

The scripture-story indicates that the exiles were wrong. Common wisdom was wrong. It is not more important to do anything at all other than restore the temple. Our assumptions about what is "logical, prudent, and rational" are based on a set of values that are not the same as the values of our faith.

This may be the most difficult point for us, living as we do on the change-point of the centuries. We are so practical. We must see the usefulness of a course of action. We want to justify activities, actions, or programs by their "outcomes" and "productivity." These stories from the scriptures remind us that when dealing with the things of God, we are not dealing in our familiar world. The world of Jeremiah and Zechariah is a world in which two plus two may add up to *apple*, not just *four*. The world of faith makes strange leaps from one thing to another. Disciples criticize a woman for wasting expensive lotion on Jesus, and he rejects their social-action concerns. Temples are not very productive. I can understand why the exiles left that until the "real" work was done.

Too many of us are not comfortable with the suggestion that such priority be given to that which is "religious" as opposed to that which is "efficacious." Indeed, that very distinction is questionable. But the point is that *what the church is is more important than what it does.*

And the heart of the church's being is the deep conversation between God and God's people that the community works out in its life of worship—in its temple. That is why it is critical to restore the temple. And this comes first. It comes before improving our institutional framework; it comes before training our clergy; it comes before organizing programs for feeding the hungry or housing the homeless; it comes before establishing nonsexist, nonracist relationships.

The life of worship and prayer is absolutely first. It is not an optional extra. That is the difficult message from scripture for us. I think we need to allow that reality to confront us and challenge us and our rationalization.

Every bone in our bodies yearns to recruit new members, raise more money, revise our rules of order, and learn how to market our church as well as others market theirs. We want to develop better education programs. We want our judicatory to restructure itself. We want to do some really basic long-term planning. Strategic planning. I do not downplay the importance of these many ministries we have developed over time. Nothing I say takes away from the fact that people are often called to reach out in response to urgencies that demand their response.

But those who care for religious institutions need to square up to the fact that restoring the temple is top priority.

CONCLUSION

Churches I have known for more than six decades and served professionally for nearly four are in a serious storm. The storm is most obvious in the collapsing structures of some of them—the ones we ironically have called mainline. If I am right, those signs of stress and strain are only symptoms of the larger storm that will engulf people of faith in many other religious families in the next decades. The churches we have known have been nurtured at the heart of our society. In our time we are moving into an exile from the heart of our society. I believe the movement is irreversible. The triumphalism of the conservative churches today becomes them no better than did the similar attitude of the mainline churches in the fifties. I doubt that the triumphalism will last much longer for the one than for the other.

My concern is to seek to help congregations of any kind—conservative, liberal, or what have you—reclaim the essential task of making disciples, one by one, and launching each of them as an apostle into the society he or she faces, wherever it is and whatever it may be like.

To do that, congregations need to transform their inner life so that their community reflects the *koinonia* of the early church's congregations. They need a sense of community that transforms the lives of members. They need to develop a ministry of *kerygma* where the story of the people of God comes alive in the power of the Spirit through the proclamation of the gospel. They need to develop a ministry of teaching, *didache*, that presents the age-old story fresh to new generations and with transforming power to those called to be apostles. They need new power to understand and reflect on their serving in the world, their *diakonia*.

That looks inside congregations, to the transformation we must make in them so that they may transform us into disciples. But the end of becoming a disciple is to be transformed into an apostle. Discipleship is the passive, but necessary grounding for the life of faith. Apostleship is the active voice for faithful living.

I want every congregation feeding apostles into the towns and cities, the agencies and the structures, the families and the neighborhoods of our society, I want every member of every congregation to know him- or herself to be called to a servant ministry, the apostolate, and I want each to have help discerning his or her gifts and to be trained and nurtured in his or her vocation. That calls for congregations that can transform ordinary people into apostles. I look for each congregation to be that kind of a transforming congregation.

For that to happen, I want to see the structures that surround congregations—the judicatories, the national structures, the seminaries, and educational institutions—building skills in new ways, ready to help transform congregations from what they are to what they must be as centers of apostolic ministry. I want all those structures working at transforming congregations.

There are more roadblocks than I have listed in Chapter 5. And each impediment is formidable. There are some things we can do to dismantle the roadblocks, things I have described in this book, and things that others are working on and learning about. But transformation occurs one person, one congregation, at a time, uniquely.

There is great good news in that fact. Every congregation is on the front edge of possibility and can begin its work of transformation. There is not a special kind of congregation or people that has the answer. This is not a task cut out for only the big congregations with high steeples and large staffs. This is not an invitation only to Baptist or to Episcopal or to independent congregations. The call is open to each and the opportunity for discovery is there for each. Each is called to start where it is.

Each congregation can begin now to commit itself to following God's purposes, come what may—bigger budgets or smaller ones, more members or fewer. Each can make a commitment to sending apostles in service to its world. Now.

The future is genuinely open. None of us has all the wisdom or the resources we need to rebuild our churches. But all of us have enough to start. In the end, I can summarize what I know into two statements:

- The time is right for us to make the commitment Jeremiah made— a commitment against all reason to the future and to God's promises.

- The tasks before us are the tasks that faced the exiles returning to Jerusalem—to rebuild the walls of the city and to restore the temple.

What lies ahead is a storm, indeed. The winds are strong, and we cannot know all that is to come. But in and through this storm, a transforming Power is at work to build an apostolic church. To be called to participate in that transformation is our life.

The Good-News/Bad-News Quadrilateral: A Design

INTRODUCTION

The following design is based on an educational model I have used in many different situations. It helps people get in touch with the many ways people and groups conceive of their special call to serve. I find it helps people understand the diversity of their congregation; it legitimizes different responses to the gospel; it helps people get an overall sense of the ministry of their group; and it raises helpful questions about the function of the larger group in relationship to the ministry of the individual. My experience with this design and comments of hundreds with whom I have used it lie beneath much of what I say in chapters 2 and 3.

THE BASIC THEORY

I see evangelism not as a "program" or organized activity but as a basic human response to God's continuous vocation to each human being. I see that continuous vocation to be almost like a gravitational pull to each of us to respond as cocreators of God's kingdom. The more conscious we are of God's grace in our lives, the more conscious and intentional we may be in responding. On the other hand, whether or not we are conscious of the call in any rational way, we may still be pulled into response at a level deeper than our minds. Those of us with the gift of articulation can name the good news. But many of us proclaim the good news without using the words of explanation. We may not even understand why we are impelled to act, and some who are evangelists may not even know in whose Name we perceive bad news and in whose Name the good news flows. Where it is God's will, the action of witnessing to the good news elicits the response of the one leper who returned to Jesus from among the ten who were cleansed. I always hope that "the ten" will return, but remember that for Jesus one was enough.

I see evangelism as profoundly situational. I see it as profoundly individual. I see it as being generated within each of us as God opens our eyes and sensitivity to the hurts of the world around us. I see the focus of each person's evangelism as shifting from time to time, driven by inner sensitivities, a sense of Grace, and the leading of God. I see our congregations as the places where our sensitivities are nourished and our evangelism fed, primarily by Word and Sacrament, but also by the community itself (*koinoia*) and the teaching (*didache*).

This design invites people to read their own evangelistic location within a map of evangelistic possibility. It helps them reflect upon that location in relationship to the location of others in the group and to the overall picture of the strengths and weaknesses they perceive in their community's openness to need.

THE PROCESS OF THE DESIGN

Step 1: Introduce the activity with a brief bit of theory, generally a description of the important good news and bad news, as described in chapter 2. The examples of Martin Luther King, Jr. and Billy Graham help people connect the idea with their experience.

Step 2: Cautions. I invite people into the exercise as an experiment in perception, noting that it is not a scientific study. I particularly press the point that I am asking them to respond in terms of where they are today, at this moment. I note that yesterday and tomorrow they may well be in different places, I visualize it as a still photograph from a moving picture.

Step 3: Two forced-choice questions. I invite—no, I push, press—everyone to make one choice for each of two continua. I urge all to be simplistic, to indicate just where they see themselves as being at this moment, ignoring complexities. Then I give them the first "command":

The continuum ranges from number 1 to number 10. I will describe number 1 and I will describe number 10. If what I describe is exactly where you are right now, then write a 1 or a 10. Probably you are somewhere between, so just guess. If you're close to 1, maybe you are at 2 or 3; if you're close to 10, maybe you're at 7 or 8, just make a choice. Place yourself on a line between these two statements.

Number 1: The *only* way to know God is in a one-on-one, direct relationship. That's the *only* way to know God.

Number 10: The *only* way to know God is in the midst of God's people, the church. That's the *only* way.

After a minute or two, during which I quell the grumbling and push them to go on and make a choice, I give them the second continuum. By now they know the ropes, so you don't have to give as much explanation. This time I make the choice in terms of the alphabet, and the choice ranges from A to J. I describe A and I describe J, and they choose their position in relationship to the extremes.

Letter A: The end and purpose of life is so to live that I am reunited with God at my death.

Letter B: The end and purpose of life is to participate with brothers and sisters in building a human society of shalom, where peace and justice and love reign.

Step 4: If I am working with newsprint, I draw a graph with the two continua as the axes. (A copy of the graph is appended, suitable for copying onto an overhead transparency if you prefer that method.) Then I call on members of the group to call out their own coordinates. As they do so, I make a mark at the appropriate spot on the map. The faster, the better. (If you have a conspicuous religious leader of this group present, I usually ask that pastor or bishop or president not to call out his or her coordinates. This is so that people will not stereotype their leader.)

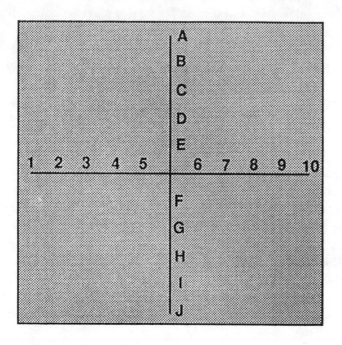

Step 5: Reflection and plenary discussion. Some of the areas in which I invite discussion:

1. The variety of responses. *All* points on the grid are legitimate positions, positions that have been held by great saints.

2. Reflect on where "clumps" of people show up. What does that mean?

3. Reflect on where there is a dearth of responses. What does that mean?

4. What does the overall pattern say about possible strengths of this particular group in ministry? What things are they most likely to be aware of ? Most likely to care about?

5. What does the pattern say about the blind spots of this group?

6. Invite people to respond to how their personal choices felt. I particularly invite those whose coordinates were "far out" from the center, or in a quadrant with few or no others, how it felt to call out their locations. (You can sometimes help the group understand the emotional pressure we exert on one another to conform.)

Step 6: Interpretation. I summarize what the group has learned in the exercise. I sometimes use more material from chapter 2, the descriptions of the quadrants, for example. I usually refer the group to the similar typologies developed by Roozen, McKinney, and Carroll. My major concern at this point is to help them think of the function of the pastor and of the congregation not to bring the congregation's "center" to where the pastor wants it or to where the majority "clump" of the congregation wants it, but to "hold the center," nourishing and feeding all the diverse ministries. I try to help them identify "lacks" in their congregation or consciousness that, if added, might increase the overall strength of the ministry. The stronger the center, in my opinion, the greater the extremes that can be supported.

Step 7: Wild applause.

NOTES

1. David Roozen, William McKinney, and Jackson Carroll, *Varieties of Religious Presence* (New York: Pilgrim Press, 1984). See especially the graph on page 87. If you use this graph, point out that it is somewhat reversed from the one I have suggested. Also point out that their grid is graphing congregations, while the one I present is graphing people.

The Statistics Behind the Graphs

The graphs of the memberships of the Episcopal Church, the Presbyterian Church, the United Church of Christ, the United Methodist Church, and the Evangelical Lutheran Church in American were based on data from Table A1.1 of the Appendix of *Church and Denominational Growth*, edited by David A. Roozen and C. Kirk Hadaway (Nashville, Abingdon, 1994). The graphs plotting the U.S. population were based on figures reported on page 361 of *The World Almanac and Book of Facts: 1994* (Mahwah, NJ: World Almanac Books, 1993).

The specific numbers used are listed on the following page.

Population of the United States

1950	151,325,798
1960	179,323,175
1970	203,302,031
1980	226,542,203
1990	248,709,873

Membership by Denomination

	Episcopalian	Presbyterian	UCC	UMC	ELCA
1950	2,417,464	3,210,635	1,977,428	9,653,178	3,982,508
1960	3,269,325	4,161,860	2,241,134	10,641,310	5,295,502
1970	3,285,826	4,045,408	1,960,608	10,509,198	5,650,137
1980	2,786,004	3,362,086	1,736,244	9,519,407	5,384,271
1990	2,446,050	2,847,437	1,599,212	8,904,824	5,240,739

Denominational Membership as a Percentage of U.S. Population

	Episcopalian	Presbyterian	UCC	UMC	ELCA
1950	1.60%	2.12%	1.31%	6.38%	2.63%
1960	1.82%	2.32%	1.25%	5.93%	2.95%
1970	1.62%	1.99%	.96%	5.17%	2.78%
1980	1.23%	1.48%	.77%	4.20%	2.38%
1990	.98%	1.14%	.64%	3.58%	2.11%

Five Challenges
for the
Once and Future Church

To
The members and staff of St. Alban's Parish—
ministers, every one of them

and especially to
the Tuesday morning eucharist group

CONTENTS

I wonder if we have the time.

Do we who love our religious traditions and systems have the time to redesign, reinvent, or redevelop them for the next generation? Can we, who have inherited such riches from earlier generations of faithful people, pass on an even stronger heritage of faith to the next generations?

These are the kinds of questions that have led me to write this book. Let me be specific. As I look at the future of the church, I see extraordinary challenges lying ahead of us. I honestly do not know if we—as a set of institutions—can survive the difficulties we face.

I often feel very lonely in this concern. I find many of my colleagues going on as they always have. I see people and institutions making plans for tomorrow as if it will be a replica of yesterday. Where I do see energy for facing difficulties, I find little sense of urgency. I get the sense that people hope it will all go away if we just keep our heads down and keep putting one foot ahead of the other. Where I sense energy for change, I too often sense an inadequate understanding of the depth of the issues we face; maybe a few minor adjustments will put things back on track.

I get angry when I hear those who tell us that all we need to do is turn back the clock to a time they remember as more peaceful, settled days for the church. I remember the times they talk about, and they were not better times; they preserved many kinds of injustices and inequities.

Several dimensions of the life of the church make me wonder whether or not we have time. Here's what I see.

First, those with the most at stake in preserving the status quo are the ones who have most of the power to change our systems.

Second, our leaders have short tenure in leadership roles. Most of the changes needed require facing critical controversies. Most leaders in our society—secular and religious—seem to want to leave the hard issues for the next generation. It is the Marie Antoinette version of leadership. Remember that the deluge did not wait until after Marie Antoinette! She lost her head. I am clear that the change ahead will be hard to carry out. We have no chance if we do not have leaders who can look further down the road and make hard choices for the future.

Third, I see a progressive erosion of the financial resources that have supported our institutions. With a short-term approach that hopes only to balance the current budget and has no care for the future. Almost no attention is being paid to the financial crises that are ten or twenty years in the future.

Fourth, I note an increasing lack of trust among the people, the agencies, and the institutions that make up our denominational systems. Our religious institutions follow the lead of our political institutions in having lost any sense of patience or civility with one another. Each person or group seems to be in competition with all others—for scarce resources, for supremacy of one point of view, sometimes for vindication or pure revenge for past losses.

John Kotter of the Harvard Business School has worked with many institutions attempting to be more successful in a changing environment. Although the church is not exactly the same as other organizations,[1] several of Kotter's impediments to organizational transformation fit our challenge in the churches.[2]

Not establishing a great enough sense of urgency. Within my experience churches are denying the reality of the threat around us. As long as church leaders—pastors, bishops, executives, theologians—continue to talk about "bottoming out" and cover up disastrous truths with language about "really exciting missionary opportunities in spite of unexpected reversals," we continue to infantalize the laity of the churches, assuming that they are too weak to take straight talk. What about the denomination that promised to open several hundred new churches but ran out of money in the first six months? What about the denomination that expects to have to close a thousand churches in the next decade? Who is talking straight to members about these things? And if the truth is soft-pedaled, who can be surprised that there is little urgency about the need for transformation?

Lacking a vision. You have a hard time nowadays finding a self-respecting church organization or institution without an engraved vision statement. Problem is, it's hard to distinguish one from any other. And most of them confuse a vision with a dream or with public relations. The dreams tend to be all-inclusive, having global scope and just a bit of triumphalism. The public relations visions represent what feels like a "positioning" of the church's image in terms of appealing to a particular market. Many of the visions give evidence of hard work over time by hundreds of people who have engaged in data gathering, assessing feedback, and all the other processes we consultants can think up. But what comes out at the other end rarely seems to express the passions of a people.

I know of one exception, one that rang so true to me that I still remember it two years after I first heard it. It is the vision the Church of the Brethren articulated to say who and what they are and what they want to be:

Continuing the work of Jesus.
Peacefully.
Simply.
Together.

As is the case with other vision statements, a lot of time and hard work went into the construction of this profoundly simply declaration. But what separates it from the others is that it rings especially true. It is not ostentatious. It makes no unreasonable claims. It toots no horns. It expresses something between a reality and a hope and is clearly built upon the traditions of that family of the church. No one but the Brethren could have said that. I am sure the Church of the Brethren is facing just as difficult a period of transformation as any of the other families of faith, but I think this vision will give them a touchstone for their transformation.

The real power of a vision is that it can put you in touch with who and what you truly are, even as you articulate that which you intend to be. Without a clear vision, Kotter warns, transformation is difficult. What I would add to his warning is my experience that visions are gifts. They represent an intuitive leap from one's historic identity into the future.[3] There is more listening than talking in discerning visions. Discerning visions depends more on waiting on the Lord than on sending out questionnaires.

Declaring victory too soon. Kotter suggests this third warning churches need to heed. It may be that churches are just too impatient. After the first effort, even before the effort is evaluated, a victory is celebrated. Indeed, all too often I have found churches celebrate as a victory an idea that has just been invented, even before it is tried out. In my experience this is caused by the necessity to garner lots of energy to try something out. So the new thing is trumpeted as the solution to all the problems facing the church—even before it is tested. Church people want to fix things. The problem? I don't see anything facing the church that is likely to be fixed in our lifetimes, if then. Some things may never be fixed. Yet if we do not sell our approach as a way to fix what's wrong, we are not likely to get a chance to try it out.[4]

Do we, then, have time? Is the crisis such that we face an inevitable collapse of the familiar and comforting supports that our religious congregations have provided in the past?

I honestly do not know. Assuming the best—that we do have time—I have tried to identify five key obstacles we face if we would leave a church for future generations that is stronger than the one we have been given. These obstacles are not sequential. We face all of them all at once. Some will press upon us more powerfully than others. Some of us will be seized by one of two of the obstacles, and we may spend our whole lives struggling with them.

Two things encourage me. First, the churches have a tradition of laypeople and clergy who rise to challenges. Second, the churches have solid grounds for facing hard things.

Time and again in its history, the church has come to what seemed to be a dead end. From the early controversies between Hellenistic and Judaistic leaders to the crises of the reformation, the church has discovered that God somehow raises up the new people, the new ideas, the new energy with which to address whatever it is that comes down the road. I see all about me today church leaders with incredible commitment to the future of the church, often with little support from those in the structures. I honor the faith of Catholic women who build for a new church in spite of opposition. I am uplifted by the laymen and women of hundreds of congregations who keep on keeping on in the face of clergy indifference to their concerns. I am humbled by the sacrifices I know some clergy make to try to do their work in a new way. I am inspired as I see bishops and executives taking their careers in their hands to open doors for change. Many of these people—clergy and lay—pay a considerable price for standing against the status quo, but they stand in a long tradition of such leaders. I trust in God that more leaders will come.

I am also encouraged because our religious tradition is not grounded on winning. Time and time again, we discover that it is in weakness we are made strong, in foolishness we are led to wisdom. This understanding is the cornerstone of who we are. We know that darkness comes before the dawn, not as some sentimental saying, but because that is how it has been in our encounter with God. When we as churches worry about whether or not we will "make it," we give in to the success-oriented philosophies of this world. We know that God's presence is with us through the valley of the shadow of death, yes, but we also know that that presence goes beyond death.

In this book I discuss the obstacles we need to address in building the church of the future. I do so with humility; I expect to be proven wrong many, many times. But I do so also with considerable confidence in what lies ahead.

In the final analysis, the outcome is in the hands of God. For now, here are the five challenges I see we have ahead of us:

To transfer the ownership of the church.
To discover new structures for the church.
To discover a passionate spirituality.
To make the church a new community and source of community.
To become an apostolic people.

NOTES

1. I have frequently argued the equally false opposite of this statement—that churches are not entirely different from other organizations. Both are true. In many ways they do interact quite similarly to businesses, schools, etc. The problem is overidentification or overdifferentiation.

2. John P. Kotter, "Why Transformation Efforts Fail," *Harvard Business Review*, March-April 1995, 59ff.

3. A friend gave me an unelegant image of this: "Some people think you can replicate a mocking bird's song if you stuff enough mockingbirds in a sausage machine. You don't get a song. You get an inedible, useless mess."

4. Kotter's eight points are all useful, but the three I have presented seem most directly applicable to the churches.

Chapter 1

Challenge 1:
To Transfer the Ownership of the Church

In America the church is owned by its clergy.

That is what *clericalism* means.

I don't know of any church that would formally agree with my opening statement. That is why I have stated it so baldly; I want us to think about what we do, not what we say we do.

As with any "ism"–sexism, racism, ageism–clericalism is not about what we say we believe. It is not about how we want to believe. It is about what we do. An "ism" is not about particular actions or conscious intentions. It is about a pattern of action, a stance of life that is under the control of larger systems of power that run counter, often, to what the individual genuinely believes he or she intends. This is why good-hearted, well-intentioned people can vote for a measure that will damage the rights of African Americans or Hispanic Americans and then say, "But I'm not a racist." Similarly, few clergy or laypeople would claim to approve of a system of clericalism that maintains clergy as a privileged caste. "Isms" are about people–both perpetrators and victims of discriminations–getting trapped by the power systems around them.[1]

Clericalism is an all-embracing assumption that shapes how we think about churches and how we think about the roles each of us plays in the life of the church. It is about how we expect each other to act–a powerful expectation that we rarely talk about. Clericalism, for us in the churches, is like the water in which a fish swims. To the fish the water is invisible, its existence unacknowledged, but it constitutes the world in which the fish lives; it limits what the fish can do and be.

I'd like to tell a story to make my point clear. Even if we cannot see the water we swim in, we may get some hunches about what clericalism is and how it sneaks up on us.

A Simple Fable

Once upon a time in a kingdom far away there was a wide valley between two high mountain ranges. The valley had rich farm land and abounded in game. The river supplied an ample variety of fish. The lavish valley tempted vagabonds. Almost every spring the farmers and householders faced armed groups intending to steal from the fields, carrying home livestock and sometimes even children. They king lived a long ways away, on the other side of the mountains. Hearing of the troubled times, he asked a trusted ally to oversee the valley—to restore the peace and prosperity.

The new lord of the valley drew on the practices and skills he had learned and then perfected defending the people of other valleys. Many thought they were ancient skills, first used by Arthur in the days of Camelot. He established orders of knights and squires skilled in martial arts, and he called on them to protect the valley from outsiders. In battle after battle he led them to victory. Gradually peace returned to the valley.

In the peaceful reign, the knights and squires came regularly to the lord's castle to practice their arts; while maintaining their leadership, they taught younger candidates the intricacies of the skills and customs. As the knights aged, they inducted the younger trainees into responsible positions. All over the kingdom stories were told of the valley between the mountains and how peace had returned to it through the strength of the lord and his knights and squires.

It wasn't long before the farms flourished, with harvests far richer than ever before. The serfs and freemen were able to till the soil without fear. They nurtured the fields and tended the crops. In time they were able to build the trading ships to carry produce down the river to distant ports. Every year the valley became more secure and stronger. The taxes the lord required for the upkeep of the castle and the knights and squires seemed inconsequential. It was a fair exchange for the peace and security the people found.

In time the external threats disappeared, and the memories of pillage became remote. As that happened, new questions arose. Was there really a need for a new wing on the castle? Did all the knights need new swords every other year? Were the costs of the lord's stable getting out of hand? Do we really need as many knights in training this year? Was it necessary for people of the valley to send finances and even some troops to help the far-off king fighting battles in other valleys? Couldn't taxes be trimmed?

The heart of the valley's prosperity was the productivity of the farmers, but the decisions about the life of the valley were left in the hands of the lord and his knights who held conferences and retreats from time to time to rethink how their skills could be improved or the castle made stronger. At great conferences in the castle, the lord called upon his knights for advice and counsel.

Granted, great care was taken to see that the valley was secure against any and all possible enemies, but the farmers and other citizens eventually grew restless. The praise for the lord turned to complaint.

The lord spoke to his knights: "I hear the valley people are restless. You know, as I do, that we ordered our life here to preserve the peace of the land. We have made many sacrifices to bring security and peace to the valley. We must have strong knights and squires and an impregnable castle. So long as we keep these strong, the valley will be peaceful and the farms prosperous." Although the knights agreed to a man, the unrest spread. People in the valley continued to ask why so many knights were necessary and whether their upkeep needed to be so expensive. They made suggestions about how costs might be reduced.

The lord of the valley reassured the people: "We who have been trained in the skills of diplomacy and warfare know more about the threats to our peace than you can know. You must understand that the society we have formed is the one that best protects your prosperity."

Over time, the lord discovered two ways of dealing with farmers who insisted on verbalizing their complaints. The most reliable method was to recognize the questioning as a sign of potential leadership. The most difficult questions reflected really thoughtful analyses of what was going on. Farmers asking such questions (there were not too many of them) were invited to become special trainees in knight school They studied diplomacy and philosophy; they learned to wield the weapons of the knights and were given swords. Upon graduation, they were invited to sit as squires first; if they did well, finally they were knighted. They sat in the councils of the lord of the valley. Interestingly enough, their questions about the rights and wrongs of the exercise of power tended to disappear. They came to discover that the way the knights thought was right after all. And, yes, the language of debate and discussion nurtured in their training did seem more useful than the language of the farmers. The farmers were pleased to see some of their own "making it" among the knights. They cheered lustily for the ex-farmer knights in the annual castle tournaments.

The lord used another, quite different approach with other articulate critics. If one was particularly impassioned, the lord would invite the critic to address council meetings, giving special honor, asking the critic to repeat the most appalling things about the inequities of the system. Council members listened carefully, asked penetrating questions, and took notes. They then sent the critics home with strong applause and statements of genuine gratitude. The critics earned a kind of fame as critics. Their farmer colleagues were proud of them and their outspokenness, "telling it like it is" even to the powers that be. Those who spoke their criticisms most forcefully were celebrated and even sent by the lord to speak in other valleys where both they and their lord became known for their challenging approach to change. Some of these critics were even invited to the king's court to there give witness to their convictions.

But not much changed.[2]

LESSONS OF THE FABLE

This fairy tale connects us to the issue of ownership. In the story the lord and the knights formed a power group that made the rules for the good of the community, a concept in which they genuinely believed, having used it as the basis for rescuing the valley from chaos and returning it to safety and prosperity. Similarly, "for the good of the community," they created the rules that, at least in the beginning, were needed for an orderly society. But the rules did not change as the situation changed. And over time, those who benefited most from the rules were the least likely to advocate change. Yes, the knights and the lord believed the rules to be right, but they also were accustomed to them and knew how to enforce them.

If, by chance, it were also true that the knights and squires loved all the pageantry, the tournaments, and the castle life—and if they were not fully aware that their decisions just happened to support their own privileges—who could deny them those small things?

And the lord's strategies for dealing with dissent are pretty transparently the strategies evident in clericalism as I have experienced it: In the church the articulate, challenging lay leader is either encouraged to go off to seminary—to understand the rules and learn the language—or informally ordained as the church's "pet prophet," riding the lecture circuit from judicatory to judicatory to the crowds' applause. And so we see evidence of the lord's two methods for handling dissenters: either co-opt them into the power system or encapsulate and "sponsor" their activities outside the power system, thereby diluting their effectiveness.

This fable illustrates, albeit obliquely, the institutional ways in which the ecclesiastical power system inhibits the church's ability to respond to the needs of the current and future age.

EVIDENCE OF CLERICALISM

What characteristics of clericalism indicate the present ownership of the churches?

1. Churches Spend Their Money on Clergy

Almost all the professional salaries paid by churches are paid to clergy. Most laypeople who work for the institutional church receive nonprofessional salaries and work at the lower, nonpolicy-making levels of the institution. After World War II several denominations with a strong history of giving lay pastors full responsibility for a congregation moved rapidly to replace those lay leaders with seminary-educated, ordained clergy. Although some denominations now face an oversupply of clergy, those denominations continue to worry about employing clergy. I see no similar organized concern for unemployed laity.

Probably, and without meaning to do so, the churches have encouraged clergy to feel that a church job is an entitlement. A lay friend once expressed it caustically: "Sometimes it looks to me as if the church is just an employment agency for clergy!"

Clergy receive the lion's share of all the laity's contributions to their churches. In many cases the churches get a bargain—because of the outstanding quality of the clergy. But the fact remains that this is where the money goes. And we do not say so very clearly. Three investigators, trying to discover how many dollars clergy actually "cost" the average congregation, unearthed another side of the problem: Churches report the actual amounts spent on clergy in such convoluted ways that it's almost impossible for an outsider to compare what one clergyperson costs as compared with another, even within the same denomination.[3]

2. Decisions are Made Primarily by the Clergy

Most decisions in churches are made primarily by clergy even though they have a high personal stake in many of those decisions, especially about the use of money. Minimum salary scales are voted in church meetings that clergy are paid to attend. Laypeople are not paid to attend such meetings. Over time decisions increasingly reflect the thinking of the clergy. Thus, the decision-making process becomes responsive to the self-interest of the clergy. (The knights truly believe that knightly leadership is in the best interest of all the people of the valley; knights do not seem to realize that they may be influenced by what is best for them more than by what is best for the farmers.)

Clergy often cite recent patterns (in the last three or four decades) of rotating congregational lay leadership to point to the strength and breadth of lay ownership of decision making. In fact this pattern has had quite the opposite effect. Rotating lay leadership has actually increased clergy power and ownership in most congregations. When lay leadership rotates every three or four years, the lay leaders are "evicted" just about the time they learn the ropes. I do not have a good alternative to offer, but I do point out that rotating leadership among a large group of laypeople effectually eliminates the strength and ownership of the lay voice.

3. Standards Are Determined by the Clergy

Denominational books of order and canons reflect clergy power in decision making. Specifically, most denominations have written into their rule books a definition of a "first-class" congregation that generally includes leadership by a full-time clergyperson serving at a denominationally determined minimum salary. This is more than a rule-book statement: By dint of long practice, this has become a self-evident standard.[4] Congregations unable to afford clergy understand themselves to be "second class." The standard norm is reinforced in that a congregation's becoming "fully self-supporting" (on the basis of these financial indicators) is cause for judicatory-wide celebration. Congregations that can no longer maintain the standard are seen to have "fallen behind," failed in a substantial way. Their "failure" is deplored by the judicatory staff and boards, and such congregations are given less voice in judicatory meetings. The standards of effective ministry are defined primarily in terms of the congregation's ability to employ a full-time clergyperson. This leads to the corollary standard that a congregation is somehow deficient if it does not have a resident clergyperson. A congregation even temporarily without a full-time pastor is considered "at risk" and becomes a worry for the judicatory executive or bishop. Such congregations are often described as being vacant. Bishops have told me that they have to hurry to get a pastor installed because otherwise "it will all go to pot." The standard is clear and self-enforcing, in spite of any demonstrable proof that many congregations do well even during extended periods without ordained clergy leaders.

4. Denominational Decision Making, Skewed to Smaller Congregations, Emphasizes Clergy Voices

Within denominational decision-making processes, power often remains predominately in rural, small congregations, with larger congregations disproportionately underrepresented. The standards of the books of order and canons (set by generations of clergy-dominated meetings) affirm that "true" congregations must have a full-time pastor who, as such, is expected to attend the decision-making, policy-setting meetings of the judicatory. This is one more reason why every congregation, no matter how small, works sacrificially to find a way to support a pastor. And those pastors, representing the concerns of their small congregations, overrepresent the rural population when compared to the number of clergy representing the larger congregations which have fewer clergy per capita. This results in underrepresentation of large-congregation laity *and* underrepresentation of large-congregation clergy.

Of course this reality varies according to the denominational polity, but the weighting occurs in practice even when the written rules contradict that intention. Early in the nineteenth century, representation in Britain's House of Parliament was found to have followed a similar pattern, with rural areas having become vastly overrepresented in proportion to the population of the growing cities. "[Rotten] boroughs" had full representation, while urban areas had virtually none. Significant issues arose because of the gulf between the rural and urban needs. Dramatic political changes resulted in redrawing constituency lines, and the predominately rural House of Lords was stripped of its power. The change was significant enough that it was called revolution. Such redress has not happened in the churches.

5. The Clergy, Not the Laity, Is Trained in the Language of the Institution

Debate about what is and is not important to the institutional church is often couched in language of historic controversies and issues; the language of academic theology is the approved medium of conversation. Few laypeople have been educated in the language and history of the controversies, so they enter the debate significantly handicapped.[5] Clergy insist that important issues be given "rigorous theological reflection," often without defining what that means. Laity are asked to play that game if their ideas are to be taken seriously. In my experience working with clergy and executives making important decisions, I cannot remember ever actually having "rigorous theological reflection" brought into the decision making. The decisions seemed to be made with the same view of pragmatism, hope, and values that was used in nonclergy decisions.[6] The term, however, is used to invalidate nonclergy input to the conversation. It reinforces the power of the clergy in making important decisions.

6. Education for Clergy Is a Major Financial Investment

All of the major denominations invest heavily in the training and education of clergy. They invest modestly, if at all, in the education of the laity. This disparity is dramatic in the churches' very large investment in institutions of theological education. I see no institution of lay education in any denomination that represents the kind of spending of the most modest seminary. Seminaries of some denominations have far more endowment than the entire denomination. The long-term investments earmarked for future education of clergy suggest that the policy of focusing resources on the clergy is being set for generations to come. Per capita education costs for clergy have escalated as have other costs in higher education. Costs per year of pastoral service have multiplied much more rapidly as older seminary students look forward to shorter and shorter periods of professional service.

7. The Clergy Controls "How One Changes the Rules"

A friend moving from one profession to another once told me, "I've decided to go to law school because lawyers write all the rules. They even write the rules about how you change the rules."

In the institutional church, the same could be said about the clergy. To facilitate institutional change one must be prepared to contend with the clergy–the group with the strongest voice in church councils and deep-rooted knowledge of institutional language.

My colleagues who consult with congregations acknowledge one rule of thumb: Clergy cannot make change happen by themselves, but they almost always have veto power.

The power of the clergy–I have described it even as ownership–is far-reaching. Over the generations the voice of the clergy has built and sustained many of the familiar and useful structures of religious life. This is true in all denominations, not just those seen as hierarchical. In some cases that power is located more locally; in others the power resides in clerical hierarchies. Several things need to be said about this power system.

THE ISSUES

Conflict of Interest

We need to recognize that a classic conflict of interest is at work here. Clergy-dominated institutions make many decisions in which clergy have a direct stake: salaries and job security, for example–sometimes involving prestige and preference. In our society we generally feel that institutions that nurture "conflict of interest" frequently make bad policy–policy that supports the welfare of those with the conflict of interest not the welfare of the entire institution.

We have discovered that although many principled people are able to make selfless decisions, it is wiser to ask a legislator not to vote on a bill in which he or she has a substantial financial interest. We ask judges to excuse themselves from making decisions on cases in which they or their families are directly involved. We urge doctors not to practice medicine on themselves or their close kin. Aspirin, yes; surgery, no. In our country we long ago made the decision that the basic policy decisions about war and peace should be made by civilians not generals.

The Anticlerical Option

In the churches we have built a system of ownership and decision making that institutionalizes conflict of interest. At various times Christians have tried to get around this problem in the church by eliminating clergy. The answer, these people say, anticlericalism. Some denominations have attempted to install this answer. Most attempts to redefine or eliminate the clergy role have not been successful; time and again the role of the clergyperson has reemerged functionally, perhaps in a new form. Even John Milton, after a generation of experience with a newly defined "presbyter," was forced to admit that "new presbyter is but old priest writ large." Since World War II many denominations (United Methodist, Baptist, Brethren, Mennonite) that traditionally encouraged laity to carry leadership of congregations have systematically replaced them with professionally trained clergy. Even most Quakers now have chosen to have ordained clergy leadership.[7]

Religious Authority and the Clergy Role: Constructive and Demonic

As I have worked with many congregations of many denominations, I have found those trained and ordained into clergy roles generally to have had enormous ability to facilitate religious growth. (I must admit some bias—perhaps conflict of interest—because I have been an ordained clergyman for forty years.) Not all of those ordained are wise, not all use power well, not all are open to change or even to criticism, but for each I characterize negatively, I know dozens if not scores who simply and directly work to lead people to God, stand beside those in pain and suffering, encourage men and women to their best, lift them up when they are broken and lost, walk with them in the valley shadow; they raise questions about life-denying public or private actions, and in their own lives witness to the following of a higher calling. Most clergy I know understand and accept sacrificial living as their personal vocation. I am genuinely proud to be numbered with them.

I have noted in the dialogue between clergy and laity something far beyond rationality and pure expedience. The relationship has deep psychological and religious dimensions and powerful emotions dwell there. Over many generations this dialogue has had enormous capacity to foster growth and spiritual development.

Twenty years ago when I met Bruce Reed of the Grubb Institute of London, I first found some of this mystery and wonderful depth explained in a way that made sense.[8] Drawing insights from anthropology (especially Victor Turner), psychology (W. R. Bion and John Bowlby), and developmental theory (D. W. Winnicott), Reed analyzed the role of clergy in relationship to the spiritual life of the individual Christian and the life of the institution. In short, the "religious person" carried great emotional authority. The role of the person or place habitually associated with the presence of the holy had a critical part in how a believer appropriated the benefits of any renewed sense of identity and purpose.

In more recent years the issue of the authority of the clergy role has become more familiar to us for the worst of reasons; we have discovered in very public ways that many clergy have misused that role, abusing those around them in many ways, often, tragically, for sexual exploitation. The authority of the role is so great that it can be used manipulatively for selfish purposes, victimizing others. The authority of the role can turn the dialogue between clergy and lay into demonic and destructive patterns.

The demonic use of the role of the clergy demonstrates the *potential* for positive growth. In healthy dialogue between clergy and the laity, the authority inherent in the clergy role has the potential for healing, for nurture, for challenge, and for self-discovery. The novels of Graham Greene go further, suggesting that the power for good in the role of the clergyperson is present even in the most undeserving carriers, echoing a traditional belief of the church that the power is not limited by the virtue (or lack of it) of the person bearing it.

It is not unlike the power inherent in the role of a father or mother—which has the potential for permanently infantilizing the child or conversely calling the child to maturity. One does not argue to abolish parents because some parents use the role poorly. People I know see the creative potential in parental roles and seek to grow better parents. So it is—or should be—with the clergy.

Creative dialogue between clergy and laypeople has enormous potential for being the locus for pastoral care and development. It can be an important tool in the equipping of the saints for their ministries.

Another View: Clergy as Overfunctioners

Edwin A. Friedman[9] and his colleagues[10] in the field of family process have given us language and a framework by which we can visualize another danger to the potentially creative dialogue between clergy and the laity. Family process describes how those in helping relationships are tempted to assume responsibility for others' lives. In attempting to help someone out of a bad patch of one kind or another, the helper makes decisions or directs behavior that should be made and directed by the person in trouble. By rationalizing his or her actions as "help" for one who is "helpless," the helper only serves to create dependency and provide the person in trouble with an excuse to abdicate personal authority. Friedman defines "overfunctioning" as taking over from the person in trouble; "underfunctioning" is the dependent behavior of that same person. Continued over time, these patterns of behavior create a class of overfunctioners and an underclass of underfunctioners, and the conditions themselves become chronic and self-replicating.

The relationship between clergy and the laity over the years has built chronic overfunctioning into the role of the clergy and underfunctioning into the role of the laity. The clergy has come to expect the laity to underfunction, and the prophecy is self-fulfilling. The laity has come to expect the clergy to overfunction, and this, too, is self-fulfilling. Neither finds it easy to challenge the depressingly self-replicating pattern of dependence.

A Prophetic Role:
The Interim Pastor—Powerless but Having Authority

More than two decades ago colleagues and I began exploring an alternative without at first realizing what we were dealing with. Our driving purpose at the time was to discover how to make a creative change when one pastor left a congregation and another was installed. We knew that some such changes were unusually traumatic for everyone involved. When there had been a particularly bad fight, perhaps with a long history of contentious relations between clergy and laity in a congregation, we discovered that the congregation's next pastorate was often short and miserable, even disastrous, replicating all the negatives of the previous experience. Similarly we found that a particularly long pastorate—fifteen years or more—was often fairly creative, but that the church's subsequent pastorate was marked by an unusually large number of unsatisfying experiences. As we identified these special cases where problems seemed to arise when one pastor was quickly replaced with another, we saw a need for a time of healing or pausing. We also discovered that the churches were raising up a few pastors whose instincts made them a natural to go into such situations for the "in-between time."

From this special cadre of pastors we identified needed skills and learned how to train what we started calling the interim pastor. This is a title and a role now widely established and used in many denominations. We have trained talented people specifically for short-term pastoral leadership roles. These pastors have become specialists in clearing out the underbrush left over from former experiences, helping congregations get ready for another long-term pastoral relationship. Our research showed that when the interim role was done well, the next installed pastor seemed to have a higher chance of success.[11]

In identifying this new role of interim pastor, we had stumbled onto a kind of religious leadership and pastoral authority that circumvented the "ownership" issue. By being intentionally a short-term actor in the congregation's life, the interim pastor was freed of the long-range responsibility for the future of the congregation—a responsibility generally felt deeply by pastors installed permanently. Ownership was not an issue to or with the interim pastor.

The interim pastor understood that he or she was to provide limited, temporary help in a congregation by entering a system in which ministry with integrity was already "happening," in which there was a long history of ministry. The assumption and the contract of the interim pastor called for the position to be temporary.

Within the interim period the psychological contract of both pastor and congregation changed. The interim pastor was understood to be the religious leader, encouraging and strengthening local leadership. The responsibility for the life of ministry in that place did not belong to the interim pastor but to the laity.

I must admit, however, that the old model of pastorate is so deeply ingrained in the laity and the clergy that most "permanent" pastors, when installed, resurrect the old patterns of overfunctioning clergy and underfunctioning laity.

Without fully understanding what we were doing, my colleagues and I had developed a model of ministry that was not locked into the "overfunctioning" standard model. Simply by acknowledging the temporary nature of the role, we placed the pastor and the congregation in different roles of ownership, different relationship of authority, and opened the doors to fully functioning roles of laity in ministry and of clergy in ministry.

Since I have understood the dynamics of what we did, I have been trying to teach all pastors that they are interim pastors, even if they stay in place for thirty years. On this point I have won a few battles—and lost many more. The old pattern will not change easily. The standards set and the instincts trained in the clericalist model are resistant to change.

This "interim mentality" is the most direct clue I have had as to how we can change the ownership issue. Where it has worked, the clergy have found new freedom and authority to be the religious leaders they want to be and the laity have discovered new ways in which their ministry is fully owned by themselves, not continually dependent upon the clergy.

CONCLUSION

I began this chapter calling for a change of ownership in the church. Such a call is not a function of anticlericalism; it is simply a statement that the churches cannot be fully and effectively in ministry in the twenty-first century by continuing patterns inherited from the twentieth.

I believe there must be a new dialogue between clergy and laity, a dialogue in which neither seeks to lord it over the other, neither defers to the other, but both give their best to the relationship. It will be a relationship in which the historic power of the role of religious authority is claimed and taken on without apology by those we probably will continue to call clergy. It will also be a relationship in which those we now call laity will see themselves as fully functioning colleagues, standing on their own feet and assured of the authenticity of their witness and work.

In the process of building religious institutions, we have created a power and ownership structure in which the clergy wields most of the power. They are now trapped in that role by history and by the arrangements locked in place by customs and laws intended to preserve the institution. In fact, the "arrangements" keep the clergy in institutional power but make it increasingly impossible for individual clergy to carry out their mandate to be bearers of the religious mystery, to have religious rather than institutional authority.

The task of the next generations will be to shift the power and ownership structures of the churches to allow laypeople to fulfill their apostolic ministries and, in so doing, free the clergy to be the catalysts of religious authority.

NOTES

1. "Isms" are the way most of us get in touch with what Paul calls "powers and principalities" (Eph. 6:12). They are demonic powers larger than the individual, and they influence and shape us in ways we are usually not aware of. Christians can recognize the power of these influences and realize that just to name them is to gain some power over them. We also must acknowledge that even these powers are subject to the One in whom we live and move. Indeed, knowing all this allows Christians to know that we *are* racist and clericalist and sexist—but that we are working to recover! And we are praying for the overthrow of the demonic powers. Our hearts are attractive targets for the demons' powers. We do well to maintain our vigilance and humility in the face of them.

2. I first tried this fable out on my friend and mentor Verna Dozier—to try to articulate why it seems so hard to change from the clericalism that characterizes the church both of us know and love.

3. See Dean Hoge, Jackson W. Carroll, and Francis K. Scheets, *Patterns of Parish Leadership* (Kansas City, MO: Sheed & Ward, 1988).

4. The work by Hoge, Carroll, and Scheets (ibid.) was done in four denominations. In all of those denominations it was clear how normative this standard has become for the laity. When asked what form of leadership lay leaders needed in their congregations, the answer was overwhelmingly "fully trained, full-time clergy." The answer was the same regardless of the possibility or impossibility of funding such leadership.

5. I remember a classic illustration from my work with churches in New Zealand. The indigenous Maori people in the churches had denominational differences described in terms of the difference between the Greek words *homoousious and homoiousious.*

6. I am aware that this is a controversial comment backed only by my observation. The only empirical evidence I have seen was compiled in the early seventies by a consultant to Internet Seminary who tried to determine how administrators at theological seminaries made decisions about their institutions. He found no instance of basic seminary planning in which administrators applied any theological concepts or criteria to the program options. Decisions were based on budget and political influence.

7. Parker Palmer, speaking of the experience of a small group of Quakers in the eastern U.S., suggests that their ability to change the pattern resulted from a decision not to eliminate the clergy, but to eliminate the laity.

8. The simplest statement is the brief piece, Bruce Reed and Barry Palmer, *The Task of the Church and the Role of Its Members* (Bethesda, MD: The Alban Institute, 1975.) Reed's fuller treatment of these issues, published in the late seventies, is now out of print: The Dynamics of Religion (London: Darton, Longman, and Todd).

9. Edwin A. Friedman, *From Generation to Generation: Family Process in Church and Synagogue* (New York: Guilford Press, 1985).

10. I note particularly for its accessibility Peter Steinke, *How Your Church Family Works* (Bethesda, MD: The Alban Institute, 1993).

11. The Alban Institute published a number of pieces about the interim pastorate. It also helped launch the Interim Pastor Network, which meets annually and continues to train interim pastors. Several denominations have their own groups of interim pastors. My own statements about the ministry are found in Loren Mead, *Critical Moment of Ministry: A Change of Pastors* (Bethesda, MD: The Alban Institute, 1986).

CHAPTER 2

CHALLENGE 2:
To Find New Structures to Carry Our Faith

The institutional framework of our churches is no longer working. So far, we have not been able to build a framework that is adequate for the years ahead.

The second challenge in building churches for the future is to construct new institutional structures that can carry the faith to generations yet to be born.

In my first book about the future of the church, I described many places in which our institutions do not work, and I described some of the historical reasons for the breakdown.[1] In my second book on the subject, I said little about structures.[2] There I focused on the functions the church of the future needs to embody, not the form of the embodiment. Now I want to return to structural issues, believing them to be one of our critical challenges.

Note that I make a big assumption here: I believe that structures are necessary to carry truth from one generation to another. I am aware of some "movements" (such as Alcoholics Anonymous) that perpetuate themselves with seemingly little or no structural form. And I am familiar with the argument that faith is more a movement than an institution. But as I review the history of the church, I see that most new insights that have survived to a second or third generation have found enough structure to outlive the one who generated the insight. And I note that my own generation received the faith through structures that, though flawed, had the ability to pass on truth from former generations.

It is also true that every generation is tempted to preserve the structures rather than the insights of the previous generation. When that temptation wins out, the critical task is to break through the structures and help the insights—if they are still viable—find structures more adequate for a new time.

That is the task we now face. The forms and structures of our churches have served well to bring the truths of the faith to this generation, but they have also become so calcified and rigid that they block communication of the insights of faith.

Many kinds of structures are needed to carry any movement from one generation to the next, and the church is no exception to this. The church must find organizational structures and structures of community that can enhance communication with the new generation—any new generation.

Our effort to meet this challenge of new structures is made more difficult by the fact that we are used to changing our structures very slowly, if not almost imperceptibly. We have grown accustomed to a pace that allows a decade or two—or even three, if necessary—to change a hymnal or book of worship. We have never before lived in a rapidly changing world where societal changes demand a quick response. We have never dealt with the need for rapid structural change, so we do not have very good adaptive mechanisms. We are in new territory.

UNDERLYING PROBLEMS WITH OUR DENOMINATIONAL STRUCTURES

Today we are experiencing obvious pain in the organizational structures that make up our denominations: relationships among congregations, between congregations and their regional bodies (judicatories), between congregations and national bodies, and between regional and national bodies.

Issues of Trust

Many of us who are older remember when our denominational structures represented trusted, effective ways for different groups and interests within the denomination to work together for the mission goals we shared. Those denominational structures, led by bishops or executives, made it possible for the concerns or needs or one part of the denomination to be connected to concerns and needs in other regions. The structures made up a skill and resource delivery system that brought the whole life of the denomination to bear at the point of missional need. So trusted were those networks that people gave sacrificially to keep them operating, even when those networks were never able to do all the churches wanted to do. Most of us felt considerable loyalty to those relationships, and we were proud to be part of it all.

That sense of trust in the structures evaporated a long time ago. To be truthful, it evaporated in many other segments of our society—medicine, law, higher education, government, business—at about the same time. (What we are talking about is not just a phenomenon of the churches; we are experiencing a paradigm shift that touches every corner of our society in terms of an erosion in the authority of social structures or a loss of loyalty.)

Today's bishop or presbytery executive, district superintendent or area minister often has to pacify a rebellious or angry constituency before beginning to work with them. An assumption of suspicion has replaced the assumption of trust. Congregations are now predisposed to resist whatever initiatives those in the "upper" structures propose, even when the proposals are first rate. This climate of distrust and suspicion severely handicaps communication and effective collaboration from the top down or from the bottom up.

No matter how hard the "upper" levels try to listen to the "grassroots," they are not perceived as being very attentive. The assumption of distrust makes neither party willing to allow the other to change behavior. Organizational paralysis can be the result.

I see the church already experimenting with new structural relationships. In many places individual congregations are taking on functions judicatories used to perform, such as program development and training. In some cases this is done almost in an adversarial stance to the judicatory. ("Anything you can do, I can do better," as Annie Oakley put it.) But I also see congregations collaborating with their judicatories, taking initiative and providing resources the judicatory does not provide. Networks of "training congregations" are emerging, providing a variety of educational programming and innovative liturgical and musical resources, much of it first class. Training initiated by these congregations usually reaches across several denominations. Such efforts to find new structures link our concerns to one another and allow us to help others and be helped by them.

Loss of Interdependence

Different levels within the same denominations do not work together as easily as they once did. The middle judicatory—diocese or conference or presbytery—stands awkwardly in-between the local congregation and the national structures. Lines of power and finance get tangled up. Congregations, heavily presured by their own finances, try to respond to the judicatory's needs while the judicatory is "squeezed" by the responsibility for national needs. From time to time totally new agencies of groups, some of them regional or ecumenical, enter the competition seeking support and participation. The congregations' cries for financial relief or program assistance grow louder, yet the national structures are importunate in demanding resources and money to meet emerging new mission issues. In fact, the needs at each level have great legitimacy, but often far outstrip the resources available. Unhealthy competition and feelings of betrayal and abandonment are more frequent than one would wish. There is little sense of interdependence upon one another.

Denominations do not work easily with other denominations at any level. The happiest relationships are probably local, where numbers of congregations seem able to get together to take on local initiatives without worrying about all the denominational furniture. Food banks, homeless shelters, Meal-on-Wheels, retirement home ministries–all are ways in which congregations of different denominations collaborate regularly. Regionally, judicatories of various denominations seem intent on running duplicative efforts that frequently seem worse than useless.[3]

Because of budget constraints and staff cutbacks in most so-called mainline denominations, program production and resourcing from the national offices have become almost nonexistent.

Regional and national judicatories have major changes to make if they are to be part of the picture of the church in the middle of the twenty-first century. Elsewhere I have argued for the critical importance of the middle judicatory,[4] but the case for the true and necessary functions of the national structures is yet to be made. Clearly such a case must be made before we can determine how much or what is needed in national organizational structures. It is unfortunate that the shortage of money adds to the pressure on these levels. The need to redesign and cut back at the same time has pushed for short-term adjustments and the defending of turf. Little time has been available for the basic structural redesign that is needed.

Perhaps the most difficult task of all will be to build trust among the elements of the structures we develop. This will take time, but it will not begin until the "higher" levels learn to listen to the "lower" levels or until each level quits making the others the perennial scapegoats.

Financial Issues

One other element of our problem of organizational structure needs to be noted, and I suspect that this element is behind most of the trouble. The financial system undergirding our denominations is in catastrophic trouble. If the church is to be a church in the future, it will need to build a new financial model. Let me name two specific financial issues that we must work through.

1. Our method of funding regional, national, and other structures depends upon gathering resources in the local congregation, then freely giving them to the various offices in loyalty and in support of the wider mission of the church. Thus from the flow of resources toward mission, each level of the church received enough funding to cover its essential costs. But as funds get tight, that flow is impeded, slowed, and in some cases stopped. In a new paradigm of mission in which the local mission is expanding in importance, there is no longer the compellingly obvious need to send funds "up the ladder." More funds are being kept locally, while everything outside the congregation loses income. Funds held locally are not all held for local mission; costs of local congregations have been rising much more rapidly than other church costs. If that weren't enough, all the agencies that used to be strongly supported by regional or national funds—seminaries, mission agencies, even church program units—now go directly to congregations to make a pitch for support. The result is "designated giving," often another name for cutting the contribution to the regional and national budgets. Here is the structural challenge: How do we determine the *essential* functions of regional and national judicatories, and how do we pay for them if that "bottom-up" financial system no longer works? Should those services be provided only when and where they are paid for by the user? What about congregations that cannot pay? How much of the regional and national structure do we need, and for what? Is this a new reason to develop regional and national endowments? How do we determine what is essential regionally and nationally, and how do we pay for it?

2. The economic model of the local congregation is already out of reach for half the congregations in our country: the cost of upkeep for a "standard-model" congregation far exceeds the means of half our congregations. In spite of this, many judicatories have plans afoot to open new congregations as rapidly as possible on this "standard" model. I am reminded of the story of the man who found it cost fifty cents to make a

widget that he could sell for no more than forty cents. His solution to the problem was to increase the output of widgets so as to increase sales. Yes, he went bankrupt faster than he otherwise would have. But he had great sales for a while. Let me show you how this model works in real life by caricaturing what we do. You might call this sketch "How the Church 'Really Works.'" Please remember that this is a caricature; it exaggerates reality far beyond what any of us have experienced so that we can recognize what we often do not want to see.

I will describe a mythical judicatory. (If you are Episcopal or Catholic, call this a diocese; if Presbyterian, a presbytery; if United Methodist or United Church of Christ, a conference; if Lutheran, a synod—you get the idea!)

The Diocese of Midlandia (as I'm an Episcopalian, we'll use my language) is like lots of their judicatories. It covers a geographic region that includes several cities and towns and the suburban-exurban areas like those that are in your own judicatory. As a religious structure, here's how it works. There are half a dozen really big churches. Everybody knows them. They are the "plums" that most of the clergy are dying to get called to. They have big budgets and fine buildings. They have excellent music, imaginative worship, and their educational programming is first rate. Each has a strong staff. Some of them, over the years, have been on the conservative side of a lot of issues; others much less so. These are the congregations you can count on. Strong, vibrant. (I don't want to be romantic about it; one or two of them may, from time to time, treat their clergy or their bishop just awfully, and they can be stubborn and mean-spirited, too, but on the whole they are fine places.)

But Midlandia has a lot of fine smaller congregations, too, They are the "ordinary" variety: one pastor on the staff, sometimes a full- or part-time secretary. Many of them are marvelous places for worship and education, places where the members have a great sense of community with one another. Like the "plums," some of these have problems from time to time; indeed, several years of conflict may almost break their backs. But week by week, good stuff happens—people are nurtured and go about trying to make a difference in their community. Some of these congregations struggle every year to come up with the resources for the annual budget, but usually they make it.

Midlandia also has a flock of quite small congregations that never quite seem to "make it." Although they have marvelous members, as a group they are always feeling a bit put-down because they have to ask for grants from the diocese and sometimes they aren't able to meet their obligations. Most of them have to share a pastor with another place, or, what may be more common, they have to make sure their pastor does not stay too long. If a pastor stays more than two or three years, they run out of funds to pay the salary. During the gaps between pastors, they put money in the bank to help pay future bills. Most of these congregations are used to hand-to-mouth existence. Although they are aware of the way the rest of the diocese tends to look down on them, some of them take pride in being "different." I remember going to the anniversary of one of these congregations, celebrating two and a half centuries of being a subsidized congregation.

As I draw this caricature of Midlandia, you may want to give name to the congregations of your judicatory who fit the categories.

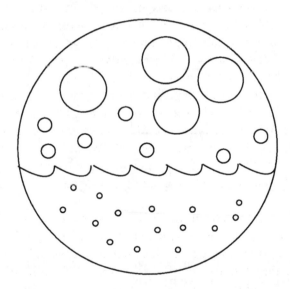

Note the wavy line I drew across the picture. It represents financial solvency.

Above that line, congregations "make it," Below it, some form of subsidy is needed to keep the congregations going. It is almost as if that wavy line is a "water line." Above it, the congregations are in the fresh air. Below it, the congregations are "under water."

How do we tend to manage this problem? We have discovered that the plums and the midsized congregations have some "extra" resources. If we use the air analogy, they have a bit more—some of them have lots more—than they need to sustain their own existence. That's where regional judicatories come in. We have come to see judicatory offices as places to which we can send the excess air from the stronger congregations, a kind of pumping station. We set up a "hose" from the judicatory office down to the tiny subsidized congregations, and we pump just enough air down to keep them alive.

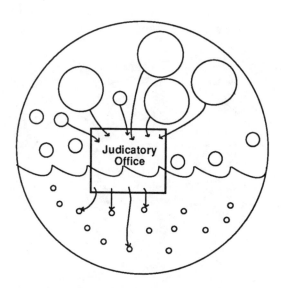

Of course this is absurd, but bear with me. And to tell the truth, doesn't it point to some of the ways we behave?

This caricature is kept alive by two fictions.

The first is our official party line: We say that all the tiny congregations really can grow up to be like the plums. But we know in our heart of hearts that this is not true. We have rarely seen this happen to dependent congregations. Occasionally one may explode, perhaps when the suburbs of the nearby city stretch in, or when a major corporation sets up a new plant in the community. But we know it is very rare for this to happen. In fact, only one person doesn't know this whole thing is a fiction: the young seminary student sent out there, encouraged to believe that by her or his efforts this little village mission can become a cathedral. Too many young pastors' hearts and spirits have been broken by trying to do that.

The other fiction is destructive on a larger scale. It says that the congregations above the water level are not affected by the water; that the water inevitably will dry up and the small and large congregations will flourish together. Operating under this fiction, the large and middle-sized congregations often feel very philanthropic and religious, "helping" all those "poor congregations." That is, they feel that way until they have a few tight budget years and begin murmuring about all those "subsidies" and muttering about "closing down some of those dead beats." The fiction encourages those that are making it to separate themselves from those that are not. The fiction keeps large congregations from understanding that they, too, are genuinely threatened.

You see, the fact is that the water is rising. In some places it is rising fast. The issue is not how to make small congregations grow into large, self-sustaining congregations. The issue is that many of the fine middle-sized congregations that today are struggling to stay above water by tomorrow will themselves be under water. If I had to guess, I would predict that at least 20 percent of those single-pastor congregations will be threatened with insolvency in the next decade and a half. Others tell me the proportion may be even higher.

The caricature I have drawn is a blunt instrument. It is not very subtle. By exaggeration it points out implications of the organizational structures congregations count on. It is a dead-end system. Right now perhaps 40 to 50 percent of our congregations are under the water line. More are going under every year.

I trust this caricature helps readers recognize the organizational dead end we face. You see, there is no way out of what I have described. To survive in the next century, most congregations will have to learn to *breathe water.* Continuing to spend energy learning better air-breathing methods, continuing to start new congregations on the old economic model—both of these are dead ends.

Breathe water? Impossible? Of course it is. I mean there is no way that creatures such as we can learn in our lifetimes to grow gills and webbed hands and feet and learn to live underwater. There is no way we can make it by learning to hold our noses and take deeper breaths when we get to the surface.

A whole new kind of existence is called for if we physically were to learn to breathe water. That's precisely what this caricature calls for in terms of our basic church structure. I am not talking about our learning how to tinker with our congregational system, to find out how to make it work a bit better. The organizational structures we now have are broken irreparably, and things of a totally new order need to be developed. New church planting, so long as we are planting the same kind of things that's failing now in more than half the cases, is not enough, and it may be wrong.

One thing I like about the caricature is what it can do to our perception of the small, dependent congregation. As things are now, of course, they are the drag on the system. The failures. The ones that can't quite make it.

But if we are serious about learning how to breathe water, look at what some of those congregations have been doing! Most have been experimenting with water breathing for years. Many have learned to maintain fine congregational life and life-affirming ministry without full-time staff. They have learned to generate financial resources out of nothing. They know how to get blood out of turnips, or at least how to get enough turnips to trade in on a blood transfusion.

No thanks, however, to the rest of the churches! They system we have is not helping these congregation. Rather, it is training them in dependence. Many are being damaged by the efforts of the rest of the church to "help" them, which amounts to leaching all of their imagination out of them. The longer we continue the dependency system I have caricatured above, the more damage we will do them and the less they will have to offer as pioneers in breathing water.

I do not want to be romantic about these congregations. With their tenacity, they have the potential to be pioneers for us—if we have not damaged them too badly. Those congregations in the midsized range that will slide below the water line in the next decade are going to need a lot of help. So far, I see no initiatives that have wholehearted denominational backing by the denominations to help with that problem. Some individual regional judicatories are experimenting, but they are swimming against the current.[5]

We desperately need pioneers to search out new economic models for the work of the church. We need local congregations operating with less than full-time staff and congregations that see that as the best way to do mission and ministry. We need congregations with the courage to merge their operations with others, not necessarily of the same denomination or even faith group. We need more pioneers who will help congregations learn to use and provide services on an entrepreneurial basis and teach us how to get help to those who cannot afford it. We need to learn how to help a self-sustaining congregation adjust to a lesser role without losing its sense of integrity and mission.

THE ECUMENICAL PART OF OUR STRUCTURAL CHALLENGE

Researchers are telling us that fewer and fewer members of our denominations are content to be dyed-in-the-wool members of their own denomination, come what may. There is a fairly constant flow of ordinary members from one denomination to another. Younger Americans seem to have more ecclesiastical wanderlust than their elders. (Clergy remain pretty consistently denominational, perhaps influenced by the difficulty of switching credentials and pensions from one denomination to another.)

Let's be honest. Most of our denominational differences represent territorial and theological feuds now three or four hundred years old. Relics of those feuds have been preserved in our organizational structures the way an insect may be preserved in a bead of amber. The reasons for the feud were very real, and the arguments we use today to defend our positions are genuine, but in most cases the arguments have to do with what happened a long time ago. In the life of the Catholic Church of his time, Martin Luther saw some practices and beliefs that caused him to start a revolution that resulted in the formation of the Lutheran churches. But to tell the truth, one would be hard put to find a region of the Catholic Church today (certainly not in the United States) where Catholic practice and belief is what it was when Luther took offense. I have not heard of the sale of a single indulgence in the past decade! Nearly every Catholic service I attend uses the hymn "A Mighty Fortress Is Our God." I hear it more there than I do in Lutheran churches. Indeed it would be hard to find a nickel's worth of difference between most of the denominations in basic theological principles today. Practices? Oh, yes, Catholics play bingo and Anglicans have bazaars. And customs? Yes, again, Assemblies of God put a high stake on tithing and Presbyterians "pledge."

I do not mean to trivialize the genuine differences that remain (the issue of ordination of women truly is a significant difference), but the ordinary church member finds the rationale for those differences increasingly trivial. The differences are much less central to the faith community than they were in the past. Our institutional structures formed around an "allergic reaction." We seem to have lived long enough to have become desensitized to what caused the original reaction. Meanwhile we have not and do not change our behavior.

What is true of the Lutherans and Catholics is true of most of the other denominational groupings. You sometimes find a Presbyterian who still goes apoplectic at the word *bishop*, and you will find Episcopalians who still mutter about "the enormities of the bishop of Rome," but you will not get a war going. And remember—most of the differences that started our denominations started physical combat in their time.

Look at the more important goals of the denomination today—their mission agenda. Each is struggling to rethink international mission agenda in light of a changed international scene and shortages of funding. Each is concerned for caring for the homeless and hungry in our society. Each worries about those who are excluded from society. Each is working on what "ministry of the laity" means and what that has to do with the role of the clergy. Each is trying to find out how better to educate its clergy.

Each is trying to learn how better to deal with ethnic diversity. Each is struggling to come to terms with major changes in human behavior—particularly sexual. Each is trying to overcome the built-in racism in its community. Each is struggling to find how to distribute power more justly and to recognize those who have been disenfranchised in the past. Each is trying to learn how to balance modernist and traditional theological articulations. Each is living with an internal civil war between "liberals" and "conservatives" with the terms defined in terms of the American political agenda more than theological positions.[6]

In terms of basic belief and practice, the differences among the denominations are more and more negligible. In terms of what the denominations are trying to do, the differences are even more negligible.[7]

What's left to be different about, except aesthetics and memory? Canadian, Reginald Bibby suggests that our denominations may become more like families or clans, places where we can celebrate common history and tradition, communities in which we can express our special kinship with one another and even do those things we have done peculiarly over the generations, such as Anglican chant and Presbyterian psalmody, Baptist gospel songs and Methodist "fellowships." We may come less and less to need our denominations as bastions from which we defend ultimate principles from the satanic forces of the "others."

Compared to where denominational differences were just a half century ago, we already are "like family." Protestant pastors in training read

Catholic theologians, and Catholics return the compliment. None of that would have occurred fifty years ago.

The structures that separate us denominationally do not yet reflect the lowering of boundaries that has already happened. In the next generation we need to find ways to increase our communication across those boundaries. This is one area in which deregulation is long overdue. It might have happened already if those with the greatest stake in the status quo–the clergy–were not the primary speakers in the ecumenical dialogues between denominations.

INTERFAITH STRUCTURES?

The boundaries between denominations are nothing compared to the boundaries between Christian churches and other faith groups. I believe those interfaith boundaries also need to be redrawn in the next generation.

Relationships between Christian churches and other faiths were set in stone in a period I have called the Age of Christendom.[8] That age assumed that history was moving toward a consummation in which all humanity would be united in the church; all the other faiths would wither away. Even in the earliest times, Paul struggled with this assumption when others asked him "What of the Jews who have not accepted Christ?" Paul's stumbling answer indicated his quandary. He did believe that all were called to become part of the church, but he also recognized the empirical fact that many Jews chose to continue a faith-life within their own tradition. Paul never solved the issue, nor did successive generations of Christians. At the time of the Enlightenment, the Christendom assumption that all would eventually come into the church came to be linked with Western European political economic power. The result was the integration of cultural, political, and religious triumphalism into what we called imperialism. The militaristic hymns of the late nineteenth century cast interfaith relations as warfare, with the power of God leading the church's armies against the heathen.

We are heirs to an understanding of the church that is filled with all kinds of cultural imperialism. Even though the world view of Christendom no longer holds sway, its relics remain in our thinking. Emotionally we believe in and sing about a triumph of the church over all the "lesser" faiths. Many of us do not want those militaristic hymns removed from our hymnbooks–because they are familiar, because they were taught to us when we were young. But we also sing them because they reflect the only relationship between Christianity and other faiths that our parents knew. It represented an honored—if flawed—world view. Those hymns expressed a fairly universal consensus of the churches that all other faiths were in retreat before the conquering hosts of the church, and that we would see the end of those faiths, probably in the "Christian century."

Many of us brought up on the militant hymns and a nineteenth-century model of mission simply compartmentalized our brains. With one part of our consciousness we hold on to the mission schema we learned years ago; with another part we register the fact that reality certainly has changed! Americans do not see the Moslem world fading away in the face of a triumphant church; they see a vigorous, diverse community of Moslem faith expanding in Africa and Asia and claiming more adherents in the United States than Presbyterians or Episcopalians! We see strong movements within other world religions that do not wither away as we, in our pride, might have thought they would. Americans are getting accustomed to seeing new religious buildings, e.g., mosques and Hindu temples, as they travel around the country.

In "Christendom" the relationship of Christians to those of other faiths was clear. "Convert them or kill them." Not many people I know today are content with that model. It may be analogous to how sixteenth-century Lutherans felt about Catholics or seventeenth-century Presbyterians felt about Anglicans. In the denominations we no longer act on or even believe the hostility we once felt. Is it possible for Christians to move beyond nineteenth-century models of relationship to other faiths?

How can we discover a new way that affirms living alongside people of other faiths?

I believe there is room for hope in the way Christians and Jews have made the first, fateful steps toward mutual engagement. Perhaps triggered by the trauma of the Holocaust, Christians—not all of them, to be sure—have begun to reach toward a new and creative relationship with our Jewish cousins in faith. Christians have come to recognize how they have contributed to anti-Semitic thinking and actions. They have discovered deeply hurtful elements in their thinking and scriptures that have to be identified and confessed before new relationships can be built. But pioneers have been working on this boundary for several decades now. Today you can find rabbis and pastors meeting weekly to study the scriptures for mutual enlightenment.[9] Laity of the two faiths are beginning to gather together for Bible study.

Participants in the interfaith conversations, the study groups, and the formal conferences affirm new learnings and new depths of understanding of their own faith family. The conversations that seemed risky by an old understanding of our mission have proven to be spiritually enriching to both families of faith.

The challenge of finding new structures for the future includes finding structures that build new nonimperialistic relationships with the resurgent world religions. As churches we must put behind us a model of mission that has strong emotional ties to our past—a model of mission built in and nurtured by the Age of Christendom, which is no more. The church of the future is called to stand beside and with other world faiths, not over them. That will not come easy for us because we have identified so much of who and what we are with a triumphal stance in society, a stance that could be understood in the terms of the Age of Christendom, but which makes no sense in the age that is emerging.

In the past we understood our role in the world to be "ruler." Can we embrace a role in which we stand in solidarity with those of other faiths? Can we understand our own faith to be large enough and secure enough not to have to lord it over others?

CONCLUSION

Building new structures is the second challenge to the future.

The challenge for new structures touches the commonplace: how we put our organizations together in new ways, how we find ways to finance those structures. Our challenge is to rethink how we engage one another within the denominational structures we have now and how we adapt those structures.

At a deeper level, as we consider our life with those of other faiths, we realize that we are being called not just to tinker with structures, but to dig into the heart of what we have called "mission" and to find new reality for that old word, perhaps letting go of our favorite things.

Our ability to open ourselves to this conversation with God and to trust God's leading will be a measure of our willingness to take on the role of pioneer for the church of the future. Please remember. Many pioneers get lost. But if they do not go out in front and blaze trails, other people will not find their way.

This is the second challenge I am laying before us: finding new structures to carry our faith.

NOTES

1. Loren Mead, *The Once and Future Church* (Bethesda, MD: The Alban Institute, 1991).

2. Loren Mead, *Transforming Congregations for the Future* (Bethesda, MD: The Alban Institute, 1994).

3. I am personally aware of many regional judicatories that sponsor "resource centers" to help congregations get better access to educational and program resources. Very few of these are much more than a gloomy closet in an office building, containing poorly catalogued educational materials stuffed onto poorly lit shelves. This continuation of duplicative, inadequate denominational effort comes in spite of a few brilliant examples of resource centers that specialize in delivering help. I think especially of the group of Parish Resource Centers created by Douglas Whiting in Lancaster, Pennsylvania, and now including similar centers on Long Island, in Dayton, Denver, and South Bend. Judicatories also wastefully duplicate the use of outside resources. At the Alban Institute we often found that three different consultants had been contracted to lead an educational event, such as conflict management, within a fifty-mile radius in a period of two months. Waste!

4. See Mead, *Transforming Congregations for the Future*, ch. 4.

5. I am aware of the work, now well over a decade old, being done in Nevada by Episcopalians. Other pioneering has begun in the Episcopal Diocese of Northern Michigan.

6. See Robert Wuthnow, *The Restructuring of American Religion* (Princeton, NJ: Princeton University Press, 1988). In this fine book, Wuthnow makes a case that the political conservatives of many denominations and the political liberals of those same denominations may be moving toward functional coalitions despite the denominational differences.

7. Those *do* remain substantial differences, one invisible, the other visible. The *visible* difference is between those who view the scriptures as inerrant and understand faith by "fundamentals" and those who do not. The invisible difference is the cultural difference between premillennialists and postmillennialists. What I am talking about as the diminished difference between the denominations is especially true of the "mainline" denominations, but not restricted to them.

8. See Mead, *The Once and Future Church*.

9. This illustration comes from work of the Institute for Christian and Jewish Studies, a remarkable coalition in Baltimore. In Washington, DC, the Interfaith Council annually hosts an interfaith celebration in a great concert of music from seven faiths.

CHAPTER 3

CHALLENGE 3:
To Discover a Passionate Spirituality

I expect that most readers of this book will find the title of this chapter startling, if not offensive. There is a story behind it. I genuinely believe that the churches must discover a passionate, even charismatic, spirituality. Stay with me as I tell my story.

CONNECTING KNOWLEDGE OF GOD WITH EXPERIENCE OF GOD

I grew up in a wonderful parish, although in later years I could recognize its faults. The congregation sustained me and many others. The life of the place taught many of its worshippers truths beyond what was actually said and done. That ability of a congregation to proclaim more than it consciously knows is a bedrock of my monomania for congregations.

In that parish I rarely came across the word or the idea of *spirituality*. It was assumed that any needed nourishment was provided in the ordered structures of worship and preaching. On Christmas and Easter that ordinary, ordered worship "ascended" to a heightened intensity. I lived with a "cool" spirituality. It had a depth and power that helped people through enormous trials and carried them through long hard journeys that tested them in every way. It was a spirituality that held them together in the face of tragedy and went with them into the valley of the shadow. It was a real spirituality. A real sense of firsthand communion with God. But it was a spirituality that nobody much talked about. What I learned about this kind of growing into God was surrounded by "oughts": how one ought to pray; how one cleanses oneself for communion with God. The way to God was a long, difficult road that I learned about. It was a road with many detours—on which I seemed to be most of the time. There was not a lot of joy associated with the walk.

My experience in theological seminary reinforced this view of spirituality. Knowing and being close to God was described and analyzed but rarely witnessed to or experienced. I got more detailed road maps and a clearer sense of the blocks we set up to spiritual growth. I learned several different approaches to spiritual growth—what steps to take and the characteristics of different ways. With all the description and analysis, however, I remember only one teacher who said to me—in a one-on-one conversation—"Let me tell you what I do." Even in seminary, spirituality—being connected with God—was similar to that which I had experienced in my parish. It was the "understood," the "assumed" piece that everyone knew to be at the heart of the religious enterprise but that nobody talked about directly, except in a lecture.

I think that would not have been enough for me without a parallel range of experiences that connected my head with my heart. I look back on a number of critical moments and turning points in my childhood and young adult years. They often occurred when least expected. Outwardly they were not very remarkable. I remember moments in the middle of the ordered Sunday worship of my parish when I was seized by something beyond myself. And other times when I was simply blown away with feelings I could not voice. I remember as a child discovering what absolution meant in the presence of a black Baptist woman who cleaned our house. I remember moments during evensong at church camp when the Voice I heard was not that of the campers and other counselors. I remember moments of quiet when I experienced "being-outside-myself" and in a greater Presence. I remember a time of great fear in which Someone gave me hopeful words from a psalm. I remember learning to pray as a young clergyman with two men who were each three times my age. (If my memory is selective, so be it—there were and are so many moments in which the Presence was present.)

Years later I found some colleagues who shared a fascination with the spiritual dimension of life. Three of them were intrigued by a research concept I floated by them in 1972—that we try to discover, on an empirical basis, what "spiritual growth" looked like.[1] Unbeknownst to us, Jean Haldane was pursuing a similar research project within a single parish. Our complementary projects involved one-on-one interviews, asking people to tell the story of their religious life. Both reports were published, with the Haldane document remaining in print for more than a decade.[2] What did we learn?

First, that everyone we talked to could describe powerful, personal experiences with God. The experiences were unique to the individual but all very real. Some of them had occurred in a "religious" setting, but most had not. Many had been life-changing events. Second, we learned that none of the people who told us of these experiences had ever been asked to tell his or her story to his or her congregation or pastor, and none had ever thought of bringing it up. It was as if the churches and parishioners had an implicit understanding that experiences did not matter in the church or to the church. It felt to us like a collusion of silence.

We researchers found it strange to discover such a gulf between people's experience of God and the congregational structures—even though the congregations had given the people words to explain those experiences, the images with which to recognize whom they had met, and even opened them to receive the experience. They used images they had learned in church to describe their experiences to us. Yet at the same time, knowledge of God and experience with God had somehow become completely different realities for these people. There seemed to be two worlds—the world in which one relates to God formally and another in which one is personally touched by the Spirit of God in the midst of ordinary life.

The Holy Spirit has always represented something unruly to the people of the church. People who love God and love the church are always discovering that the Holy Spirit paints outside the lines we draw to order our church life.

For two thousand years the church has staunchly organized and structured itself. It has engaged in complex theological struggles to clarify what it meant about God and who Jesus was and how he related to God. But the Holy Spirit remains the unacknowledged guest at the feast, at least partly because things get unpredictable when the Spirit is around.

What I have described—both my personal experience and what we saw as the experience of those who told us their stories—is related to the discomfort of structured religion around the unpredictable power of the Spirit who comes and goes without regard to our plans.

HISTORICAL PERSPECTIVE

Throughout the history of the church the activity ascribed to the followers of the Spirit has caused contention and uncertainly. Writing of those who had the "gift of tongues," Paul gave such mixed signals that we suspect he would have been happier if he hadn't had to deal with them.[3] Paul clearly recognized the gift of tongues as a gift of the Spirit, and even though he claimed the gift himself, it seems he didn't particularly like it. He implied that almost anything else would have been better.

Rational plans and organizational structures always conflict with spontaneity. Where the Spirit comes and goes, spontaneity is to be expected. Organization wonks need to have things clear and orderly. Where the Spirit appear, the lines of demarcation get broken down; what is so carefully defined and structured seems to be a way for us to attempt to limit or control the urgent purposes of God.

Harvey Cox brings this age-old dilemma of the church into the twentieth century, describing the explosive impact of the contemporary charismatic movement across the globe.[4] He claims that Pentecostalism may be the one religious phenomenon that touches more Christians today than any other.

In the early years of this century a small church in Los Angeles became the location for the beginnings of what Pentecostals view as a new pouring out of the Spirit upon the world in our time.[5] This Azusa Street Revival quickly affected and challenged the ordered denominational systems of America and soon ignited a great global spiritual explosion.

At Azusa Street, and elsewhere as the movement spread to many parts of the country and overseas, men and women seemed able and willing to set aside conventional social barriers; black and white, male and female, young and old found common cause in the enthusiasm of their new-found exuberant faith—with the ancient practice of speaking in tongues as a common bonding experience. People danced and sang and praised God. The primary manifestations of the Spirit were explosive expressions of ecstasy, worship that did not fit the patterns of rational liturgies, healings, and singing and dancing—anything but the familiar, staid decorum most Christians knew to be the "correct ways" to address God.

This occurred at the very moment in history when Americans were moving toward more separations: Jim Crow laws were expanding; the distance between the sexes was widening. But in Los Angeles a whole new experience was born. As it spread across the country, it shattered the barriers polite society was trying to erect. No wonder it seemed revolutionary.

It was too much. The denominations and churches drew back from this vitality. Some who tried to bring the Azusa Street Revival into their denominations were not welcomed there. The Pentecostal denominations grew, sometimes splintering among themselves, finding it difficult to overcome society's divisiveness even among themselves. Mainliners scoffingly spoke of them as "holy rollers" and joked about their passionate expressions of faith.

Late in the sixties a new, somewhat sanitized version of charismatic renewal occurred within the mainline denominations. First reported in an Episcopal parish led by Dennis Bennett, this movement has spread into many of the denominations that rejected the Azusa Street experience. The second movement has been somewhat similar to the first, with considerable suspicion from "regular" churchgoers of these "far-out" people. The earlier denominational "blanket rejection" of the charismatic has not occurred, but I fear there lurks in both camps—charismatic and traditional—a hope that each could get rid of the other. Each seems to feel that the other is not only different, but wrong in some fundamental way.

I propose that the third challenge the churches must meet to build a church for the future is to find ways to bring this charismatic expression of spirituality into the heart of the Christian experience and bind it fully into the very structures and systems of the religious world of the churches. This will not be easy. Both "parties" seem to generate an allergic reaction in the other. Each acts as if the other is an essential threat.

INTEGRATING THE GIFTS

Contrary to the behavior of the traditional mainliners and traditional charismatics, the challenge is not for one group to eliminate the other, but that the gifts of the ordered, structured approach to faith may be integrated into the vital, enthusiastic, Spirit-filled approach. The challenge is to move beyond the war between religious sensibilities and experiences to discover a new expression of faith that incorporates the gifts of both traditions.

Clearly there is tension between these forms of spirituality. Here I delineate their differences in list form, even though to do so oversimplifies reality and probably does injustice to both:

Traditional Spirituality	Charismatic Spirituality
Form is central	Experience is central
Structure is important. There are steps, procedures, practices to follow	Life is shaped by the free-flowing, free-moving Spirit; structures get in the way
Rational; subject to analytical thought	Emotional; analysis is irrelevant
Disciplined, ordered, patterned	Spontaneous, surprising
Measured, rhythmic (Mozart)	Profligate, multipatterned (jazz)
Self-effacing	Self-affirming
Can be diagrammed	Free-form, finger-painting
Unobtrusive	Overwhelming, obtrusive
Deep, often intense, quiet, private	Explosive, shattering, erupting, communal
Tenacious, steady	Unpredictable, mercurial
Frequently silent	Frequently loud, even raucous
Slowly and deeply burning (like long-lived underground fire in a volcano)	Explosive (like a pipe bomb)

These are more than lists of differences. Think of the people or groups you have known who express the best of each.

Followers of traditional spirituality have been people of great influence in my life. I think of people whose daily practice of disciplines of prayer sometimes seemed artificial to me but never to them. People who attended the mass daily before going to work. I find I am moved by essays and meditations that have grown out of weeks and months of thought and study, papers that witness to slow, steady growth in depth and meaning. I am entranced by the careful, sometimes laborious statements of great theologians about the nature of God and humanity. I am enlightened by the scrupulous work of anthropologists and scholars who by painstaking analysis of bits and pieces of ancient cultures bring new insight to my reading of the scriptures. I am moved often by the careful liturgical planning and organization that lies behind a great occasion of worship or celebration. Some are great moments of inspiration, built upon long, sometimes dry periods of reflections and study. I am excited by the language gift of those who can take an old truth and turn it inside out—finding a new way to say it. I am grateful for the hands and knowledge of those who fix broken bones and cut out diseased tissue. I enjoy the laborious work of the poet or hymnwriter whose art nourishes me in reading and worship.

The best of the charismatic spirituality is equally life giving. There is a "now-ness" to their perception of the presence of God that we traditionalists do not know well. I welcome the simple openness of the charismatic to what God is and can do. What a power of expectation is evident in hands uplifted in prayer and verbal affirmation in worship. I am grateful for the wonderful charismatic woman who taught me from her death-bed that one does not have to get well to be healed. I remember moments that were great and dramatic because someone seized an opportunity no one else recognized, sensed the need of a situation, sensed the call and power of God , and acted on faith, not on a predetermined plan, not knowing for sure what the outcome would be.[6] As a "traditional" Anglican deeply imbued with the power of the Eucharist, I have felt the new power released in the sacrament when the gift of tongues was breathed over a large group as they sang after Communion, I have seen lives transformed by God in places where I did not expect it to happen. I have seen barriers broken down—separates brought together—when it seemed impossible.

A church that does not find a way to include the liveliness of both of these ways of spirituality is likely to miss something that God has in store for us all. I venture further to say that neither side can be truly healthy without the other in counterpoint. Each side deteriorates if left to itself. The health of the one is dependent upon the health of the other. I think that we see that as we look at what is happening in the churches today.

When the traditional way of spirituality decays it become a stuffy, dry, lifeless formality. Many members of the traditional churches have lived in such a straitjacket of their tradition that they have never found the power available in that very tradition—consequently their lives quietly go rigid and dry. Outsiders looking to the church as a place to know God and be known by God see a spiritual desert, where people go through the motions of religion. Many members hold on and carry on, knowing they have had and hoping they may again have some of the experiences of grace that mark traditional spirituality at its best. And many others drift away, having given up hope. The younger generation, unwilling to pack its emotions in dry ice, simply opts for other venues in which to find vitality.

When charismatic spirituality decays, it goes in another direction. As in the case of traditional spirituality, it becomes a parody of its strengths. Charismatic spirituality at its worst degenerates into spiritual pride. It "puts down" any other experience of God as counterfeit. This characteristic of decayed charismatic spirituality often makes for severe conflict within congregations. This spirituality can also become uncritically supportive of any strong, assertive voice and can make peace with dictatorial leaders. It can deify the patterns of the past, both social and religious, forgetting the central promise that the Spirit will lead us into new truth. It sometimes moves beyond emotional vitality to an irrationality and a suspicion that are close to paranoia. The wholehearted dependence on God that characterizes the best of the charismatic life sometimes is unable to recognize gifts from God that do not fit what these believers expect God's gifts to be. They are not willing to admit that God paints outside the lines they recognize.

Two parallel lists, then, delineate two kinds of spirituality. Each can decay into something much less creative.

Our usual way of managing such differences is to see them as opposites and to treat them as a conflict of values or lifestyle, attempting to find out which is "better" and eliminating the other. We assume an either/or stance.

But both of these types of spirituality are essential to us. The machinery of the mainline denominations has been in the hands of the traditionalists for centuries with the result that the charismatic has been relegated to the fringe. To face the future, the church must find ways to bring the gifts of charismatic spirituality to the heart of the church life without denying the gifts and contributions of traditional spirituality. My hunch is that the presence of both, living in tension but not in opposition, will increase the vitality of both kinds of spirituality. Can we do that? Can we learn not only to tolerate each other (that's hard enough for many of us), but also to affirm and even sometimes love each other?

A colleague, Barry Johnson, has proposed a new way of looking at what we perceive to be opposites, a new way of bringing opposites into conversation with each other. In his challenging book *Polarity Management*, Johnson suggests that many differences are not true matters of conflict, where one must be eliminated for the other to survive.[7] He suggests a new "polarity" or "polar opposites," to describe a pair of differing realities that are both necessary. Like inhaling and exhaling, each is different from the other but both are essential to health.

I suggest that traditional and charismatic spirituality are polar opposites, and that the health of the body depends on our finding a creative way for them to coexist within the churches.

Johnson describes the way polar opposites need each other to maintain health. When traditional spirituality and charismatic spirituality are healthy and producing fruit in the lives of people, churches, and society, there is no problem. Neither will need to be negative about or defensive toward the other. Neither approach will be imperialistic, seeking to overthrow or undercut the integrity of the other.

The problem arises when either form of spirituality begins to decay. When the traditional decays into the dry, lifeless spiritual void, it grows more vulnerable and defensive; that's when it is most likely to fear or make enemies of those who approach spirituality in a different way. Similarly, when the charismatic approach decays into irrationality and sheer energy, it grows imperialistic, proud, and least able to live with anyone who has a different expression. Either spirituality under threat or sensing its own decay becomes defensive and least open to proponents of the other.

Johnson notes that as each pole degenerates into its lesser form, it grows more convinced that the only way "out" is to commit itself to its tradition and to try harder to make it work. The traditional form of spirituality, when it decays, assumes that the way to health is to reinforce traditional forms, patterns, and disciplines that once made sense and worked; when the formal structure stops providing sustenance, the best course is to try twice as much formal structure, spend more time in the forms that used to make sense. Johnson observes that it never works. Such thinking drives the decayed truth deeper and deeper into decay and even into depression.

The same is true for the charismatic side of the polarity. The more it goes into decay, the more its worst characteristics come to the fore, and the more the unspoken command is given: Do it more; do it better. Again, it does not work. The decay goes on and "life" moves further and further away. The charismatic version of depression seems to be guilt.

Johnson's very helpful insight is that the way out of the decay of one polar reality is to be found only in the opposite pole. For example, as the traditional spirituality decays, it cannot be healed by working harder at the traditional way; it only digs itself deeper into its hole. Hope lies in seeking the positive gifts of charismatic spirituality, opening itself to experiencing the strengthening presence of the Spirit. Similarly, the decayed charismatic spirituality is not likely to find renewal simply in repeating the experiences that once gave life, but in seeking the gifts of the ordered, patterned, structured ways of spiritual development so familiar in the traditional forms.

Johnson's theory suggests a surprising prescription for someone for whom the traditional has become pedantic, dry, and routine: Seek out the totally different experience of charismatic spirituality. Immerse oneself there for a while and discover renewed vitality in the old forms. Similarly, for the charismatic beginning to feel guilty because that spirituality is not "working" very well: Take a silent retreat or meditate on the stations of the cross. In either case, the new experience can renew the vitality of one's spiritual path to God.

In Johnson's theories and research, I hear an affirmation of the debate in Paul about the nature of law and grace. Somehow the law holds us in bondage tighter and tighter, always making us think that the only way out is to try harder and harder to do what the law requires. The universal human experience is that this is a dead-end route. One either gives up in despair or cuts the law down to a manageable size. On their own, both forms of spirituality convince us that the only way is to go deeper in the way that has led us to despair.

Paul points to the fact that the answer is not to be found in the law, but in the reception of grace from outside. So those who have found life in either traditional or charismatic spirituality but have continued on to emptiness need to give up the hard-nosed attempt to overcome their emptiness by force of will. They need to allow another path to lead them back to health and wholeness.

Johnson describes a continuing oscillation between poles as the path of health. The Johnson theories give a framework for my proposal that the church is challenged to develop a larger spirituality than it has. As one whose home is in the traditional churches and forms of spirituality, I see an urgent need for those churches to open themselves to the charismatic dimension that they have kept at arms' length for two thousand years. For many in those families of churches, the aridity of the experience of religion is palpable. Those churches, while still mediating life to many in their pews, have generally ceased to be able to communicate to outsiders that they are repositories of living water.

It may be that the other need is as urgent: for those with the charismatic identity and experience to renew their connections to the traditional systems and structures of religious life. As one whose life has not been primarily in that community, I cannot judge its inner reality. But I see signs of what seem to an outsider to be a pride and narcissism that may represent a decay in portions of the charismatic community.

The long-term issue, regardless of who needs most at the moment, is whether or not we can build a sense of spiritual growth that embraces a wider spectrum of styles and methods, of experiences and structures. Because we cannot begin to imagine the challenges that will face those who will live in the twenty-first century, the spirituality we have—traditional or charismatic—will not suffice.[8] Perhaps those two great languages together can communicate living water in the deserts of the future.

NOTES

1. Parker Palmer, Tilden Edwards, and James Simmons—all later better known for teaching and writing. Tilden is the founder of the Shalem Institute for Spiritual Formation in Washington, DC.

2. Jean Haldane, *Religious Pilgrimages* (Bethesda, MD: The Alban Institute, 1975).

3. Paul clearly recognizes the practice of *glossalia* as fairly widespread in the early church. In contrast to a literal reading of Acts 2, in which speaking in tongues is taken to mean speaking in the languages of different nationalities, glossalia is ecstatic utterance, often within worship.

4. Harvey Cox, *Fire from Heaven* (Reading, MA: Addison-Wesley, 1995). A fascinating and sweeping story of Pentecostalism and the charismatic movement in the twentieth century.

5. There is some cultural chauvinism in this remark. Since beginning this chapter, I have become aware of strong "charismatic" outbreaks in many other parts of the world in this and earlier centuries.

6. I do not say this very clearly because it is too close for comfort. Being aware of a pressure from Someone beyond myself, I have found myself called to do something that breaks all the rules. Such impulses are not always from the Spirit, I ruefully note, but there have been moments when my impulse was from the Spirit and lives changed as a result. For *me*, those moments have tended to be in situations of community, often in worship.

7. Barry Johnson, *Polarity Management: Identifying and Managing Unsolvable Problems* (Amherst, MA: HRD Press, 1992).

8. Corrine Ware, *Discover Your Spiritual Type* (Bethesda, MD: The Alban Institute, 1995), has provided us with a new framework for understanding spirituality in a wholistic way. She gives a model for understanding the relationship of different kinds of spirituality, and she also provides tools for people and congregations wanting to explore the full dimensions of spirituality. I am particularly grateful to her for building on the idea of the late U. T. Holmes, Jr., whose tragic loss in 1981 still hurts.

See also Donald Hands and Wayne Fehr, *Spiritual Wholeness for Clergy* (Bethesda, MD: The Alban Institute, 1993). They explore a wholistic approach to spirituality, starting with clinical studies of clergy who had burned out spiritually. The learnings of this study of clergy spirituality have much to teach about building healthier, more comprehensive models of spirituality.

CHALLENGE 4:
To Feed the World's Need for Community

WHAT AND WHERE IS COMMUNITY?

It was the summer of 1964. For ten months my family and I had been in England where I was an exchange pastor in a parish near London. We had enjoyed a warmth of hospitality that I have rarely experienced. I had attended family celebrations, and I had mourned with parishioners in their losses. When "our" president, John Kennedy, was assassinated, the entire village mourned with us, and many dropped by the house to bring flowers. We had worshipped together, and yes, we had pushed each other's understandings in many areas, not least of which was faith itself.

It had been a good year, but I was never able to let go of the sense of "home" I felt among the people of my family in South Carolina and my church family in North Carolina. High points of the year had been opening packages: My mother had air-mailed two pounds of grits to help us face the cold mornings of November. And my back-home choir had sent a tape of Christmas music that included a folk-song carol I particularly loved, "Jesus, Jesus, Rest Your Head," arranged by John Jacob Niles.

It was August. I was at a "pops" concert at Albert Hall in London, and I found myself sitting in that public place with tears streaming down my face. The music was a folk tune I knew from back home—the tune to the song "Going Home" (and the largo movement of Dvorak's "Fifth Symphony in E Minor").

The yearning for "going home" is deep and universal. It is a feeling that is larger than the geography of home, often deeper than our actual relationships with anyone there. Even those who have experienced "home" as a very dysfunctional place or community yearn for what the word points to.

The tug to find or return "home" triggers a hope for a network of memory and relationship, sometimes romanticized with time. That network is what the word *community* reaches for. For most of us, those memories of home—its places and people, its notion of "the way things were" and the values that lay beneath that world—remain the mental image of what community is about.

We need to belong—to be part of a larger world. The need to belong drives us to community, a place where we know we belong. It is also a place where we will be safe—a kind of "home base" in the world's chaotic game of "tag." It is a place where you are valued for what you are in yourself, but also a place that often sees more in you than you see in yourself. All of this is wrapped up in the word *community*, and all of it is a mix of people and places, memories and values.

This chapter is about community and our continuing search for it. I base this discussion on three assumptions: (1) that in this society one has fewer and fewer opportunities to find community, (2) that congregations in the past have been important sources of community, and (3) that a major challenge to congregations everywhere is to feed the world's need for community of meaning and relationship. I present this challenge as the fourth we need to address if our congregations are to be as creative in the world of the future as they have been in the past.

"Where is the community I knew as a child?" What a tiresome refrain that has become. Politicians use it to plug their programs; advertisers use it to flog their merchandise. I am suspicious of the nostalgia that circles like a vulture around the concept. I remember the times I grew up in, and I know now how many injustices were a part of that world. My nostalgia blots out things I'd rather not remember—such as living on the "right" or "wrong" side of the tracks, the systemic devaluation of women and girls, the inability to cope with ethnic diversity, the economy that favored me at the expense of many others, the racial phobias we breathed.

Right from the start we need to remind ourselves of the mixed character of our memory and the ambiguous images to which it may lead us.

But John Gardner gives reasons why "community" is a bedrock of society:

> Families and communities are the ground-level generators and preservers of values and ethical systems. No society can remain vital or even survive without a reasonable base of shared values—and

such values are not established by edict from the lofty levels of the society. They are generated chiefly in the family, school, and other intimate settings in which people deal with one another face to face. The ideals of justice and compassion are nurtured in communities.

Where community exists it confers upon its members identity, a sense of belonging, a measure of security. Individuals acquire a sense of self partly from the continuous relationships to others, and from the culture of their native place....

A community has the power to motivate its members to exceptional performance. It can set standards of expectation for the individual and provide the climate in which great things happen.[1]

John Gardner's contention, and mine, is that whatever faults that traditional form of community had, as a "web of interdependency and mutual obligation" it was a powerful influence in our society. It had a central generative force in shaping our personal lives and our sense of self-esteem; it had impact upon our understanding of the role of families; it influenced the values we sought to live by and shaped many of the structures in which we live.

There may be no consensus on exactly what *community* means. My use of the "going home" image indicates how each of us in our different experiences of home has a deep but unique perspective on what community means. Each of us has had experiences in which that "web of interdependence" was truly there for us—perhaps in our families of origin, in a sports team or a school group in which we felt alive and connected. For some of us it may have been a situation in which we, with others, experienced pressure, opposition, challenge, or even persecution; for others it may have been moments of group engagement in a task. The experiences of the web of community may have been the pain of exclusion from another community—looking over the wall, as it were, to a joy that was denied us.

Many of us have found powerful experiences of genuine community in our congregations, or in some group associated with our churches. Tragically, many of us have also been in congregations in which we had to look over the walls of exclusion to see community that others experienced but to which we were outsiders.

Wherever we have found it, community leaves its mark upon us. Evidence is accumulating that people deprived of a sense of community in early years carry deprivation through life. Evidence also indicates that where the framework of nurturing community has been violated and become abusive, victims often perpetuate similarly abusive relationships in future generations.

Community is much more than something for which we have nostalgia. It is clear that it is a matter of life and death. Because it is so important, we have tended to seek community in many places in recent history. And in most places where we used to find it, it seems in increasingly short supply. That may be why we feel so nostalgic about it!

LOSSES OF COMMUNITY

The Idea of Neighborhood

Right after World War II a national obsession with finding a community fueled middle-class America's migration to the suburbs.[2] The move to the suburbs—to the expanding Levittowns of America—was a search not only for a house and a plot of ground, but also for the myth of a close—knit human community, a place where one could belong. What these seekers found rarely matched their romantic image of community. They found that houses in suburbia can feel as isolating as apartments in a city; suburban people were busy and hard to get to know beyond superficiality. They found that communication with neighbors was impeded by the roar of lawnmowers. They found charcoal smoke and commuter traffic but not always a sense of community.

Today neighborhoods continue to be thought of as sources of community, but fewer and fewer actually deliver the goods in the city or in the suburb. *Neighbor* is often the new word for *stranger*.

Today's migrations take several forms. From the suburbs many are moving to the bucolic outlands of exurbia or small towns, any place on the current list of the "fifty best places to live." But there they are rapidly re-creating what they don't like about suburbia. Many nonwhite middle-class populations are repeating the white suburban migration of the fifties and sixties, with about as much hope in discovering community. (Their churches are moving from inner cities to the suburbs, following the example of mainline denominations. Those that have stayed in the inner city provide genuine hope for community,[3] but they need to pay attention to the problem mainline churches have had, preserving the vitality of their church communities when many members move to suburbia.) Then some of the migration has reversed itself back to the city, where it is hoped that new structures of community can be built. The operative work is *hope*.

Recent migrants to the more affluent suburbs live in isolation from one another within developments walled off from the outside world and protected by armed guards. These wealthy ghettos may well be safer than the urban ghetto, but the jury is out as to whether they actually provide the life-giving qualities that result in a deep sense of grounding and belonging. Does community really live there?

Finding a sense of life-giving community in one's neighborhood has proven to be a search for a will-o'-the-wisp as the twentieth century moves into the twenty-first.

The Idea of Community in the Work Place

Within American society, many others have traditionally found their basic community in the work place. For generations many corporations and businesses nurtured the sense of the work place as more than just a place to make a living. Such businesses genuinely fostered loyalty; mutual caring coexisted with annual profit. At times worker loyalty to the company led both worker and company to make significant sacrifices for that relationship.

No more. *The Downsizing of America* is the title of a recent book, but it is also an apt description of an experience many employees are discovering in the companies for which they work and to which they have had life-long loyalties.[4] People used to laugh about the meaning of IBM, saying it meant "I've Been Moved." But in some sense it was proud laughter—proud of the commitment of the company to its employees, a company that was willing to invest in them, willing to strengthen their careers and the company at the same time. There is not much laughter at IBM since the massive layoffs of the eighties and nineties. *The Downsizing of America* points to town after town, company after company where the workers are experiencing downsizing as a shocking betrayal—all the more shocking because of their assumptions about the company as a place of community. They thought they belonged!

Particularly poignant are stories of families that have committed themselves for several generations to an employer considered to be almost "family"–at least until the downsizing started. One such story about AT&T ends: "The corporation of my parents did, after all, pay for my education and help me become a successful adult. At times, I wish I could stay in the secure arms of Ma Bell, but she no longer exists."[5]

Discussing this corporate phenomenon, *The Downsizing of America* points to the erosion of a sense of community that goes beyond the individual to the fabric of the town itself. The sense of community in the town erodes as its taxpayers and volunteers have their lives and incomes disrupted. It is increasingly difficult to find community in the work place.

Many who did not find community with their employers came to rely upon labor unions as a rich and real community. The refrain of the old labor song "Solidarity Forever" says, "We shall not be, we shall not be moved!" What a statement of community commitment to one another.

But from their strong central role in the work life of large parts of the population in the thirties, forties, and fifties, labor unions have declined sharply in number and in influence. Part of this is no doubt due to the changing face of the American economy, shifting as it has from manufacturing to the service sector (in which labor can sometimes be more easily exploited, but in which workers do not seem as ready to join unions). Fewer and fewer people turn to unions and their union halls as sources of community.

The Idea of Group Activities

Other realms of living express losses of community. Many activities that formerly gathered enthusiastic groups of people who knew one another and acted together for the fun of it have become professionalized and distanced from ordinary citizens. Sports, music, theater, and the arts were once home-made activities engaging the creativity of all sorts of people. There was spontaneous group singing around a piano, guitar, or accordion. There were high school teams and pick-up sand-lot games. Perhaps the only remainder of this from the past is the urban neighborhood basketball scrimmages today. Almost all have become spectator activities.

Even though spectator sports are once-removed from personal participation, they still build a kind of community such as that known by the die-hard Red Sox fans.[6] But even this residue of community seems to be ending. The New York Times describes the phenomenon in a headline: "Owners' New Strategy: Take the Team and Run."[7] Fans, for whom the team has become an icon of their city and a focus of their sense of community, are forced to go to court to try to keep owners from chasing dollars to another town.

This sense of a loss of community seems to be pervasive. The theme and image of a Harvard professor's January 1995 essay titled "Bowling Alone: America's Declining Social Capital"[8] was picked up by countless columnists, speechmakers, and preachers as a cogent statement of the American predicament. Robert Putnam's image was a simple one: that America had until recently been a nation of bowling leagues, where thousands regularly gathered with teammates in bowling alleys to take on another team in an evening of beer and pretzels, pizza and laughter. Putnam's research had led him to an unsettling discovery—"more Americans are bowling today than ever before, but bowling in organized leagues has plummeted in the last decade or so."[9] People, Putnam suggested, are taking a communal activity and making it a profoundly private experience. People, he concluded, are bowling alone.

The dramatic simplicity of Putnam's point probably was what led to the quick spread of his idea, which appeared even in President Clinton's speeches. The truth is much more complex, of course, than the sound byte "bowling alone." Putnam put his argument in a context of many other phenomena of society in which there are increased personal commitments to group concerns.[10] And yet the overall impression that emerges from his analysis is that in spite of some positive movements toward community (environmental groups, for example) there is trouble in River City in terms of community values. William Raspberry, the distinguished columnist of the Washington Post, succinctly calls it "our crisis of community."[11]

More than a decade ago, Robert Bellah and his colleagues[12] documented what they saw to be a shifting of ground in American society away from commitment and community to a more raw individualism and an individual pursuit of happiness. Although their analysis was a limited sector of the public, the book became a bestseller among a wide group of people who seemed to have identified Bellah's thesis as something they recognized in their world.

Bellah's hope is for "social transformation," a theme consistent with John Gardner's passion for the rebirth of community within society. There is little specific direction for those who seek to build community for the future. The problem may lie deeper than these analyses, in the very way we have structured our social relations.[13]

Again, my thesis in this chapter is that the church of the future must become a center within society that feeds and supports the human need for community. The challenge is made more important because of the increasing experience of deprivation of community. The challenge is made more difficult because of the church's loss of credibility as a source of community in our time.

THE CHURCH: ITS ROLE, PAST AND PRESENT

Historically Americans have looked to our churches for community. Realizing the erosion of a sense of community in modern congregations, one reads almost with astonishment of the powerful community in congregations of just a few generations ago. Extraordinary immigrant congregations supported people from "the old country" while they were finding their bearings in a strange continent. Even today new generations of immigrants discover the life-giving power of faith-communities critical to their assimilation into the society. Powerful faith communities among slaves in the eighteenth and nineteenth centuries brought spiritual growth and personal strength in the midst of dehumanizing conditions. Congregations formed on the frontiers strengthened the generations that built a nation. Congregations in our cities challenged the powers that be, the builders of towns and industries. Congregations built colleges and universities and invented forms of social service to the poor and neglected. Congregations provided a support system for families, the locus in which most people found their most critical expression of community. Congregations were centers of education before public education was invented. While these religious communities were doing all that, they went about their more routine but perhaps more important functions–giving people a challenging place to belong, a place that stood by, witnessing to large purposes and a call to serve others. They generated people who built the structures of society.

More than that, and closer to home–I expect that any reader of this book has felt the power of community in a congregation. There are moments like the one described by Isaiah–when he saw God in the temple and discovered his life's vocation–moments when ordinary people find themselves powerfully moved by the Spirit to reevaluate their lives and families and vocations. (Such moments sometimes occur when the person sitting next to them in the pew is thinking, *What an ordinary Sunday service this is!*) Whole congregations have discovered themselves to be a people, a community, in biblical stories of the people of God. Many people have there heard a new call to themselves or to their world and have begun to respond to it. There are moments when a person's intense sense of lostness and isolation is broken through in ordinary things like making music with a choir. Or even hearing music being made by others. There are times when broken relationships are healed in congregations—God knows how! There are congregations—you and I could name some of them—where, among quite ordinary folk, some are inspired to become quite extraordinary, to see the thing that needs doing, the word that needs saying, the hurt that needs sharing. There are thousands of congregations—obsolete though the experts think them to be—where people simply find the strength to keep on keeping on. There are minds wandering through the innumerable words of a tired, retreaded sermon that are suddenly electrified by a phrase, a note, a hint in which the Word appears with conviction and power, frequently without the knowledge of the preacher. There are individual lives and ordinary families fed and sustained in acts of worship or of being together. This is the stuff of congregational life. The power of community is born again in us and around us.

That has always been one of the functions of congregations.

You see, most of the stories of life-changing community are distinctly anonymous; they occur without fanfare. Britton Johnston and Sally Johnson participated in a four-year effort by congregations in the Midwest that wanted to reach out beyond their parish bounds with their sense of community. The authors tell scores of stories, many of them of only a page or less, each describing the impact of these "nonheadline" moments in which community comes alive.[14]

The fact is, however, that congregations today are rarely seen as centers of genuine community. Catholic theologian John Linnan says very directly that congregations are obsolete as centers of human support and growth.[15] His comment reflects the feeling of many. The extraordinary power of community that congregations of the past have shown and that we have experienced from time to time is not very evident in our world. The congregations that "outsiders" see do not seem to express the presence of the kind of community that those people are hungry for.

For all too many, congregations appear to be self-satisfied conglomerations of like-minded people. Non-Christians often use the word *hypocritical* to describe what they see in congregations. A Midwest conference of the United Methodist Church did a courageous piece of work in focus groups asking nonchurched people to describe the public perception of the church.[16]

Almost no comments indicated an attraction to churches because of the sense of community found there. Instead people said: "I have yet to find a church where people want to be there because of shared values instead of just being cliquish and judgmental."

People of our time, whose common value is sometimes "what's in it for me?" have a hard time seeing congregations as the source of genuine community.

Reginald Bibby, a sociologist who has studied churches across Canada and their relationship to the public, documents the way people in Canada seem to be looking for the benefits—including a sense of community—that the church has traditionally tried to provide. He points out two things he learned: that people are not looking for the church and that the churches are not looking for people but focus instead on their institutional survival.[17] Hoge, Johnson, and Luidens make a similar point in their study of unchurched Presbyterians.[18]

People are finding less and less sense of community in their world; they seem to be looking for it, but one of the very institutions that has traditionally met the need for community (and still does for many) simply is not on the radar screen of many who really want community. People simply do not look to the churches for that which is supposed to be one of its great values.

That is why I see this as a major challenge for the church: (1) to discover how to be and to support authentic community and (2) to see that those hungry for community in our society can find it. Being such a community is itself a tremendous challenge, but the more daunting task is to change the perceptions of people who have come to think of the church's expression of community in terms of hypocrisy. Neither part of the dual challenge will be easy.

We must begin where we are. The church of tomorrow will evolve from the churches we have. The challenge to develop authentic community is a challenge to each congregation, building on whatever community is already in place.

We begin with enormous handicaps. Our society has lost many traditionally strong sources of community, giving rise to an isolating form of individualism. Congregations, one of the sources of community in previous generations, are themselves beset by the same demons that inhabit our society. Their own resources for "being community" even for members are severely eroded. And, more tragically, congregations have lost public credibility as potential sources of community.

Where do we begin?

I will first identify three modes for approaching both the tasks noted above (being community and helping people connect with it). Then I want to note some strategies by which we can move out from where we are.

THREE MODES OF BEING AND GENERATING COMMUNITY

Congregations as Community

Analysts of congregations rightly point out that different cultural situations have different needs and possibilities for being community. Urban, suburban, and rural settings all call for different kinds of congregational life that in itself provides the community people need.

In some rural situations congregations can still offer the kind of experience of community that embraces almost all of life. Work life, family life, public and private life—all are lived out in such a way that Sunday worship does reflect a unified world. There all the congregation's children go to the same schools and everyone goes to the same movies. There congregations can still be a focus in which the whole life of the whole neighborhood is celebrated and offered to God in the community of faith. Fewer and fewer of our rural communities reflect this almost romantic view of what rural communities may have been a century ago. Even in the most rural of areas today television brings fragmented values and the presence of a whole outside world that dissipates the sense of togetherness with one's neighbors. Consolidation of schools may mean that the community children are spread out in schools located in several counties.

A few urban congregations also have some of the feel of rural congregations—a sense of being an enclave in which the whole of life is shared. This is particularly true for ethnic groups, but it is also true for small congregations of Episcopalians or Presbyterians, Baptists or United Methodists who have maintained their historical presence in urban locations.

In many urban, metropolitan, and suburban congregations, the ability to be community as a single entity is severely circumscribed. Moments of community in great occasions of worship can be nurturing and dramatic. I have known great pastors who, by preaching and leading worship, bring the gift of community to incredibly diverse groups. Indeed, the great preachers of the nineteenth and early twentieth century built real community through preaching. Dr. George Docherty, retired pastor of New York Avenue Presbyterian Church in Washington, D.C., used the Sunday morning service announcement period to bring people into community with one another. Community can also be achieved as a group cooperates in great mission tasks or even–God help us–building projects! For the most part, however, urban congregations have to seek ways in which subsets of the whole congregation can find community and also ways in which the congregation can support the development of human community in larger society.

As our nation embraces diversity, congregations of people with the same background are likely to be essential "home bases" for people overwhelmed by strange language and cultural values. Such congregations retain a role they have played for centuries as new Americans have sought sometimes to integrate themselves into this new world, and at other times to maintain an identity. Our challenge will be to help those who depend on this sense of community move into the wider society. Will ethnic congregations remain as isolating islands radically separated from society, or will they become places of safety encouraging and facilitating engagement with the wider culture? Will the remnant congregations retain their identity until the last member dies? The churches themselves will need to struggle with this question: At what point–if ever–does a community of "apartness" begin to be at war with the community in Christ?

All congregations must explore what it means to be a congregation within a particular heritage and faith story–honoring both the large faith story and also the local flavor of that particular place and people. The genuine community they have to offer society is not a simple togetherness, but a being-together out of commitment, a common story, and shared values. It is a working out of the meaning of the biblical story–that we are brothers and sisters of one another, children of a purposeful God. Community is not just a nice product we have to sell to society; it is what we are as Christians. To the extent that we have forgotten that, we must rediscover the biblical grounds of our being in community and articulate that larger sense of community in a way that leaves space for the necessary "safe places" many of us need in order to deal with diversity and change in our lives.

Congregations as Generators of Community

The extent to which a congregation can or should actually "be community," as described above, differs depending on its setting. But wherever it is, a congregation has a function of being a generator of community—an institution that seeks by what it does to stimulate opportunities for people to find community with others. Let me name a few ways that congregations are already working to make that happen, both within their own structures and also within the society outside the congregation's bounds.

The image of the house church comes to mind first. In widely disparate forms house churches have been around forever. (Many of the congregations described in the New Testament were probably house churches.) Basically house churches are an attempt to do all that a "standard model parish" does without the focus on buildings, staff, and budgets that other congregations find so confining. Characteristically a group of families covenant together to become a church, and they build the structures and patterns of life they need. House churches often fulfill a need for intimacy and closeness that ordinary congregations cannot sustain. They permit a clarity of life that other congregations trying to meet requirements of the institutional church seem to get distracted from. Such churches sometimes are "stand alone" entities. Others understand themselves to be special "subdivisions" of the parent congregations.

A house church often begins from an impulse to find more authentic community, a more authentic sense of church. This need must be affirmed and supported. Many congregations see the establishment of a house church as a threat—loss of members and loss of pledges! That may be true. Yet local congregations need to have a deeper understanding of their task. The task of generating community includes listening for times to start house churches. A less well understood fact is that most house churches have a limited life-span; in our society they rarely become permanent institutions. This means that congregations need to be ready to help the people who are called to launch house churches, but they need also to stand by to give support when it is time for the house church to die. Without such help, the death of a house church is a long-drawn-out experience with a deep, painful sense of failure. With real help, such a death often leads to a resurrection of faith and vocation in the congregation and for the former members of the house church.

Congregations need to understand the rich opportunity for generating community that already exists in ordinary congregational groups. Established groups, such as Sunday school classes, choirs, teachers groups, guilds, even committees, can get so focused on their assignment that they simply overlook the chance to help generate genuine community (in spite of voluminous research showing that most tasks are performed best if the participants have a sense of community and caring with their fellow-workers). Every congregation has such groups. Some care for the altar; some arrange the music or perform it, some attend or teach weekly classes; some make sandwiches for the hungry; some plan how to change local politics; some take care of the church garden. Each of these ongoing groups is full of people yearning for the experience of community; each of these groups has the potential to become more of a community than it is. Somebody in each congregation and in each group needs to be aware of the potential for community available within the group. Part of the church's task is to recognize these opportunities to generate community in the ordinary interactions that make up congregational life.

Across the denominational spectrum I find people increasingly trying to find out how the church board—long the home of interminable meetings and grinding debate—can become one of those places in which community happens. Church boards have a special calling to transform themselves from places noted for slogging, depressing work to places of community and spiritual growth. Charles Olsen has provided us with insights and resources for helping a congregation do just that. He wants boards to undertake what he calls "worshipful work."[19]

The term *small groups* covers a wide range of efforts to generate community within congregations. As I look back over my life, I see that I spiritually and personally grew most when I was involved in a small personal group, experiencing intense community and building relationships that have fed me through the years since the group came to an end. The groups varied widely: a two-year group of ten (five seminary couples infatuated with personal therapy and trying to understand marriage); a six-year group of seven to ten (couples and single parents in a parish); a five-year group of eight long-in-the-tooth clergymen; a two-year group of three men trying to learn to pray together....So what I have to say here is based on a personal witness to the power one can experience in such small groups, however they are organized and run.

Local congregations need to be in the business of generating small-group opportunities for their people—small groups tasked with no specific purpose other than "being community" with one another within the context of faith. Experts suggest different strategies, courses of study, methods of managing the groups, of supervising or not supervising leaders. I have found many of their insights helpful, but I get nervous about experts who approach small groups ideologically, as the only way to be church. Yes, I know how much I have gained in small groups. But I also know that there have been seasons in my life when small groups "did not fit." And I do not believe congregations need to be in the business of "cookie-cutting" everybody into small groups. Generating small groups and helping them to nurture–that is the task, not coercing people into small groups. If the congregation does not work hard at generating small groups, they probably won't happen. If the congregation gets high and mighty about them, they can generate an explosive reaction. That's the tension. We must face the tension and move ahead. If you are pushing too hard, you'll soon find out.

The world of small-group advocates includes at least three different types of small-group development, each with its true believers.

The Asian model assumes a small group exists for the purpose of expanding the church's membership and expanding lay leadership. Such use of small groups has been part of the explosive growth of Korean churches. In this model a church automatically assigns each new "walk-in" member to a small group. Most new members are brought in by the small groups themselves, each of which "splits" when it reaches a certain size. The theory is that church members cannot genuinely "belong" if they are not in a face-to-face group for spiritual nurture and growth. As adapted in America, this model is also seen as a primary way to lead laypeople into full ministries as apostles of the church. Here in the States I have seen this model work in a few places–primarily in new church starts. It is problematic in long-standing congregations where "small groups" is brought in by a pastor or leadership group in spite of significant opposition from church members. In American churches this model also runs into problems in that groups do not, on the whole, seem able to "split." Indeed, small groups have a hard time being able to assimilate new members easily. In this culture, groups seem to become effective in pastoral care of group members rather than in church extension. Churches that start small groups hoping for membership growth often find not membership growth but a quality of caring and nurturing that has enormous impact upon the spiritual growth of group members and their families.

A second small-group model is from the tradition of human relations training; the interpersonal power of these small-group experiences has revolutionized many lives. At one time characterized as "sensitivity training," these groups have become standard fare in helping managers learn how to work with other people. These face-to-face groups encourage authentic communication and the direct facing of human dynamics that get hidden in ordinary discourse. They encourage people to "tell it like it is." These small groups can be deeply introspective and long-lasting, becoming a primary focal point of members' lives. Children of the "T-Group" experiences of the fifties and sixties, these groups find it difficult to incorporate new members or to let old members move on when they need to. Many of these groups include an explicit or a tacit concern to help members build more healthful personal and interpersonal relationships. They help people get clear and direct feedback on their behavior. As a source of personal growth, these groups many be unmatched, but I have known plenty to bomb out.

The third small-group model is based on South American Catholic lay groups called "base communities," which have become centers of powerful movements for liberation, both in politics and the church. They center in biblical study and engage with the important issues of people's lives and communities. Primarily lay-led, they have spread across South America wherever the Catholic church is found. In North America the attempt to generate base communities has not been as contagious as in South America. Here, even Catholic congregations considered to be centers of base community work rarely claim more than a model membership participation. Within the Catholic Church in the U.S., these groups are known as Small Faith Communities. (The acronym SFC appears frequently in Catholic conference advertisements.) The energy the South American base community movement finds in South America may well come from that particular cultural situation; until the past two generations, Catholics in South America had no access to the Bible in the vernacular. The energy of base community life may be analogous to the experience of laity in Northern Europe in the sixteenth century when they first had access to scriptures in common languages.

The point is not that all the models have flaws, but that all the models provide very practical ways for the churches to be generators of community. If these models are not adequate, we should be about developing better ones.

Churches have much to offer as generators of community in a society that is increasingly deprived of "community." Members of congregations have a right to call upon the church to help them connect with community.

Congregations as Support for Community

The ability of a congregation to *be* community depends on the world in which it exists. But even in places where the congregation has a limited ability to be community, as may be the case in large metropolitan areas, it can still have a strong role *generating* community. Here, I want to address the challenging role of the congregation in *supporting* community within society—another important dimension of its calling in today's world.

Despite the breakdown in family life deplored by society's leaders, it is clear that most peoples' primary experience of community occurs within the family. More and more people experience that community in diverse family systems—single-parent families, groups of singles living as families, empty-nest families, and extended families. Statistics on the increased number of single-parent families, of traditional families without children, of nonmarried people as family units—all continue to point to the changing character of what we call "family" and its impact upon our society.

And it is in families that most ordinary people find that sense of closeness that fosters the growth of identity. Most people go to "family" when hurt or damaged by life experience. And, for many people, "family" is where they can count on being taken in, no matter what.

Even the enormous potential for abuse and manipulation in no way detracts from the life-giving potential of family life.

The congregation is one of the few family back-up systems in our society. *Simply being there* at the critical events that make and shape families is a central function of congregations—the bonding of two people,[20] the birth or adoption of children, the milestones in children's lives, celebrations of new stages of life or work, the trauma of illness, the encounters with guilt, depression or despair, the uncertainties of new challenges, the farewells of death. Most of the churches have liturgies and traditions that help to bring many of these transitions and crises into perspective with a creative and redemptive sense of purpose modeled in our credal statements.

I sense that, over the generations, the churches have allowed their participation in these events to become routine performances. I am impressed with the way many of those same churches are struggling to bring those life-transition ministries back to life. Perhaps the most visible of those struggles has been in the churches that practice infant baptism. Only half a century ago, baptisms were routinely private affairs to which parents and close friends gathered with a pastor engaged to "do" the child. That still happens in some places, but more often baptism is a major public affirmation of identity in community. Marriage itself is being renewed as a rite as a result of many forms of marriage enrichment available through congregations. Family crises–including those we have ignored in the past (retirement, divorce)–need to be explored as ways to undergird the strength and health of the family. The debate about "marriage" of same-sex couples may be beneficial to the churches if it leads to affirmation of the larger purposes of and need for human community and gets beyond matters of genital behavior.

Congregations have another function in supporting the experience of community in our society. They need to encourage people to look beyond their own personal life or even family life. Congregations produce the people who commit themselves to the public–who work on community boards, who help the schools, who volunteer where society needs assistance. Congregations also support community by challenging people to generosity and to become philanthropists outside their own family and congregational life.[21]

The Dilemma, the Challenge, Some Beginning Clues

We begin with a difficult dilemma: Our society has lost many of the ingredients that made for community even as a new individualism has appeared that divides and separates. Congregations, caught up in their own survival and enculturated in the larger societal trends, have lost much of their ability to be community, to generate community for their people, or even, in some cases, to support community. All too often our congregations have become another part of the problem–just one more organization competing for the attention of people, hawking its wares as superior to those of others, and, in effect, further fragmenting whatever experience of community remains. The public all too frequently has recognized us as a part of the problem and has increasingly stopped looking to us for answers or help in their search for a sense of community.

The gift of community, so badly needed by society, so longed for, has not been nourished within the church. We have lost touch with it ourselves. It is doubly ironic that we are the people to whom community was especially revealed, whose theology articulates God as God-in-community, and who came onto the world's stage as a people noted for how they loved one another. Who can wonder that the world does not look to us for answers when we have been so prodigal in the waste of our gifts?

In the face of this dilemma, the fourth challenge to the churches is that we must once again become a wellspring of the experience of community within our world. Within a generation or two we must reshape the life of the church so that this world will be shot through with nourishing, provocative community that excludes no one from a sense of belonging. Within that life-span we must also make strides to be that place that is known to side with, encourage, and generate community throughout our society. If we address these imperatives we will be known once more as the place to go to discover what it feels like to be in a community, cared for, forgiven, and—yes—challenged!

In the Beginning

The greatest single resource we have for rebuilding vital community in our congregations is the one that is closest at hand. Who we are and what we are about is the heart of what every congregation does whenever it meets for worship. Who we are is the community of God, the community for others. What we are about is being that community living within the Power from beyond ourselves and witnessing to God's love and forgiveness for all. Every time we gather to worship God, that reality lies all around us. It is there for the taking. It is there to be soaked in, whether we understand it fully or not. In worship we grasp for that which is beyond our comprehension. The act of worship itself is a cry to God for community, but it is also paradoxically an opening through which God's power to give community gets into our lives and into our inadequate community. Worship reaches out for community and is at the same time a means by which that for which we pray comes to us. The opportunity comes so regularly and routinely that we often overlook its power to change us and our congregations.

Worship is our definition of ourselves in relationship to God and our side of a dialogue that is God's definition of us. There is no other one place in which the congregation tries to express itself before God—who it is, what it needs, what it values, what it believes in, what it grieves, what it celebrates. Attention to the quality and content of worship is the central resource for rediscovering our identity and reconnecting to our roots.

I do not mean to say that worship is valuable primary as a means to develop community, although I admit that it can be used that way to great effect. I do not mean to say that sacraments and ordinances, music and liturgy, preaching and prayer themselves serve primarily to constitute a solid human community, but, again, I admit that they can help do this.

My point is that the central moment for every congregation is its moment of worship. That is where it most defines itself in dynamic relationship to that Power that is the source of its identity. That is where it seeks to draw on the Spirit of that Power to bring new life to the individual and to the community. It is dynamic. Something happens there.

Worship is the place at which the identity of the congregation is dramatically acted out and also discovered in relationship to and in dialogue with God.

Great worship does build community. Great worship opens hearts to hear the cries of loneliness and joy of the congregation. Great worship places us with the great pain of the world and of our neighbors, and it sharpens our commitment to making a difference. Great worship helps us celebrate the grandeur and the misery of existence. Great worship makes and should make great demands upon us—to be committed to serving God's people and God's world. Great worship brings healing where there is illness, strength where there is weakness, forgiveness where there is guilt. It is the doorway through which God tells us who we are and empowers us to be what God calls us to be. It is not something to fool around with or treat lightly.

As we use all the resources at our command to build the community that the world needs, worship remains our central resource.

But What Comes Next?

In pursing community, we must begin by recognizing that there is no one answer to the problems we face. Each congregation starts at a different place; let's agree that no starting place is better than another. It also means that the answers we come up with will be specific to where we are and who we are. Our direction may be different from others. No national program, no ideological commitment to "the correct way" is likely to give us more than some initial direction, some hunches. Indeed, answers will have to be home-grown. Trial and error must become our standard operating system. That, in itself, may be one of the most important clues to moving ahead.

The technologically astute among us call this trial-and-error approach "action research," a method in which action is taken after the best insight is gathered from as wide a spectrum as possible; the results of the action are sifted and evaluated in preparation for the next step. Most church "programs" propose a series of actions that make logical sense, but they don't take into account the fact that the first step never goes the way it is designed. Each step then gets further and further from what was intended. The program ends as a disappointment or disaster that usually is blamed on "the program" or the church agency that sold it to them. I am not talking about something terribly complicated. I'm suggesting we pay attention to what happens every time we try something, then make adjustments. Frankly, that's all most consultants worth their salt help us do—pay attention to what has happened and learn from our experience.

Starting where we are means that we are dealing with slow and incremental change, change that will take years. Let me be honest. I am saying that meeting this and the other challenges I am describing puts us on a course that does not end. It does not "get there"; it will never be done. We are embarking on a journey into God's future. Given this reality, if we are willing to accept it, what then do we do first?

I think the most promising first step is to think about and work on boundaries. In their hearts congregations have a story, an experience with God, a heritage—one that is different from that of the general society. Unfortunately, congregations have become enculturated to the extent that they are unable to differentiate themselves from the society around them. They have "gone native." This has happened gradually, over generations, and continues as society's values and stories and heritage infiltrate our lives and congregations. Through exposure to media we assimilate values from a culture that puts little value on human caring. The models of acceptable behavior that we see in our towns and cities—in private citizens and political leaders—also conflict with what our faith and the scriptures tell us. Behaviors to which our children are exposed are the antithesis to what we want them to learn.

There are congregations that see (and try to practice) a severe disconnection from the outside world as a cure to this enculturation. If our Amish and our fundamentalist brothers and sisters sometimes act in ways we do not understand, it is this distinctive difference they are defending. And celebrating. I do not choose or recommend that way, but I have enormous sympathy for it.[22]

I suggest that we mainline churches rethink the issues of boundary. When the boundary between a congregation and the world outside is so blurred that we can no longer tell the one world from the other, one's identity takes on the coloration of the dominant society. The church then operates by society's standards without reference to its own story, heritage, and values, and the individual has no community compass to determine true directions for life.

We must pay attention to boundaries between the church and the community. That means rethinking what it is that makes us a special community. It means rediscovering and rehearsing the story of where we came from and whose we are. It means reconnecting with the power of our heritage. It means redefining our values in today's world. This is an internal task—one we must do for ourselves and with ourselves. It calls us to become a learning community in brand new ways.

Most churches think of education as being synonymous with Sunday school. That is totally inadequate even to help us relearn our own story.[23] Accepting the challenge of becoming a center of community for tomorrow's world commits us to massive new efforts for adult education about the faith. We need to face the facts: that most of us in the church today have forgotten our story; we maintain our heritage only by habits we learned form those who knew the story by heart. Each generation has to reappropriate the story and connect with the experience of faith. It does not suffice to be able to repeat what parents told us a long time ago. Adults of this generation have remedial work to do before they will be able to communicate the story to their own children and grandchildren. That is what is called for—not just an hour on Sunday mornings.

Our congregations can be wonderful associations of people, but they cannot become the kind of life-giving community we need unless we reinvest ourselves in the story of faith—remembering and experiencing again our slavery in Egypt and our release from captivity, experiencing the power of false gods and of judgment, experiencing the surprise of the appearance of the Promised One, and discovering the power of the Spirit. Second-hand faith is not enough for the kind of community we need.

Rebuilding the boundary of the congregation means building a community of faith within the congregation that knows itself and can differentiate itself from the spirits of this age. It involves the life of the entire body. This is not a step that happens all at once. Rebuilding such a boundary is what I'd call a boot-strap operation, experimentally moving ahead, testing, then adjusting direction and speed. Let me give some specifics.

The act of entering a congregation is an act of leaving one world and set of values and entering another; it is an experience of crossing a boundary. Church leaders need to help people crossing that boundary recognize it as a passage from one kind of life to another. We cannot do that unless we ourselves become more conscious of who we are in this community and how we are different. Again, I see this as "boot-strap change." At this point in history, church members really have forgotten much that makes the church distinctive. That means every entry of every outsider becomes a double opportunity for building a new community: It provides the congregation with an opportunity to understand itself more deeply (or to deepen that community). It is also an opportunity to help the newcomer learn what this community actually stands for and is.

Every entry must dramatize that move from one life to another. Above I discussed recent changes in baptismal practices. They can be a useful image of boot-strap change. The initial attempts to change baptismal practices involved a tortuous process of pastors arm wrestling individual families. The first step was to make baptism part of the Sunday morning public worship. The practice was enriched by a sometimes furtive effort to educate godparents and parents. Eventually the forms of liturgies began to change, giving congregations a more active part in baptism. I now go to a parish in which baptismal "classes" are scheduled, and candidates are prayed for for weeks before baptisms, which are important festival events. Clearly, what has happened did not happen all at once. Indeed, I don't think we knew where it was all going when we started. We made one step, and then the next followed. Different congregations did it different ways. Who knows what the next steps will be? But all these signs point to a growing sense of what it means to belong to this peculiar community, to what it means to cross this boundary. Each step can lead to the next. Each step starts where people are.

There are other entry points.[24] Every one of them—new membership, transfer from another congregation, confirmation or other affirmation of membership, return from a sabbatical, return after a long journey or years of living elsewhere—provides opportunities for the boot-strap process I have described. Anyone crossing the boundary provides an opportunity to reinforce the meaning of the community to members and to those entering it.

Increasingly, congregations are adopting more stringent training for new members, but rare still is the congregation that genuinely owns standards for membership, takes responsibility for modeling those standards, and is prepared to enforce those standards upon new members. Some ten or fifteen years ago, my own denomination made a decision (in spite of all the dangers of top-down decisions, this was so done, but not without considerable grass-roots agitation!) to make tithing the standard of giving for the denomination.[25] The national board argued and fought and then decided to accept tithing as their personal standard and to recommend it to the parishes. Parish after parish argued about it. Some "accepted" and did nothing. Others decided it was not for them. Others said no, then a few years later changed their stance. In time, most members were exposed to the idea that tithing is one expectation of the members of this particular denomination. The impact on per-member giving has been most positive; but that is irrelevant to my point about setting standards of membership. That brief story illustrates a boot-strap operation of identifying what we are and what our standards are. It also points out that standards should be set by leaders who will live by them.

What actually distinguishes people who are part of your congregation? Or what should distinguish them? Who should be involved in determining that? How can the congregation affirm and support those who try to live by those standards?

These questions about setting standards can help you get clarity about what the community wants to stand for. The specific standards are legion. What should being a member of this congregation mean about attendance at public worship? What should it mean in terms of relationships to spouses and children? What should it mean about involvement in the economic and political world surrounding the congregation? What does it mean about how members relate to their resources?

Having developed standards for being in the congregation, how do we then help each other to live by those standards? How do we train new members of the community about the standards? Working on the boundary means working on issues such as these.

Some congregations are beginning such training for new members, but most "transfers" from other congregations still bypass the training. Maybe we need a congregational immigration service and training program, one that reflects the values and standards of the congregation. It should not be primarily the task of the clergy. Such a program would call for continuous work in the congregation, reviewing and rethinking (1) what that congregation understands membership of this church to mean and (2) how an individual demonstrates those behaviors and trains for them.

I have described a process of developing community by delineating the boundary one must cross to enter the community. We begin with what's left of an identity that may have been distinctive several centuries ago but which has become overwhelmed by the identity of the social environment. Genuine community in the church can come only with a new clarity about identity with the Christian faith and a willingness to make that identity central to the congregation.

Every human crisis point is an opportunity for the congregation to rediscover itself and for the person in crisis to experience a deeper dimension of faith-identity in that community. Ministries to one another in those crises give new and concrete meaning to our identity as a community of faith.

I have already noted the potential of the many groups in every congregation to become centers of life-giving community. Applying bootstrap action-research methods can also help them achieve more of their potential. Beginning where it is, each group can revise its own life in relationship to the deepening sense of identity that the congregation has, and each group can contribute to that identity. Similarly, the congregation that encourages house churches and small-group life will find that those laboratories of community will be able to receive and give much to the congregation's growing sense of identity.

The fourth challenge for the church to face and overcome in the next few generations is to become the place that feeds the world's need for community.

NOTES

1. John W. Gardner, *Building Community* (Washington, DC: Independent Sector, 1991), 5. Used by permission.

2. Gibson Winter captured the meaning of this migration for American churches in his analysis, *The Suburban Captivity of the Churches*, (Garden City, NY: Doubleday, 1961).

3. See Samuel Freedman, *Upon This Rock: The Miracles of a Black Church* (San Francisco: HarperCollins, 1993), the story of a great African-American congregation in Brooklyn.

4. *The Downsizing of America: Millions of Americans Are Losing Good Jobs. This Is Their Story* (New York: Random House, 1996). This book is a compilation of articles printed in the *New York Times*.

5. "For an AT&T Brat, the Anguish of Letting Go," *New York Times*, 14 January 1996, 12.

6. One can see the frightening reality of such communities when they go to war with one another, as they do regularly at European soccer matches!

7. "Owners' New Strategy: Take the Team and Run," *New York Times*, 14 January 1996, sec. 8, p. 1.

8. Robert D. Putnam, "Bowling Alone: America's Declining Social Capital," *Journal of Democracy* 6, no. 1 (January 1995), 65-77.

9. Ibid., 70. Putnam indicates the size of the phenomenon he's talking about: "nearly 80 million Americans went bowling at least once in 1993, nearly a third more than voted in the 1994 Congressional elections."

10. In fact, his basic contention is refuted sharply by Robert J. Samuelson in an op-ed column. "'Bowling Alone' Is Bunk." *Washington Post*, 10 April 1996. Samuleson marshals impressive data of his own while questioning a number of Putnam's conclusions. What may be the most fascinating element in this exchange is the way the Putnam thesis seems to have touched something the public recognized as a felt reality. My hunch is that people will remember "Bowling Alone" a lot longer than "'Bowling Alone' Is Bunk" because the former seems to explain something Americans both fear and sense to be happening to them and around them. The fear and anxiety may be more "real" than the statistics.

11. William Raspberry, "Crisis of Community," *Sewanee*, January 1996.

12. Robert Bellah, et al., *Habits of the Heart* (Berkeley: University of California Press, 1985).

13. Garrett Hardin, in a provocatively simple paper now nearly three decades old, points to a basic problem we have in seeking the experience of community. In "The Tragedy of the Commons," *Science* (1968), Hardin suggests that our society is constructed by assumptions in which individual self-interest is in conflict with being in community. He argues that genuine "community" has to be based in a larger view of life than simple self-interest. The strengths of his article are its simple statement of profound truth (analogous to Putnam's article on bowling) and its basis in economic analysis–a dimension often overlooked by those who try to engineer society to provide community.

14. Britton Johnston and Sally Johnson, *Saints and Neighbors* (Chicago: Center for Church and Community Ministries at McCormick Seminary, 1991). The project from which these stories come was productive in other ways: Carl Dudley, director of the project, wrote two other books on the experience–*Basic Steps to Community Ministry* (Bethesda, MD: The Alban Institute, 1991) and the more recent *Next Steps in Community Ministry* (Bethesda, MD: The Alban Institute, 1996).

15. John E. Linnan, as quoted in *National Catholic Reporter*, 31 May 1996, 6. Linnan is a teacher at the Catholic Theological Union in Chicago.

16. *Research Project: Attitudes and Perceptions about the Church.* The study was done for the United Methodist Church, Kansas West Conference, 1994).

17. Reginald Bibby, *There's Got to Be More* (Winfield, BC, Canada: Wood Lake Books, 1995).

18. Dean Hoge, Benton Johnson, and Donald Luidens, *Vanishing Boundaries* (Louisville, Westminster/John Knox, 1994). See especially 132-144.

19. See Charles Olsen, *Transforming Church Boards* (Bethesda, MD: The

Alban Institute, 1995). Olsen has been following the issue of church as community for years. I first knew him through his 1970s research on house churches in Project Base Church. His new book comes from the conviction that congregations will not become spiritual communities until church boards themselves become spiritual communities. The book details his research on the subject but also gives practical help to those who want to help their church boards in this critical transformation.

20. It is tragic that many churches are having such a struggle separating out "valid" from "invalid" forms of human family—with distinctions based on sexual behavior. Clearly the function I am describing here requires the churches to support human community wherever it is exercised to the spiritual and personal growth of persons. The affirmation of community is essential: the form of it may be argued.

21. Research by the Independent Sector and others indicates that people who belong to churches and religious congregations are much more likely than non-members to be volunteers and donors to community causes.

22. Although I do have difficulty when a denomination denounces Walt Disney and others boycott Proctor and Gamble for alleged cultural sell-outs.

23. C. Ellis Nelson, beloved wise man of Christian education in the Presbyterian Church, puts it bluntly: "Let's face it, friends. Sunday school will no longer cut it!" Unpublished quote from an address to Presbyterian educators and pastors, 1996.

24. One of the first books published by the Alban Institute was titled *A Way to Belong*. In that book, Celia Allison Hahn explored the very special way one congregation—Saint Mark's Episcopal Church in Washington, D.C. —designed and carried out a way for new members to learn the values and meanings of congregational belonging. The thesis was that all congregations need to be clear about designing a way to belong. The book is out of print.

25. Although I have tried to practice tithing for many years, I still have a lot of questions about it. I'm worried about the legalistic way it is often used and also about the crazy theological ideas that sometimes seem to grow up like weeds around it.

CHAPTER 5

CHALLENGE 5:
To Become an Apostolic People

The church we live in understands "the mission of the church" in very institutional ways. Who is "sent" and where they are sent is a function of decisions made by executives in mission agencies or denominational headquarters. The purposes and priorities of mission are outgrowths of the life of the congregations, judicatories, and groups that make up the church.

The apostolic task (the "sending" or "being sent" function of the church) is managed and directed by the institutional framework of the church. The various denominations have managed this apostolic function in different ways. Most are very serious about it, put major energy into it, work hard to build support for it, and do it as well as they possibly can. It is important to them. Because of the way those systems are structured, however, the focus is on the mission of the *church* (understood, at best, as the universal church, but often as the mission of this particular church or denomination). The central apostolic task of the church is determined by the clergy and the hierarchies, and the laity is relegated to the role of "supporter" of the apostolic work.

As its fifth challenge the church of the future must become fully apostolic. It must be an apostolic people, not an apostolic institution or hierarchy. And each member of the church must see him- or herself as *being* an apostle. You have probably heard this message before, but I say there is much more to it than we have been willing to admit or face.

How Is an "Apostolic People" Different from an "Apostolic Church"?

From the earliest days, the church's common assumption has been that its central business is to go, to be sent, to make disciples across the world. That consciousness of "being sent" has undergirded the church's sense of who and what it is, and it has defined its mission. The early life of the church was consumed by a sense of mission—of reaching out, of crossing boundaries, and of protecting itself against attacks from inside or outside.[1] To be involved in the church's mission was to be sent, to be apostolic.

Two themes dominated Jesus' message to his followers about that mission: (1) that every follower of Jesus was called to reach out as a caring servant of others, like Jesus himself; and (2) that the church itself was to be a community that expanded to the ends of the earth, bringing all manner of people into its life and embrace; the church was to encompass the world.

The concept of mission as understood by the churches of our generation has focused on the second of these themes and consequently the churches organized to accomplish it. The churches honor the first role (the servant role) as genuine and celebrate it in those individual people who live out humble service, but they have shaped their institutional priorities and structures to accomplish the expansionist model. We love Saint Francis, but we organize like Franciscans.

Our self-understanding as Christians is derived from the "Great Commission" that we should make disciples of all the nations, baptizing them in the name of the Father, the Son, and the Holy Ghost.[2] That concept of mission, however, picked up all sorts of cultural accretions as it made its way through the centuries and civilizations through which it passed on its way to us. We did not receive a pristine concept of mission directly from the New Testament; we received an idea of mission as modified by the experiences of the church over the ages. In particular, the concept of mission that dominated the thinking of the late nineteenth-century and early twentieth-century church was heavily shaped by intellectual, economic, and political currents in Western Europe and North America during those same years, years of unprecedented ferment and cultural change.

Enlightenment currents flourished in the universities in which theologians were trained. Assumptions about the superiority of Western culture infected Christians' way of looking at civilizations in which Christianity was not the norm. Missionary thinking was modified by Western cultural elitism.

People of other cultures were stereotyped as the poor, ignorant heathen or romanticized as the noble savage. In either case they were defined by Western sensibilities that rarely looked to the flesh and blood lives that were touched.[3]

Economic and political movements led European and North American nations to develop colonial empires in which they took great pride and from which they sometimes took profit. Expeditionary forces went to bring those pagan lands under the protection of the "crown," as some put it. (Americans tipped a hand to God and called it Manifest Destiny.) Patriotism and economics got mixed up with a sense of moral superiority and a deep-felt sense of a call to mission. Different actors represented different mixes of these complex motives.

The theme of mission as the extension of the bounds of Christendom carried the day within the church. In church circles, the word mission came to mean the expansion of the church to new lands and to new peoples. Honest enthusiasm for mission merged with national passions for colonial expansion. Supported as it was by cultural, political, economic, and intellectual consensus, the word *mission* became the religious side of the word *imperialism*.

In making this overly simplistic comment, I do not at all question the integrity of the impulse to mission concern that was genuine among leaders of the churches and ordinary members themselves. Some of those leaders were heroic and self-giving by any standard. There was a genuine desire to follow the great commandment of Jesus to "make disciples of all nations." But the cultural milieu in which the people sought to carry out that commandment modified how they understood mission and how they thought it should be done. Culture put a pressure behind the deeply religious convictions of mission-minded Christians.

Those understandings of mission—powerfully religious yet also greatly influenced by cultural images of Christian/Western superiority—shaped our understanding of the roles of church leadership and the design of our institutional forms.

The result was a "top-down" relationship between roles in the church and a "top-down" set of institutional arrangements for doing mission. Those arrangements continue to rule our organization for mission. The authentication of mission came to be related to validation by the higher authorities in the churches. Ministry was seen as being valid only if it was authenticated by those validated by the structural arrangements of the denominations. Hence the endless debates in the nineteenth and twentieth centuries in which ecclesiologists and theologians tried to define whose clergy had validity and whose did not.[4] Those conversations echo through many contemporary negotiations between denominations seeking grounds for reunion.

I'm aware of two ways we validate orders today: through the "franchise" system and the "trickle-down" system.

The franchise system authenticates clergy, ministry, and mission with the authority of their denominational system. Everyone authenticated in the Presbyterian or United Methodist systems, for example, may "deliver the goods"–at least to those in that system. They may not cross over to one of the other systems unless they are authenticated by it. Why do I use the word franchise? Think in terms of McDonald's. Anywhere you see the golden arches, you know you will get a McDonald's hamburger, not cotton candy. The manager has the franchise, and he or she has been checked out by the organization. Go in there, the system says, and you'll get the genuine article. In a church, if the system has the franchise, you're hooked up to a valid missionary and ministry enterprise. The company stands behind it.

The trickle-down system assumes that validity of ministry comes from knowledge. So we get brilliant people to cluster in our seminaries to teach ordination candidates. Those brilliant people pass on all they can to their students, who are no intellectual slouches themselves. Those students are expected to pick up "enough" of the professors' knowledge to preach well enough to pass on sufficient knowledge to the person in the pew; parishioners thereby become knowledgeable enough to have a valid lay ministry. Each level loses a bit in prestige, but its purpose is to channel "enough" to the "lower" levels.

Just what constitutes "enough knowledge" is the subject of considerable debate. Heated arguments occur when people try to define the enoughs. Although denominations have invested enormous energy and resources in systems to ensure that enough trickles down, some early evidence suggests that this may not be happening. The system is not producing enough theological acumen at the lower levels.[5]

These two caricatures of the churches' authentication systems have this in common: both assume that ministry is to be authenticated through the organizational system. Validation is passed "down" from those who have a level of knowledge or authority higher than those who are "lower" in the system. To put it in terms used earlier in this book, these systems are intrinsically clericalist. The power to determine authenticity of mission, the power to transmit authenticity or even define it, is reserved to the clergy, whether presbyterial, congregational, or episcopal.

The ordinary member of the church is therefore relegated to the role of "client of the clergy"–the one to be trained in mission, convinced of the clerical definition of ministry, measured by the clergy's standards. And the mission itself is defined and structured by the institution itself.

I trust my stating it this way shows how we, in our domestic ecclesiological life, play out the same game that has been played in our foreign mission approach for generations.[6] In our domestic churches the laity is treated like the overseas clients of the home church's missionary effort; the laity is the pagan, treated as a stranger to the gospel, ignorant of revelation of God, untutored in the ways deemed essential for valid faith and mission. We assume that little or nothing is genuinely of God in the experience of the laity at home or the pagan in far-off countries; God has to be imported into their lives before they can be called into active mission. In this framework the apostolic dimension of the church is obviously located in its clergy and ecclesiastical governors.

I think it is time to say that this tack is bankrupt. Wrong.

THE MISSION BELONGS TO GOD

My basic assumption is that the mission that counts is God's mission, not the church's.[7] That assumption makes us look at the world and mission in a new light. We no longer look at the world for the *gaps*, so that we, in mission, can take God to where God is not now. Instead, we look at the world as the arena in which God's care and love are already, everywhere, at work. We do not take mission out; we go out to meet the mission already there. We look for the places to which we are called to take our place in that larger, ongoing mission.

As things are now, we church people look across the world and see the church's congregations, colleges, institutions, and there we see the mission of the church. We take pride in remarkable institutional accomplishments and heroic actions for the faith.

But if with the eyes of faith we look across the very same world, we can see a much larger mission. We can see the loving, judging, life-giving concern of God for the whole of the created order, a concern that calls all of creation into life and into life-giving partnerships. We can view the mission of God as far greater than the mission of our institutions. In God's mission the church has a role, as does each of us. In such a view, many who are not of the church are part of God's mission. Many of them already show great gifts of the Spirit. In such a view of mission, the primary missionaries may be those who can claim no "valid" credentials at all. Many may not be of the household of faith. As God freed the exiles in Babylon through the agency of Cyrus—not one of the people of Israel—so God's distinct mission today is not necessarily solely directed through the church, no matter how much church people defensively claim that place in the scheme of things.[8]

In our time one can see evidence of the mission of God around the world, in movements with which the church has ambivalent relations.[9] I briefly discuss three of the movements in which I see marks of God's mission.

Freedom Movements

Sweeping changes have occurred as oppressed and colonized people have struggled to freedom from political and social bondage. Much of this I see as an expression of a power greater than ours, greater than organizations. In the power of these different movements, I see God reaching out in mission. These movements have swept across colonial nations, particularly in Africa, East Asia, and Central Asia. They have swept across Eastern Europe and the former Soviet Union.

Abraham Lincoln suggested that he saw God's hand similarly operating in the United States in the war between the slave states and free states. A power seems loose in the world, a power that does not condone slavery and repression simply because one group is stronger or richer than another. In South America the movements of oppressed people have been accompanied by new theologies of liberation—theologies that have become as controversial in church hierarchies as in political offices. In our country the civil rights movement was a local expression of this great movement of God. One has only to name these movements to recognize how often the church as an institution has been split and confused by these tides of change. The churches have not often seen these movements—at least in their beginnings—as mission. The church often has been most resistant to these freedom movements. As a matter of fact, the institutional church could sometimes be accused of having colluded with forces that caused the oppression in the first place. And yet thousands of church people have been engaged in these struggles for freedom. In that sense church members have been engaged in this mission. In Eastern Europe the role of the churches was crucial to many of the changes in the social order. As the old order has been overthrown, the churches have been slow to find a role in helping overcome the resulting societal chaos. Traditional mission efforts in many areas, such as Central and West Africa, seem paralyzed by the rapid social changes. How does the institution catch up with God's mission and with its people who are already apostolically engaged? How does the church begin to bring genuine new life to societies and people victorious but confused after casting out one set of demons? In many places the throwing off of colonial oppression has led to other kinds of oppression and subjugation. Without some initiatives that could at least partly come from the churches, we may well find the freed societies to be like the person in the scriptures who was cleansed of one demon only to have it replaced by seven more deadly than the first.

In short, these diverse movements to overthrow oppression seem to bear the mark of something God is doing in our world. That is where the initiative for mission is and always has been. If the church as an institution wants to be engaged in mission, this is a place to connect with what God is doing. Millions of caring people are already engaged in these liberating efforts. The rest of us in the church need to find how we can connect with what God is already about.

The Environmental Movement

A new spirit of stewardship of the earth has emerged in the last few generations. People have responded to that spirit in a myriad of ways. The center of the environmental movement has never been the traditional churches, although people from the churches are found in all the groups concerned for the environment. Many key leaders of the environmental movement are among those I call Christian alumni–people well exposed to the things of faith (early in life or through other people of faith) but no longer "at home" in churches. Current church efforts to establish task forces on environmental issues may be worthwhile but probably will have little impact. The task of the church is to call people and send them into those places in which God's mission is already being done. The church must also articulate and name the mission God is carrying out. In this, as in other areas, the church's task is not to control mission, but to celebrate it, participate in it, and to bring the heritage of faith into the stream of mission.

Human Empowerment

Here I may simply be giving a new "spin" to the first area of God's mission discussed above, freedom movements. But I want to call attention to a new dimension of what God is doing: God is moving to authenticate the specialness of each person and each group. I see many indications of this movement of the Spirit to claim the uniqueness of each person and group and to celebrate it. Equally important is the urgency with which they seek to gain their place at the table of society—the emergence of self-conscious pride among ethnic groups, led in our society by African Americans.[10] The largest, least completed, and most revolutionary empowerment movement has been that of women. This struggle for empowerment is against the structures—many of them church structures or structures in which church systems have colluded—that would deny women their full humanness. God's mission appears to be an affirmation of the integrity and value of every human voice.

Exploring These Areas and the Larger Mission

Churches that want to engage in mission would do well to explore these three areas in which God's mission seems to be running well ahead of our own. My pride in the fact that churches served as training grounds for many of these struggles in no way diminishes my realization of how often the churches have stood against—and still stand against—many areas in which God is engaged in a mission larger than we have on our mission plans and charts!

Within each of these three efforts for human empowerment, there is space and need for those who bear the gospel. All these efforts need the witness of those who bear in their lives the freedom of the gospel and know the ways of demonic powers. These movements, for example, have the potential to ask participants to make the "cause" into an ultimate commitment, sacrificing their own lives for the group. Some of these groups are unrelenting in their pressure on members to turn over their personalities to "the cause." Christians know to be wary of this demon.

I've here discussed three flawed glimpses of what the mission of God today looks like. The mission of God is, of course, much more than these; it is an enormous pressure of loving energy as God reaches out to the world, seeking to touch and heal all its hurts. It is a continuing outpouring of God's care for the fulfillment of hopes and possibilities, an outpouring that seeks to overcome all forces of enslavement and poverty. The mission of God is connected to God's "heart" and passion for the world and all its inhabitants. The movements of freedom, the new awareness of the environment, and the empowerment of human life are but three pulses of that larger concern.

The mission is far greater than our institutional vision of mission has ever imagined. The apostolic church has carved out only a small corner of the mission God has in mind. Mission as interpreted by the church as institution is far too small for the mission of God.

The apostolic task of the people of God is to participate in that larger mission of God. Each person is called to hear and respond to God in the here and now. Each is called to be a servant to humankind and to the world, bringing healing and life, joy and peace. This is not a mission that can be controlled or even authorized by an institution. It is not a mission that awaits the organizational skills of church leaders. It is not a mission to which the church is to deploy its members or for which it is to develop task forces. It is a mission that neither popes nor bishops nor executives nor professors have authority over or even fully understand.

The mission comes to life only as the spread-out people of God reach out to touch whatever is around them—in their jobs, communities, organizations—in their worldly commitments. The mission becomes visible in their actions as servants. Their task: to see that no pain is unshared, no hurt unnoticed, no hunger untouched, no loss grieved alone, no death unknown, and no joy uncelebrated.

Such a people would understand themselves to be apostolic. Their whole life would be sent into God's mission.

What Missional Role Remains for the Institutional Church?

I trust it is clear that the church is not in charge of—has no control over—mission. It needs to move back from thinking that it calls the shots and sets the conditions for mission. It needs to understand mission not in terms of its own aggrandizement or even growth. The mission is God's, and the task of the apostolic people across the globe is to get alongside that mission in their lives.

As for the church, I see four classic patterns for its involvement in God's mission.[11]

Receiving

Institutionally the church is called to open itself to watch and listen for signs of God's mission. This involves keeping the story alive, continuing to hear and study the great works of God in the past so we are better able to recognize God's appearance today. It involves looking with expectation at what the people of God are up to, understanding that the mission of God will be revealed in the pain and joy encountered by people as they live as apostles. It means listening, listening, listening. Listening to what gospel is discovered by the people. Listening to signs of God's mission in the world. Of course this calls the church to move away from its habit of telling and exhorting. Its mode should be receptive. If it is to support an apostolic people, the church must learn to believe what God is and will be doing in God's people. It is to open all the pores of its being to the miracles that God will do through the apostolic, servant people. And it is through this openness that calls will also come to the people.

Offering

Offering is the second mode with which the institution responds to this great mission. I use the term *offering* to mean that the whole experience of the apostolic people is received and becomes that which the church places before God. The offering is celebration and blessing. All the pieces and parts of the world touched by the apostolic people are brought together in prayer and praise. The life of the people becomes the beginning of prayer. As the church takes bread and wine to its altars and holy tables, the church is similarly called to present to God the servant life of its people. In every congregation the gathered people bring with them the worlds they inhabit: the personal—co-workers, neighbors, adversaries, spouses, in-laws; the vocational and institutional—companies, banks, and agencies, universities and offices, white-collar work, blue-collar work, and unemployment. All the realities people live with are received and then made part of the people's conversation with God; they are offered up in celebration.

Identifying

Identification with the pain of the world is the third pattern the church as an institution is to live out. The church as a body receives into itself all the tragedy and pain its people discover in the fallen world in which they serve. The church is to identify itself with the suffering that creeps into every life, every home, every community. The apostolic people bring to the worship of the church all the pain of brokenness they have encountered as they have participated in God's mission of caring for the hurts of the world.

Serving

Finally, the church will release the apostles for service in the world. Having received all that the apostles experienced as servants of the mission, having offered up the life of the world through their experience, having accepted the brokenness and hurt of the world and of change, the church is to release its people for service. It is to release them—not direct them

Those patterns are, indeed, liturgical. But they turn liturgy upside down from our usual experience. Instead of bringing stories from scripture to illuminate and direct lives we need to bring lives to the scripture to discover new visions of our calling. Instead of proclaiming answers, we need a liturgy of openness and expectation. Instead of maintaining a theology of the academy, we need an emerging theology born in the people's engagement with God's mission of the world.

An apostolic people needs a church that supports apostolicity but does not seek to define and control mission. An apostolic people sees its task as that of being servants of humanity and the world. An apostolic people undersands mission to be participation in God's mission.

The fifth challenge of the church is to become that apostolic people. This means that every member of the church is called to engage in ministry all the time, everywhere.

No small order!

NOTES

1. The best overall study of the development of consciousness of mission is David Bosch, *Transforming Mission* (Maryknoll, NY: Orbis, 1991). A provocative counterpoint to the internal tensions in the church regarding the meaning of outreach to the Jews is found in Elaine Pagel, *The Origin of Satan* (New York: Random House, 1995).

2. Matthew 28:18-20. A strength of Bosch's Transforming Mission is his careful study of biblical sources; he indicates there is a variety of understanding of

mission. Our inherited understanding of the biblical record comes from focusing for centuries on this one Matthew theme, which won the day.

3. I realize that thousands of people engaged in the face-to-face work of mission went far beyond the stereotypes and came to a deep appreciation of the uniqueness of the cultures and people they encountered. I am speaking of the popular sense of that mission and much of the motivation for engaging in it.

4. Frankly, it seems as if a lot of the discussions of church union today take their point of departure from those relatively fruitless discussions.

5. See D. Hoge, B. Johnson, and D. Luidens, *Vanishing Boundaries* (Louisville: Westminster/John Knox Press, 1994). These authors describe churched populations as having about as much "trickled down" theological knowledge as those who are totally unchurched.

6. I am deeply indebted to the work of Robert J. Schreiter, *Constructing Local Theologies* (Maryknoll, NY: Orbis, 1993). Schreiter breaks new ground in the theology and strategy of mission. This book and Bosch's Transforming Mission have the potential to blow out of the water much of our mission practice and offer a beginning place for a genuinely comprehensive picture of the mission of the future. These are very significant books.

7. I am deeply indebted in this section to the work of Schreiter, *Constructing Local Theologies*, and Bosch, *Transforming Mission*.

8. Schreiter, *Constructing Local Theologies*, points to the critical but limited role of the church in this larger mission of God, saying first that "the development of local theologies depends as much on finding Christ already active in the culture as it does on bringing Christ to the culture" (p. 29). But he goes on to say, "for a local theology to become a Christian local theology, it must have a genuine encounter with the Christian tradition" (p. 34). Between these two sentences hangs the dilemma of how any of us with faith communicate it to those who have not yet found it.

9. As I name and briefly describe these movements of the mission of God, I am very aware that I see only what I see and that final judgment on these movements will not be in for generations. "By their fruits you shall know them."

10. Consider the impact of Stokely Carmichael's cry, "Black Power," which transformed a struggle about civil rights into a crusade for racial and personal pride in identity.

11. In my book *Transforming Congregations for the Future*, I discuss another four—the four functions congregations need to carry out as they equip people to become apostolic. Those four are programmatic functions: the tasks of (1) proclamation, (2) teaching, (3) serving, and (4) building community. Here I am pointing to the church's spiritual involvement in God's mission. Old friends will detect the influence of Dom Gregory Dix.

CHAPTER 6

Can These Bones Live?

This book is actually the third in a series. (See "Postlude" at the end of this chapter.) Working on these books, I have had a growing sense of the power and relevance of the biblical images of the Babylonian exile. My question "Do we have time?" is a pale version of Ezekiel's question to God as Ezekiel stood before a graphic vision of a valley heaped with dry bones. He asked, "Can these bones live?" Let us review the historical context of the question.

The history of the people of Israel is an unprecedented and still unsurpassed story in world history. A little more than three thousand years ago, a small band of slaves somehow escaped servitude in Egypt; they preserved their memories of that moment as a point of deliverance by God—the story of the parting and crossing of the Red Sea. Whatever that story meant (the movie version with waves standing rigid as walls or the more liberal version of high winds sweeping water away from a swampy area[1]), within a few generations that small band of slaves began to turn the world upside down. They may have embellished their story, but they nevertheless took some incredible steps.

They conceived a moral code grounded in their experience of God—the Ten Commandments, a code that has not yet been surpassed. Beginning with the Red Sea story, they conceived of a God who had purpose and direction. In short, they began to invent history. All this, remember, beginning from incredibly modest beginnings, as slaves.

This band of outsiders gradually built the strength and unity with which to claim and settle some of the most disputed land in the world—the western end of the Fertile Crescent, at the crossroads of the then-known world. They overthrew the inhabitants of the land.[2] A chaotic period followed during which this new nation faced constant challenges by people passing through the area or trying to supplant them. With no political system beyond their tribal alliances, they discovered how to meet crises—by raising up heroic figures they called judges who rallied the people against their many enemies with mixed success. The need for a more dependable political structure led them to invent a monarchy.

Two of the greatest kings of the ancient world—David and Solomon—came to the throne. Under David the people overpowered the fortress of Jerusalem—Zion—and immediately started to see it as the Holy City. Solomon's building of the temple—one of the wonders of the world—was not as wonderful as what the temple embodied: the development of a comprehensive theology growing from the early experiences, crossing the Red Sea and wandering in the wilderness. The temple became a holy place, replacing the portable Ark of the Covenant; it was there in the temple that the people's dialogue with God occurred.

Remember, this all started at what to us looks like ground zero. In some three to four hundred years, these incredible moral, theological, and political inventions were made by these people—moved by their God. In all of human history I do not know of a people who came so far so fast. Of course there were problems, but even the problems were celebrated in poetry and writings that, in themselves, were unprecedented for their variety and literary quality.

During the next generations, things seemed to fall apart. Division crept in. Civil war led to a split kingdom, two monarchies. Unjust kings reigned. The people and their leaders regularly fell away from the vision of earlier years. One of the two kingdoms was overcome by a foreign power.

But even those setbacks generated new reflection on God's purposes, a new deepening of a consciousness of a moral order. Extraordinary prophets emerged from the life of the people, holding up a plumb line to call the people back to God's ways. The tradition and writing of the prophets added a richness again unparalleled in the ancient world. Out of their failures, the Hebrews produced the work of Jeremiah and Amos.

And all through these lean years, the people grew more strongly attached to the meaning of Jerusalem and the temple. These realities stood for the special call of the people before God. They became the embodiment of the story.

And this incredible story was the background for Ezekiel's question, "Can these bones live?" In 587 B.C.E. the story of this remarkable people came to an end—so far as they could see. Nebuchadnezzar's armies conquered

Jerusalem, the Holy City, and leveled the temple—the place through which their contact with God was mediated. The *only* place, they thought hopelessly. They temple vessels were even taken away to grace the altars of foreign gods in Babylon. Leaders of the nation were led away in chains to an exile far from their beloved city.

When in history has such a story been told? When has such incredible vitality and imagination, sheer inventiveness, made such a civilization in just a few centuries, then to be completely destroyed, as if forever? We can understand the people's shock, dismay, loss of hope. Exiled from the center of their life. Exiled, it seemed, even from their God. Rejected by God.

Exiled Ezekiel asked a question that was about more than whether they could ever return to Jerusalem. It included a prophetic statement that the people had fallen away from the relationship that had given them life. They had become not only exiles, but also dead and dry to their vocation to be God's people.

The situation was hopeless. No way was open.

That is precisely why I call on Ezekiel's question for us today in the churches. In spite of the fact that we are surrounded by great church buildings, theologies, and traditions, I believe the life has disappeared from many of the structures that have been so important and supportive for us. As the people of Israel were separated from the traditions that had given them life, so more and more of us in the churches are finding ourselves separated from that which gave life to previous generations. I sometimes think the people of Israel were in one way more fortunate than we are; they were physically uprooted and separated from their Jerusalem; they had no way to disguise those hard realities. They woke up every morning and saw Babylon, not Jerusalem, outside their windows.

We still wake up in the morning thinking we are in Jerusalem. Until a generation or so ago that *seemed* to be true. Bu now we wake up finding ourselves in Babylon. *We* can fool ourselves in ways they could not. We look out the window and see all the furniture of our supposed Jerusalem: churches on the corners, some of them bursting at the seams. And yet more and more of us have begun to realize that the world we inhabit is not Jerusalem. We live in Babylon. And I see no signs that Babylon is going to become Jerusalem.

How can we sing the Lord's song in this foreign land? Can these bones live? Is there time?

I take hope from what happened to the people of Israel while they were in exile. Consider the seventy years of the exile. (It is no accident when I say that I look forward to at least three generations of difficult times for us in the churches.) What did the people do in those years of exile? Having lost all the supports for their faith and community, what did they do? I see four critical answers to that question.[3]

First, they wrote the Bible. Of course that is an exaggeration. They had many pieces already written. Stories. Poems. Bits and pieces. But while they were in Babylon (not Jerusalem) the segments were stitched together, and important new pieces were written. Far from home, they set about the task of remembering who they were. My personal hunch is that they fully understood the miracle at the Red Sea only after they were exiled, far from home. And in Babylon they wrote the story, answering "Who are we and to what are we called?"

What's more, they realized they needed to study the story, to reflect on its meanings. They invented a place where they could gather for study, the synagogue.

Similarly, they invented the role of the teacher. From that time on, the religious leadership of the rabbi was a central ingredient in the growth of the people's consciousness.

Perhaps most important, the people discovered how the faith did not depend upon the temple; it could be carried from generation to generation through the teaching and witness of the family. Modes of celebration of the great events of the history of the people were developed from home liturgy and celebration.

By the end of the exile, the Jewish people had put together the essentials tools they needed for survival. Those essentials served them well for 2,500 years, holding them steady and maintaining their identity as a people and sense of vocation in dispersion all across the globe. Even if they had never returned to Jerusalem—and many never did—they had the resources to live in dispersion.

By the power of God, the bones did come to life.

There is good news for us in this story. Not easy news, but good news. I do not believe we face greater challenges than did the exiles in Babylon. Our challenge is to change the ownership of the church and involves freeing ourselves from some of the unproductive power issues. We need to find a way for the laity and the clergy to enter into creative dialogue for the growth of the body. Remember, God helped the people in Babylon to begin to define the nature of the rabbinate.

Our second challenge is to find more appropriate and workable structures for the life of faith. (In Babylon a people who had lost the locus of their life of worship discovered the life of the synagogue.)

Our third challenge is to find a way to express a fuller spirituality in dependence on the Spirit of God. What else did the people of Israel do but learn that the Spirit of God was not limited to the structure of the temple? The Spirit went with them, bringing life wherever they were called to go.

Our fourth challenge is to find community with one another and to find how to share that in our world. (The end product of the Babylonian exile was a people with a clear sense of identity and an ability to make that identity portable.)

Our fifth challenge is to become an apostolic people. (Since the exile, the people of Israel have known themselves to be marked by God, and they bear that mark, even among aliens and into persecution, because they claim that identity.)

I must state one important caveat. The great creative adaptation of the people of Israel began when they discovered that they were living in Babylon. I believe we in the churches are, indeed, in a foreign land, our own Babylon. But too many of us continue to pretend that we are surrounded by the comfortable walls of Jerusalem, safe in the shadow of the temple. Or we think we have only to make a few adjustments to the city wall or the architecture of the temple to return to the comfortable days we think we had in the past.

No. The bones really are dry.

But I have enormous confidence in the One who led the people through the Red Sea to become a great people. I have great confidence in the One who went into exile with the people and led them to a new life there, bringing dry bones to life. I have even greater confidence in the One who lived among us as our servant, died, and was raised to new life to open that life to us. And in these later days, when we seem to have strayed away from what Christ calls us to, I have confidence that he continues to call and that he will shape our life to reflect his loving will for us and for all humankind.

What will the future hold for the church? Who can know? What would you have said the future held for the band of shackled captives being driven down the road to Babylon?

What we can know is that God is faithful. We can know that in Babylon God called a lost people, and they responded. Their bones were covered with sinew and flesh and then brought to life by the breath of God. We can trust that God will be faithful to us through our times of change and trial.

When, in God's providence, these dry bones leap to life, we will discover again the powerful breath of the Spirit, bringing us and the church of the future to new life.

NOTES

1. I can live with almost any interpretation, but I do find it difficult to sing the hymn line that refers to walking through the Red Sea with "unmoistened foot," I sense it must at least have been muddy.

2. Modern biblical scholarship suggests that the story we have received exaggerates the unity and cohesion of the people in the beginning, and that numbers of people and tribes gradually were brought into the identity of the Hebrew people. If this is true, this is an even greater miracle than the biblical story.

3. In these four points I am greatly oversimplifying. Most of these elements have a more complex history, but critical, if not formative, parts took place in these years of exile.

Author's Note

This is the third book of a series I did not know I was writing as a series.[1] The books have grown out of a forty-year dialogue I have had with people in churches. The books all come out of my conviction that the way we have "done church" over the past few generations has stopped working.

The first book, *The Once and Future Church*, came out of my observations of church life and my teaching about church tensions. I was teaching some of the material a decade before I wrote it down. But during long-range strategic planning that preceded my retirement from the presidency of the Alban Institute, I was given an assignment by consultants Vance and Mary Sharer Johnson. "Your job," they told me, "is to articulate the vision that has driven this institute." I did the best I could to come up with the classic "twenty-five words or less" vision statement, but I simply could not do it. So I sat down and wrote it as a series of articles that laid out what I saw happening in the churches and how my colleagues and I at the Alban Institute were attempting to respond. It eventually became that first book.

Anyone working with congregations today knows the sheer hard work required of church leaders, lay or clergy. Anyone knows that things that worked well a generation ago no long work. Anyone knows that the local structures get out of alignment with the regional or national church structures. I observed that whatever was going wrong was generating a massive amount of anger and scapegoating. People at all levels were trying to "blame" somebody else for the pain they were experiencing.

The book was an attempt to point out that the dislocations were objective changes that were also occurring in the larger society. I believed and wanted to stress that there was no plot afoot; we happened to be living in a time of changing understandings. In terms of the modern jargon, the paradigms were shifting.

That first book offered no solutions but provided a perspective to allow us to see where we are and stop blaming each other. Apparently the book worked for many people. It gave names to some causes of pain. Though I am no historian, I received requests to teach about shifts of history.[2] The Evangelical Lutheran Church in Canada hired me to be keynoter of their conference on the subject, a conference they daringly named Holy Shift.[3]

Questions people asked pushed me to think about some of the next steps. If I could not tell what we must do to change the church that "wasn't working," could I at least try to state what kind of church we might need in the future? As I worked with and learned from others and as I reviewed the work of the past generation or two of pioneers in church change, I saw sets of functions that have marked the life of the church in all previous generations.

The second book of the series, *Transforming Congregations for the Future*, came out of that effort to describe the key functions we need to include in the life of the church in any generation. If we understood how we got to be in the fix we are in—and *The Once and Future Church* tried to provide clarity on that point—I hoped we could initiate changes as we identified some of the functions we needed to reconstitute for tomorrow's church. To survive, the church must provide answers for some very pragmatic needs. In denomination after denomination I saw cutbacks being done in a haphazard way simply to make a budget balance. Considering budget restraints and social pressures, we needed to make changes consciously—not haphazardly—in a way that would preserve vital dimensions of the church.[4]

As I continued working with people in different denominations, they asked me what we needed to do to build the church of the future. I remain very skittish in making prescriptions because I feel that the church will include many churches, many shapes of religious institutional life. I believe the church will grow organically out of the diversity and richness of the churches we have today.

In March 1995, Dr. Francis Wade, rector of my parish, Saint Alban's Episcopal in Washington, D.C., asked me to breakfast and gave me a commission: "Would you put together your ideas about what the church must face in the next generation or two to rebuild its life for the future?" He elaborated, "What challenges do we face? What roadblocks must we get around?" He then asked me to present those ideas in a Sunday sermon.

I gave the sermon and kept working on the idea. In the year since then I have worked and reworked to try to be clearer and more helpful to those who are trying to work for that church of tomorrow. I have shared these ideas with a number of audiences, with the Urban-Suburban Clergy Group of the Episcopal Church, with Hillside Christian Church, with two groups in continuing education programs at the Toronto School of Theology, and as a set of lectures for the religion department of the Chautauqua Institution in New York. Every time I have shared the ideas I have learned from those who have reacted to them. In this final shape—here in this book—they are deeply influenced by the scores of people who have asked me questions, who have argued with me and many who have shown me the error of my ways. I am grateful to them all. Where I am able to identify the contributions of others I try to give credit, but I am aware that almost everything I know and believe has been given me by this community of faith in which I work.

That community and that conversation continue to exist. I expect and welcome comments from friends and critics. That is an open invitation to you in two ways: First, take these ideas and generate your own in your life and work. Go beyond what I think and know. Second, if you feel the urge, write me to add to or to challenge my understanding and knowledge.

The most important message from me is this: Your congregation is where you touch this worldwide set of challenges. Engage them there. Give it your best. And tell us how it goes. Help build a life-giving community of faith for tomorrow.

NOTES

1. Loren Mead, *The Once and Future Church* (Bethesda, MD: The Alban Institute, 1991); *Transforming Congregations for the Future* (Bethesda, MD: The Alban Instititute, 1994).

2. See also David Bosch, *Transforming Mission* (Maryknoll, NY: Orbis Books, 1991). I continually refer people to this as an excellent introduction to the real history I skim over in my book.

3. Complete with t-shirts emblazoned with "Holy Shift" on the front and "Shift Happens" on the back.

4. Some people have found my book *More Than Numbers* (Bethesda, MD: The Alban Institute, 1993) to be a very practical help in their work in congregations. I have to admit that I wrote *More Than Numbers* before I had any plan to write

Transforming Congregations. More Than Numbers was an effort to make available some of the practical tools I had found useful in working with congregations. It was not intended to be part of this series that I did not yet know I was writing. Several other books of mine are similarly unrelated and deal with other church issues.